REA: THE TEST PREP AP® TEACHERS RECOMMEND

3rd Edition

AP® EUROPEAN HISTORY CRASH COURSE®

By Larry Krieger, M.A., M.A.T.

Research & Education Association
www.rea.com

Research & Education Association
258 Prospect Plains Road
Cranbury, New Jersey 08512
Email: info@rea.com

AP® EUROPEAN HISTORY CRASH COURSE®, 3rd Edition

Printed in the United States of America

Library of Congress Control Number 2019953139

ISBN-13: 978-0-7386-1270-6
ISBN-10: 0-7386-1270-7

A20

AP® EUROPEAN HISTORY CRASH COURSE TABLE OF CONTENTS

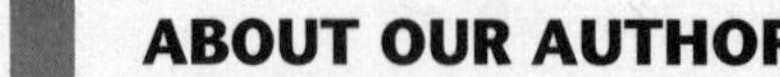

ABOUT OUR AUTHOR

Larry Krieger earned his B.A. and M.A.T. from the University of North Carolina at Chapel Hill and his M.A. from Wake Forest University. In a career spanning more than 40 years, Mr. Krieger has taught a variety of AP® subjects including U.S. History, World History, European History, U.S. Government and Politics, and Art History. His popular courses were renowned for their energetic presentations, commitment to scholarship, and success in helping students achieve high AP® exam scores. All of Mr. Krieger's students scored above a 3, with most students scoring a 4 or a 5. The College Board has recognized Mr. Krieger as one of the nation's foremost AP® teachers.

Mr. Krieger's success has extended far beyond the classroom. He conducts SAT® and AP® workshops around the country, and has spoken at numerous Social Studies conferences. In addition, he is the author of several widely used American History and World History textbooks, as well as REA's *Crash Course* test preps for European History, U.S. History, U.S. Government and Politics, and Psychology.

ACKNOWLEDGMENTS

We would like to thank Pam Weston, Publisher, for setting the quality standards for production integrity and managing the publication to completion; Larry B. Kling, Editorial Director, for his overall direction; John Cording, Technology Director, for coordinating the design and development of the REA Study Center; Diane Goldschmidt for proofreading; and Jennifer Calhoun for file prep.

We would also like to extend our appreciation to Patti Harrold for technically reviewing the manuscript; Linda Robbian for copyediting; and Kathy Caratozzolo of Caragraphics for typesetting.

ABOUT OUR BOOK

REA's *AP® European History Crash Course* is designed for the last-minute studier or any student who wants a quick refresher on the AP® course. The *Crash Course* is based on the 2019–2020 AP® European History course and exam and focuses only on the topics tested, so you can make the most of your study time.

Written by a veteran AP® European History test expert, our *Crash Course* gives you a concise review of the major concepts and important topics tested on the AP® European History exam.

- **Part I** offers you our **Keys for Success**, so you can tackle the exam with confidence. It also gives you a list of **Key Terms** that you must know.
- **Part II** is the **Chronological Review** that covers all of the periods found in the AP® European History course framework.
- **Part III** is devoted to **Key Themes and Facts** with particular attention focused on intellectual and diplomatic history as well as women's history.
- **Part IV** offers specific **Test-Taking Strategies and AP®-style Practice Questions** to prepare you for what you'll see on test day.

ABOUT OUR ONLINE PRACTICE EXAM

How ready are you for the AP® European History exam? Find out by taking **REA's online practice exam** available at *www.rea.com/studycenter*. This test features automatic scoring, detailed explanations of all answers, and diagnostic score reporting that will help you identify your strengths and weaknesses so you'll be ready on exam day.

Whether you use this book throughout the school year or as a refresher in the final weeks before the exam, REA's *Crash Course* will show you how to study efficiently and strategically, so you can boost your score.

Good luck on your AP® European History exam!

PART I

INTRODUCTION

Chapter 1

Seven Keys for Success on the AP® European History Exam

AP® European History textbooks are very thick and contain thousands of names, dates, places, and events. If all of these facts had an equal chance of appearing on your Advanced Placement® European History (APEURO) exam, studying would be a nightmare. Where would you begin? What would you emphasize? Is there any information you can safely omit? Or must you study everything?

Fortunately, preparing for the APEURO exam does not have to be a nightmare. By studying efficiently and strategically, you can score a 4 or a 5 on the exam. This book will help you understand and use the following seven keys for success:

1. UNDERSTANDING THE APEURO SCORE SCALE

Many students believe they must make close to a perfect score to receive a 5. Nothing could be further from the truth. Each APEURO exam contains a total of 140 points—55 from the multiple-choice and 85 from the free-response questions. Here is the probable score range for the APEURO Exam:

Score Range	AP® Grade	Minimum Percent Correct
109–140	5	77%
91–108	4	65%
73–90	3	52%
55–72	2	39%
0–54	1	0–38%

This chart is not a misprint. As is clearly shown, you can achieve a score of 5 by correctly answering just 77 percent of the questions, a 4 by correctly answering just 65 percent of the questions, and a 3 by correctly answering just 52 percent of the questions!

2. UNDERSTANDING THE DIVISION OF APEURO INTO NINE CHRONOLOGICAL PERIODS

APEURO test writers follow a detailed framework that divides European history into the nine distinct units shown in the following table:

Units	Chronological Period
Unit 1: Renaissance and Exploration	c. 1450–c. 1648
Unit 2: Age of Reformation	c. 1450–c. 1648
Unit 3: Absolutism and Constitutionalism	c. 1648–c. 1815
Unit 4: Scientific, Philosophical, and Political Developments	c. 1648–c. 1815
Unit 5: Conflict, Crisis, and Reaction in the Late 18th Century	c. 1648–c. 1815
Unit 6: Industrialization and Its Effects	c. 1815–c. 1914
Unit 7: 19th-Century Perspectives and Political Developments	c. 1815–c. 1914
Unit 8: 20th-Century Global Conflicts	c. 1914–present
Unit 9: Cold War and Contemporary Europe	c. 1914–present

Each of these nine chronological time periods accounts for 10–15 percent of the points on your exam. No AP® European History exam question will require students to know historical content that falls outside of these chronological periods. The 29 chapters in our Crash Course Chronological Review are designed to provide you with the key events, trends, and ideas from these nine periods.

3. UNDERSTANDING THE APEURO TOPICAL THEMES

Many students believe that members of the APEURO exam development committee have the freedom to write any question they wish. This widespread belief is not true. APEURO test writers follow a framework devoted to the following seven themes:

- **Theme 1:** Interaction of Europe and the World (INT)
- **Theme 2:** Economic and Commercial Developments (ECD)
- **Theme 3:** Cultural and Intellectual Developments (CID)
- **Theme 4:** States and Other Institutions of Power (SOP)
- **Theme 5:** Social Organization and Development (SCD)
- **Theme 6:** National and European Identity (NEI)
- **Theme 7:** Technological and Scientific Innovation (TSI)

These seven themes explain why there are so many questions on key intellectual figures, major artistic movements, diplomatic agreements, and economic policies. They also explain why it is a waste of time to study battles, generals, and specific dates.

4. UNDERSTANDING THE APEURO EXAM FORMAT

Your APEURO Exam will include four very different question formats. Here are the key facts about each of these formats:

A. MULTIPLE-CHOICE QUESTIONS

1. You will be asked to answer 55 multiple-choice questions.
2. The 55 questions will be grouped into sets containing between 2 and 4 questions. Each set of questions will be based upon a stimulus prompt. The prompts will be a brief source that could be a reading passage, a chart or graph, an image, or a map.
3. Each of the 55 questions will be worth 1 point for a total of 55 points. The multiple-choice questions will count for 40 percent of your total score.
4. You will be given 55 minutes to complete the multiple-choice questions.
5. See Chapter 35 for detailed strategies for answering the multiple-choice questions.
6. See Chapter 36 for sample realistic multiple-choice questions.

B. SHORT-ANSWER QUESTIONS

1. You will be asked to answer 3 short-answer questions.
2. The first short-answer question will feature a secondary source passage. The second short-answer question will feature a primary source. The final two short-answer questions will ask you to compare significant historical trends, patterns, and movements. You will only have to answer one of these two questions. It is important to note that these two questions will not contain a primary or secondary source.
3. Each short-answer question will include three very specific sub-points. Your answers to these sub-points do ***not*** require a thesis. Concentrate on writing concise statements that include specific historic examples. Use complete sentences; an outline or list of bulleted points is not acceptable.
4. Each sub-point is worth 3.1 points. As a result, a full short-answer question is worth 9.3 points. Taken together, the three short-answer questions are worth a total of 28 points, or 20 percent of your total exam score.
5. You will be given 40 minutes to complete three short-answer questions.
6. See Chapter 37 for detailed strategies for answering the short-answer questions.

C. DOCUMENT-BASED QUESTION (DBQ)

1. The DBQ is an essay question that requires you to interpret and analyze 7 brief primary source documents. The documents typically include excerpts from diaries, speeches, letters, reports, and official decrees. In addition, DBQs often include at least one graph, chart, map, political cartoon, or work of art.
2. Your DBQ will be scored on a scale that includes 7 specific points. Each one is worth 5 points. Taken together, the DBQ is worth a maximum of 35 points or 25 percent of your total score.
3. See Chapter 38 for detailed strategies for answering the document-based essay question.

D. LONG-ESSAY QUESTION

1. You will be given three long-essay questions. Although the three questions will be taken from different time periods, they will be related by a common theme and historical thinking skill. You will be asked to select and write about just one of the three long-essay questions.
2. Your essay will be scored on a scale that includes 6 specific points. Each one is worth 3.5 points. Taken together the long-essay question is worth 21 points or 15 percent of your total exam score.
3. See Chapter 39 for detailed strategies for answering the long-essay question.

E. TIMING ON THE DBQ AND LONG ESSAY

1. You will be given 100 minutes to complete the essay portion of your exam.
2. The College Board recommends that you devote 15 minutes to reading the DBQ documents, 45 minutes to writing the DBQ essay, and 40 minutes to writing the long essay.
3. It is important to note that these times are just recommendations. It is up to you to determine how to best allocate your time. For example, you could choose to spend 65 minutes on your DBQ and 35 minutes on your long essay.

5. UNDERSTANDING THE MEANING AND USES OF THREE HISTORICAL REASONING PROCESSES

The APEURO course stresses the understanding and use of three key historical reasoning processes. It is crucial that you understand the meaning of each skill and the role it plays on the exam.

A. HISTORICAL CAUSATION

1. This skill involves the ability to identify and evaluate the long- and short-term causes and consequences of a historical event, development, or process.
2. This skill plays a significant role in the multiple-choice questions, short-essay questions and long-essay questions.

B. PATTERNS OF CONTINUITY AND CHANGE OVER TIME

1. This skill involves the ability to recognize, analyze, and evaluate the dynamics of historical continuity and change over periods of time of varying lengths. It also involves the ability to connect these patterns to larger historical processes or themes.
2. This skill plays a significant role in the short-essay and long-essay questions.

C. COMPARISON

1. This skill involves the ability to identify, compare, and evaluate multiple perspectives on a given historical event, development, or process.
2. This skill plays a significant role in the multiple-choice questions and long-essay questions.

D. CONTEXTUALIZATION

1. This skill involves the ability to connect historical events and processes to specific circumstances of time and place as well as to broader regional, national, and global processes occurring at the same time.
2. This skill plays a significant role in the multiple-choice questions. It also generates a specific point in the DBQ rubric.

E. HISTORICAL ARGUMENTATION

1. This skill involves the ability to create an argument and support it using relevant historical ideas.
2. This skill plays a significant role in both the DBQ and the long-essay questions. The rubrics in both of these questions award points for developing and supporting a defensible thesis.

F. ANALYZING EVIDENCE

1. This skill involves the ability to analyze features of historical evidence such as audience, purpose, point of view, and historical context.
2. This skill plays a significant role in the DBQ. The DBQ rubric awards 2 points for analyzing evidence presented in the documents.

G. INTERPRETATION

1. This skill involves the ability to describe, analyze, and evaluate the different ways historians interpret the past.
2. This skill plays a significant role in the short-essay questions.

6. UNDERSTANDING HOW TO USE YOUR *CRASH COURSE* TO BUILD A WINNING COALITION OF POINTS

This *Crash Course* book is based on a careful analysis of the latest *AP® European History Course and Exam Description* as well as released exam questions.

- Chapter 2 contains key terms that you absolutely, positively have to know.
- Chapters 3–31 provide you with a detailed chronological review of European history.
- Chapters 32–34 provide you with key facts about themes that regularly appear on each exam.
- Chapters 35–39 use proven strategies and realistic practice to cover each of the four types of questions found on your exam.

If you have the time, review the entire book. This is desirable but not mandatory. The chapters can be studied in any order. Each chapter provides you with a digest of key information that is repeatedly tested. Battles, inventions, rulers, and political events that have never been asked about have been omitted. Unlike most review books, the digests are not meant to be exhaustive. Instead, they are meant to focus your attention on the vital material you must study.

Many of the *Crash Course* chapters have a special feature called "Making Comparisons." This feature is designed to provide you with in-depth discussions of key topics. The Making Comparison feature will help you develop the historical thinking skills of making comparisons, interpreting events, and developing a thesis.

7. USING COLLEGE BOARD MATERIALS TO SUPPLEMENT YOUR *CRASH COURSE*

This *Crash Course* contains everything you need to know to score a 4 or a 5 on your exam. Even so, you should supplement it with College Board materials designed specifically for studying AP® European History. Visit the College Board's AP® Central website for resources including the latest *AP® European History Course and Exam Description*, updated in fall 2019, which includes sample questions.

Key Terms

I. RENAISSANCE AND EXPLORATION, c. 1450 to c. 1648

1. **HUMANISM**—The scholarly interest in the study of the classical texts, values, and styles of Greece and Rome. Humanism contributed to the promotion of a liberal arts education based on the study of the classics, rhetoric, and history.

2. **CHRISTIAN HUMANISM**—A branch of humanism associated with northern Europe. Like their Italian counterparts, the Christian humanists closely studied classical texts. However, they also sought to give humanism a specifically Christian content. Christian humanists like Desiderius Erasmus were committed to religious piety and institutional reform.

3. **VERNACULAR**—The everyday language of a region or country. Miguel de Cervantes, Geoffrey Chaucer, Dante, and Martin Luther all encouraged the development of their national languages by writing in the vernacular. Desiderius Erasmus, however, continued to write in Latin.

4. **NEW MONARCHS**—European monarchs who created professional armies and a more centralized administrative bureaucracy. The new monarchs also negotiated a new relationship with the Catholic Church. Key new monarchs include Charles VII, Louis XI, Henry VII, and Ferdinand and Isabella.

5. **SECULARISM**—Promoted by the Humanists and the Renaissance. Trend toward making religious faith a private domain rather than one directly connected to state power. Promoted a search for nonreligious explanations for political authority and natural phenomena.

6. **COLUMBIAN EXCHANGE**—The interchange of plants, animals, diseases, and human populations between the Old World and the New World. Opened new opportunities for Europeans while at the

same time creating a demographic catastrophe for indigenous peoples in the Americas.

7. **MERCANTILISM**—Economic philosophy calling for close government regulation of the economy. Mercantilist theory emphasized building a strong, self-sufficient economy by maximizing exports and limiting imports. Mercantilists supported the acquisition of colonies as sources of raw materials and markets for finished goods. This favorable balance of trade would enable a country to accumulate reserves of gold and silver. Mercantilism gave the new monarchies a leading role in promoting commercial development and the acquisition of New World colonies.

8. **COMMERCIAL REVOLUTION**—Innovations in banking and finance that promoted the growth of urban financial centers and a money economy.

9. **JOINT-STOCK COMPANY**—A business arrangement in which many investors raise money for a venture too large for any of them to undertake alone. They share the profits in proportion to the amount they invest. English entrepreneurs used joint-stock companies to finance the establishment of New World colonies.

II. AGE OF REFORMATION, c. 1450 to c. 1648

10. **INDULGENCE**—A certificate granted by the pope in return for the payment of a fee to the church. The certificate stated that the soul of the dead relative or friend of the purchaser would have his time in purgatory reduced by many years or canceled altogether.

11. **ANABAPTISTS**—Sixteenth-century Protestants who insisted that only adult baptism conformed to Scripture. Protestant and Catholic leaders condemned Anabaptists as radicals who advocated the complete separation of church and state.

12. **PREDESTINATION**—Doctrine espoused by John Calvin that God has known since the beginning of time who will be saved and who will be damned. Calvin declared that "by an eternal and immutable counsel, God has once and for all determined, both whom he would admit to salvation, and whom he would condemn to destruction."

13. **HUGUENOTS**—French Protestants who followed the teachings of John Calvin.

14. **POLITIQUES**—Rulers who put political necessities above personal beliefs. For example, both Henry IV of France and Elizabeth I of England subordinated theological controversies in order to achieve political unity.

15. **PUTTING-OUT SYSTEM**—A pre-industrial manufacturing system in which an entrepreneur would bring materials to rural people who worked on them in their own homes. For example, watch manufacturers in Swiss towns employed villagers to make parts for their products. The system enabled entrepreneurs to avoid restrictive guild regulations.

16. **BAROQUE ART**—An artistic style of the seventeenth century that featured dramatic action, intense emotions, and exaggerated lighting. Monarchies, city-states, and the Catholic Church commissioned Baroque works as a means of promoting their own stature and power.

III. ABSOLUTISM AND CONSTITUTIONALISM, c. 1648 to c. 1815

17. **ABSOLUTISM**—A system of government in which the ruler claims sole and uncontestable power. Absolute monarchs were not limited by constitutional restraints.

18. **DIVINE RIGHT OF KINGS**—The idea that rulers receive their authority from God and are answerable only to God. Jacques-Bénigne Bossuet, a French bishop and court preacher to Louis XIV, provided the theological justification for the divine right of kings by declaring that "the state of monarchy is the supremest thing on earth, for kings are not only God's lieutenants upon earth and sit upon God's throne, but even by God himself are called gods. In the Scriptures, kings are called Gods, and their power is compared to the divine powers."

19. **INTENDANTS**—French royal officials who supervised provincial governments in the name of the king. Intendants played a key role in establishing French absolutism.

20. **CONSTITUTIONALISM**—System of government in which rulers share power with parliaments made up of elected representatives.

21. **TRANSATLANTIC TRADE**—The exchange of goods and labor between Africa, the Americas, and Europe. West Indian sugar, Chesapeake tobacco, British manufacturing goods, and West African slaves dominated transatlantic trade.

IV. SCIENTIFIC, PHILOSOPHICAL, AND POLITICAL DEVELOPMENTS, c. 1648 to c. 1815

22. **SCIENTIFIC METHOD**—The use of inductive logic and controlled experiments to discover regular patterns in nature. These patterns or natural laws can be described with mathematical formulas.

23. **SCIENTIFIC REVOLUTION**—New ideas in science based on the scientific method that challenged classical views of the cosmos, nature, and the human body.

24. **ENLIGHTENMENT**—Applied scientific revolution concepts and practices to political, social, and ethical issues. Led to an increased—but not unchallenged—emphasis on reason in European culture.

25. **PHILOSOPHES**—Eighteenth-century writers who stressed reason and advocated freedom of expression, religious toleration, and a reformed legal system. Leading philosophes such as Voltaire fought irrational prejudice and believed that society should be open to people of talent.

26. **DEISM**—The belief that God created the universe but allowed it to operate through the laws of nature. Deists believed that natural laws could be discovered by the use of human reason.

27. **GENERAL WILL**—A concept in political philosophy referring to the desire or interest of a people as a whole. As used by Jean-Jacques Rousseau, who championed the concept, the general will is identical to the rule of law.

28. **ENLIGHTENED DESPOTISM**—A system of government supported by leading philosophes in which an absolute ruler uses his or her power for the good of the people. Enlightened monarchs supported religious tolerance, increased economic productivity, administrative reform, and scientific academies. Joseph II, Frederick the Great, and Catherine the Great were the best-known Enlightened monarchs.

29. **ENCLOSURE MOVEMENT**—The process by which British landlords consolidated or fenced in common lands to increase the production of cash crops. The Enclosure Acts led to an increase in the size of farms held by large landowners.

30. **AGRICULTURAL REVOLUTION**—The innovations in farm production that began in eighteenth-century Holland and spread to England. These advances replaced the open-field agriculture system with a more scientific and mechanized system of agriculture that produced more food with fewer workers, increased food supply, and reduced the number of demographic crises caused by major epidemic diseases.

31. **INVISIBLE HAND**—Phrase coined by Adam Smith to refer to the self-regulating nature of a free marketplace.

32. **NEOCLASSICISM**—A style of art and architecture that emerged in the late eighteenth century as part of a general revival of interest in classical Greek and Roman themes of order, balance, and harmony.

V. CONFLICT, CRISIS, AND REACTION, c. 1648 to c. 1815

33. **PARLEMENTS**—French regional courts dominated by hereditary nobles. The Parlement of Paris claimed the right to register royal decrees before they could become law.

34. **GIRONDINS**—A moderate republican faction active in the French Revolution from 1791 to 1793. The Girondin Party favored a policy of extending the French Revolution beyond France's borders.

35. **JACOBINS**—A radical republican party during the French Revolution. Led by Maximilien Robespierre, the Jacobins unleashed the Reign of Terror. Other key leaders included Jean-Paul Marat, Georges-Jacques Danton, and the Comte de Mirabeau. The Marquis de Lafayette was not a Jacobin.

36. **SANS-CULOTTES**—The working people of Paris who were characterized by their long working pants and support for radical politics.

37. **LEVÉE EN MASSE**—The French policy of conscripting all males into the army. This created a new type of military force based upon mass participation and a fully mobilized economy.

38. **THERMIDORIAN REACTION**—Name given to the reaction against the radicalism of the French Revolution. It is associated with the end of the Reign of Terror and reassertion of bourgeoisie power in the Directory.

39. **LEGITIMACY**—The principle that rulers who have been driven from their thrones should be restored to power. For example, the Congress of Vienna restored the Bourbons to power in France.

40. **BALANCE OF POWER**—A strategy to maintain an equilibrium, in which weak countries join together to match or exceed the power of a stronger country. It was one of the guiding principles of the Congress of Vienna.

41. **NATIONALISM**—Belief that a nation consists of a group of people who share similar traditions, history, and language. Nationalists

argued that every nation should be sovereign and include all members of a community. Thus, a person's greatest loyalty should be to a nation-state.

42. **ROMANTICISM**—Philosophical and artistic movement in late eighteenth- and early nineteenth-century Europe that represented a reaction against the Neoclassical emphasis upon reason. Romantic artists, writers, and composers stressed emotion and the contemplation of nature.

VI. INDUSTRIALIZATION AND ITS EFFECTS, c. 1815 to c. 1914

43. **INDUSTRIAL REVOLUTION**—Began in Great Britain in the late eighteenth and early nineteenth centuries. Britain established its industrial dominance through the mechanization of textile production, iron production, and the construction of a network of railroads.

44. **CONSERVATISM**—Political philosophy that emerged after 1789. Conservatives preferred monarchs over republics, tradition over revolution, and established religion over Enlightenment skepticism. Conservatives favored gradual change in the established social order.

45. **LIBERALISM**—Political philosophy in the nineteenth century that advocated representative government dominated by the propertied classes, minimal government interference in the economy, religious toleration, and civil liberties such as freedom of speech.

46. **CONCERT OF EUROPE (OR CONGRESS SYSTEM)**—Sought to maintain the status quo through collective action and adherence to conservative principles. Metternich used the Concert of Europe to suppress nationalist and liberal revolutions.

47. **PROLETARIAT**—The industrial working class concentrated in large cities.

48. **BOURGEOISIE**—French term referring to the commercial class of urban shopkeepers and factory owners.

49. **SOCIALISM**—A social and political ideology that advocated the redistribution of society's resources and wealth.

50. **UTOPIAN SOCIALISTS**—Early nineteenth-century socialists who hoped to replace the overly competitive capitalist structure with planned communities guided by a spirit of cooperation. Leading

French utopian socialists such as Charles Fourier and Louis Blanc believed that property should be communally owned.

51. **MARXISM**—Political and economic philosophy of Karl Marx and Friedrich Engels. They believed that history is the result of a class conflict that will end with the triumph of the industrial proletariat over the bourgeoisie. The new classless society would abolish private property.

52. **ANARCHISTS**—Asserted that all forms of governmental authority were unnecessary and should be overthrown and replaced with a society based on voluntary cooperation.

53. **CULT OF DOMESTICITY**—Idealization of women in their roles as wives and mothers. As a nurturing mother and faithful spouse, the wife had a special responsibility to create a home that was a "haven in a heartless world."

VII. NINETEENTH-CENTURY PERSPECTIVES AND POLITICAL DEVELOPMENTS

54. **SECOND INDUSTRIAL REVOLUTION**—A wave of late nineteenth-century industrialization that was characterized by an increased use of steel, chemical processes, electric power, and railroads. This period also witnessed the spread of industrialization from Great Britain to Western Europe and the United States. Both the United States and Germany soon rivaled Great Britain.

55. **ZIONISM**—A form of Jewish nationalism developed in the late nineteenth century as a response to growing anti-Semitism throughout Europe.

56. **REALPOLITIK**—"The politics of reality"; used to describe the tough, practical politics in which idealism and romanticism play no part. Otto von Bismarck and Camillo Benso di Cavour were the leading practitioners of Realpolitik.

57. **SOCIAL DARWINISM**—The belief that there is a natural evolutionary process by which the fittest will survive. Wealthy business and industrial leaders used Social Darwinism to justify their success.

58. **AUTOCRACY**—A government in which the ruler has unlimited power and uses it in an arbitrary manner. The Romanov dynasty in Russia is the best example of an autocracy.

59. **POSITIVISM**—A theory developed in the mid-nineteenth century that the study of facts would generate accurate, or "positive," laws of society and that these laws could, in turn, help in the formulation of policies and legislation.

60. **IMPERIALISM**—European dominance of the non-West through economic exploitation and political rule. Imperialists justified overseas expansion by claiming cultural and racial superiority. Imperialism created diplomatic tensions among European states that strained alliance systems.

61. **SPHERE OF INFLUENCE**—A region dominated by, but not directly ruled by, a foreign nation.

62. **FREUDIAN PSYCHOLOGY**—Emphasized the role of the irrational and the struggle between the conscious and the subconscious.

63. **REALISM**—Painters and writers depicted the lives of ordinary people and drew attention to social problems.

64. **MODERN ART**—Artistic and literary movements that moved beyond the representational to the subjective, abstract, and expressive.

VIII. TWENTIETH-CENTURY GLOBAL CONFLICTS, c. 1914 TO PRESENT

65. **FOURTEEN POINTS**—President Woodrow Wilson's idealistic peace aims. Wilson stressed national self-determination, the rights of small countries, freedom of the seas, and free trade.

66. **BOLSHEVIKS**—A party of revolutionary Marxists, led by Vladimir Lenin, who seized power in Russia in 1917.

67. **NEW ECONOMIC POLICY**—A program initiated by Vladimir Lenin to stimulate the economic recovery of the Soviet Union in the early 1920s. The New Economic Policy utilized a limited revival of capitalism in light industry and agriculture.

68. **EXISTENTIALISM**—Philosophy that God, reason, and progress are all myths. Humans must accept responsibility for their actions. This responsibility causes an overwhelming sense of dread and anguish. Existentialism reflects the sense of isolation and alienation in the twentieth century.

69. **RELATIVITY**—A scientific theory associated with Albert Einstein. Relativity holds that time and space do not exist separately. Instead, they are a combined continuum whose measurement depends as much on the observer as on the entities being measured.

70. **TOTALITARIANISM**—A political system in which the government has total control over the lives of individual citizens.

71. **FASCISM**—A political system that combines an authoritarian government with a corporate economy. Fascist governments glorify their leaders, appeal to nationalism, control the media, and repress individual liberties.

72. **KULAKS**—Land-owning peasantry in tsarist Russia. Joseph Stalin accused the kulaks of being class enemies of the poorer peasants. Stalin "liquidated the kulaks as a class" by executing them and expropriating their land to form collective farms.

73. **KEYNESIAN ECONOMICS**—An economic theory based on the ideas of twentieth-century British economist John Maynard Keynes. According to Keynesian economics, governments can spend their economies out of a depression by using deficit-spending to encourage employment and stimulate economic growth.

74. **APPEASEMENT**—A policy of making concessions to an aggressor in the hopes of avoiding war. Associated with Neville Chamberlain's policy of making concessions to Adolf Hitler.

75. **HOLOCAUST**—During World War II, mass extinction of Jews by Nazis under Adolf Hitler. Part of Hitler's ruthless attempt to create a "new racial order."

IX. COLD WAR AND CONTEMPORARY EUROPE, c. 1914 TO PRESENT

76. **CONTAINMENT**—The name of a U.S. foreign policy designed to contain or block the spread of Soviet policy. Inspired by George F. Kennan, containment was expressed in the Truman Doctrine and implemented in the Marshall Plan and the North Atlantic Treaty Organization (NATO) alliance.

77. **COLD WAR**—A prolonged period of economic and political rivalry between the United States and the Soviet Union. Led to the division

of Europe, which was referred to in the West as the Iron Curtain. The Cold War began with the announcement of the Truman Doctrine in 1947 and ended with the fall of the Berlin Wall in 1989 and the collapse of the Soviet Union in 1991.

78. **MARSHALL PLAN**—Massive program of economic aid from the United States that financed an extensive reconstruction of industry and infrastructure and stimulated an extended period of growth in Western and Central Europe.

79. **DECOLONIZATION**—The process by which colonies gained their independence from the imperial European powers after World War II.

80. **DE-STALINIZATION**—The policy of liberalization of the Stalinist system in the Soviet Union. As carried out by Nikita Khrushchev, de-Stalinization meant denouncing Joseph Stalin's cult of personality, producing more consumer goods, allowing greater cultural freedom, and pursuing peaceful coexistence with the West.

81. **BREZHNEV DOCTRINE**—Assertion that the Soviet Union and its allies had the right to intervene in any socialist country whenever they saw the need. The Brezhnev Doctrine justified the Soviet invasion of Czechoslovakia in 1968.

82. **DÉTENTE**—The relaxation of tensions between the United States and the Soviet Union. Détente was introduced by Secretary of State Henry Kissinger and President Richard Nixon. Examples of détente include the Strategic Arms Limitation Talks (SALT), expanded trade with the Soviet Union, and President Nixon's trips to China and Russia.

83. **SOLIDARITY**—A Polish labor union founded in 1980 by Lech Walesa and Anna Walentynowicz. Solidarity contested Communist Party programs and eventually ousted the party from the Polish government.

84. **GLASNOST**—Policy initiated by Soviet premier Mikhail Gorbachev in the mid-1980s. Glasnost resulted in a new openness of speech, reduced censorship, and greater criticism of Communist Party policies.

85. **PERESTROIKA**—An economic policy initiated by Soviet premier Mikhail Gorbachev in the mid-1980s. Meaning "restructuring," perestroika called for less government regulation and greater efficiency in manufacturing and agriculture.

86. **WELFARE STATE**—A social system in which the state assumes primary responsibility for the welfare of its citizens in matters of health care,

education, employment, and social security. Germany was the first European country to develop a state social welfare system.

87. **GUEST WORKERS**—Foreign workers working temporarily in European countries.

88. **BIG SCIENCE**—The unprecedented combination of theoretical science and complex engineering under government sponsorship.

89. **GLOBALIZATION**—The trend by which peoples and nations have become more interdependent. The term is often used to refer to the development of a global economy and culture.

90. **EUROPEAN UNION**—Evolved from the Common Market and the European Community. Formed in 1994 under the terms of the Maastricht Treaty, its members have political ties through the European parliament as well as long-standing common economic, legal, and business mechanisms.

PART II

CHRONOLOGICAL REVIEW

Renaissance and Exploration

c. 1450 to c. 1648

Chapters 3–6

PREVIEW: UNIT 1 KEY CONCEPTS

- The rediscovery of works from ancient Greece and Rome and observation of the natural world changed many Europeans' view of their world.
  - A revival of classical texts led to new methods of scholarship and new values in both society and religion.
  - The visual arts incorporated the new ideas of the Renaissance and were used to promote personal, political, and religious goals.
- Europeans explored and settled overseas territories, encountering and interacting with indigenous populations.
  - European nations were driven by commercial and religious motives to explore overseas territories and establish colonies.
- European society and the experiences of everyday life were increasingly shaped by commercial and agricultural capitalism, notwithstanding the continued existence of medieval social and economic structures.
  - Economic change produced new social patterns, while traditions of hierarchy and status continued.
  - Most Europeans derived their livelihood from agriculture and oriented their lives around the seasons, the village, or the manor, although economic changes began to alter rural production and power.
- The struggle for sovereignty within and among states resulted in varying degrees of political centralization.
  - The new concept of the sovereign state and secular systems of law played a central role in the creation of new political institutions.

Chapter 3

The Italian Renaissance

I. RISE OF THE ITALIAN CITY-STATES

A. URBAN CENTERS

1. While the rest of Europe was still rural, a number of cities prospered in northern Italy.
2. By the late 1300s, Florence, Venice, and Milan all had populations of about 100,000.

B. WEALTHY MERCHANTS

1. In the absence of hereditary kings, wealthy merchants formed oligarchies that governed the independent city-states in northern Italy.
2. Wealthy merchant families dominated political, economic, and artistic life in the northern Italian cities.

II. FLORENCE AND THE MEDICI

A. THE PRIMACY OF FLORENCE

1. During the fifteenth century, or *Quattrocento*, Florence became the acknowledged center of the Renaissance—the rebirth of classical learning, literature, and art.
2. The golden age of Florence was based on the wealth earned by its textile merchants and bankers.

florence = birth of renaissance

B. THE LEADERSHIP OF THE MEDICI

1. The Medici family dominated Florence's economic, political, and artistic life for much of the fifteenth century.
2. The Medici earned their wealth as bankers. Led by Cosimo (1389–1464), Piero (1416–1469), and Lorenzo the Magnificent (1449–1492), the Medici financed libraries, built churches, sponsored the Platonic Academy of Philosophy, and commissioned hundreds of artworks.
3. The Florentine Renaissance reached its peak during the lifetime of Lorenzo the Magnificent.

medici family = leaders

III. THE RENAISSANCE SPIRIT

A. THE MEDIEVAL MINDSET

1. Medieval thinkers believed that God had created the world to prepare humans for salvation or eternal damnation. Human beings and their lives on earth were equally insignificant. The individual was of no importance.
2. Medieval artists did not win fame as individuals. The architects, glassmakers, and sculptors who designed and decorated Europe's great cathedrals worked for the glory of God, not for personal glory.

B. A NEW CELEBRATION OF THE INDIVIDUAL

1. Unlike feudal nobles, Italian merchants did not inherit their social rank. Success in business depended mostly on the merchants' own skill. As a result, prosperous merchants took pride in their achievements. They believed they were successful because of their merit as individuals.
2. Like the merchants, northern Italian artists and writers were eager to be known and remembered as individuals. From this time on, we know the names of people who created works of art. Fame thus became a reward for superior talent.
3. Portrait painting and autobiography illustrate the interest in individual personality and fame. Wealthy patrons wanted their portraits recorded for posterity. Renaissance artists often included self-portraits in their paintings. Autobiographies were the written equivalents of self-portraits.

↳portraits in art

4. Renaissance individualism stressed the importance of personality, the development of unique talents, and the pursuit of fame and glory. By displaying the full range of human abilities, a Renaissance person demonstrated the highly prized trait known as *virtu*.
5. In his famous *Oration on the Dignity of Man*, Giovanni Pico della Mirandola celebrated the human potential for greatness.

C. HUMANIST SCHOLARS AND THE LOVE OF CLASSICAL LEARNING

1. Petrarch and other Renaissance scholars scorned medieval art and literature. Petrarch summed up the Renaissance attitude by calling the medieval years "the Dark Ages."
2. Scholars such as Petrarch who studied the classical texts and cultures of ancient Greece and Rome were called humanists.
3. Inspired by classical authors, humanists rejected medieval scholasticism and instead advocated a curriculum based on the study of Greek and Roman literature, rhetoric, and history. Humanists believed that by studying the classics they would gain a more practical understanding of human nature.
4. Humanists played a key role in promoting the new liberal arts education, developing vernacular languages, and renewing interest in translating and preserving Greek and Roman manuscripts.
5. Humanists believed that contact with the classical past would enrich their own culture by promoting civic responsibility, encouraging artistic creativity, and rewarding individual excellence.
6. Lorenzo Valla demonstrated the power of Renaissance scholarship when he used a careful linguistic and historical analysis to demonstrate that the Donation of Constantine was actually a clumsy forgery.

D. A NEW SECULAR SPIRIT

1. Medieval culture emphasized spiritual values and salvation.
2. Renaissance culture was far more interested in the pleasures of material possessions. Wealthy Renaissance families openly enjoyed fine music, expensive foods, and beautiful works of art.

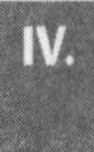

IV. EDUCATION AND THE IDEAL COURTIER

A. HUMANIST EDUCATION

1. Medieval scholastics studied the classics to understand God. In contrast, Renaissance humanists studied the classics to understand human nature and learn practical skills.
2. Leading humanists opened schools and academies that taught Roman history, Greek philosophy, and Latin grammar and rhetoric.
3. Humanists believed that their classical curriculum would teach future business, political, and military leaders how to become eloquent and persuasive speakers and writers.

B. BALDASSARE CASTIGLIONE (1478–1529)

1. For Renaissance humanists, the ideal individual strove to become a "universal man" who excelled in many fields.
2. In his book *The Courtier*, Baldassare Castiglione explained how upper-class men and women could become accomplished courtiers.
3. According to Castiglione, the ideal courtier should be polite, charming, and witty. He should be able to dance, write poetry, sing, and play music. In addition, he should be physically graceful and strong.
4. Castiglione did not ignore upper-class women. The perfect court lady, he said, should be well educated and charming. Yet women were not expected to seek fame as men did. Like Dante's Beatrice and Petrarch's Laura, they were expected to inspire poetry and art but rarely to create it.

V. MACHIAVELLI AND *THE PRINCE*

A. TURMOIL IN ITALY

1. The golden age of Florence lasted nearly a century. Lorenzo the Magnificent's unexpected death in 1492 left Florence without a strong leader.
2. In 1494, King Charles VIII of France invaded Italy with the goal of conquering Naples. Spain's King Ferdinand soon contested the French claim to Naples.

3. These invasions sparked a series of conflicts called the Habsburg-Valois Wars that involved all the major Italian city-states. Diplomacy and war became the keys to survival.

B. NICCOLÒ MACHIAVELLI (1469–1527)

1. Machiavelli was a Florentine diplomat and political philosopher. He is considered the founder of modern political science.
2. Machiavelli was appalled by the devastation caused by the Habsburg-Valois Wars. "At this time," he passionately wrote, "the whole land of Italy is without a head, without order, beaten, spoiled, torn in pieces, overrun, and abandoned to destruction in every shape. She prays to God to send someone to rescue her from these barbarous cruelties."
3. Machiavelli wrote *The Prince* to advise Italian rulers on the ruthless statecraft needed to unite his war-torn and divided Italian homeland.

C. THE QUALITIES OF A SUCCESSFUL PRINCE

1. Machiavelli had a pessimistic view of human nature. He believed that people are "ungrateful, changeable, simulators and dissimulators, runaways in danger, eager for gain; while you do well by them they are all yours; they offer you their blood, their property, their lives, their children when need is far off; but when it comes near you, they turn about."
2. Because human nature is selfish, untrustworthy, and corrupt, a prince must be strong as a lion and shrewd as a fox: "For the lion cannot protect himself from traps, and the fox cannot defend himself from wolves. One must therefore be a fox to recognize traps, and a lion to fight wolves."
3. The successful ruler, Machiavelli insisted, must be ruthless and pragmatic, always remembering that the end justifies the means.

In* The Prince, *Machiavelli suggested that a ruler should behave both "like a lion" and "like a fox." Be prepared for a short-answer essay question asking you to summarize Machiavelli's key points and apply them to rulers such as Elizabeth I of England, Henry IV of France, and Frederick II of Prussia.

UNIT 1 | RENAISSANCE AND EXPLORATION

ITALIAN RENAISSANCE ART

A. PATRONS

1. Renaissance artists were not independent contractors who produced works of art for themselves or the public. Instead, they received commissions from the Catholic Church, guilds, and wealthy families such as the Medici.
2. While these patrons appreciated the beauty of fine art, they also understood the ability of artists to create visible symbols of power. Renaissance patrons thus used art as a way of displaying their wealth and promoting their fame.

B. CHARACTERISTICS OF RENAISSANCE ART

1. Perspective

   i. A geometric method of creating the illusion of depth on a flat, two-dimensional surface.

   ii. Enabled artists to create paintings that opened "a window on the world." This way of presenting space became the foundation of European painting for the next 500 years.

2. Chiaroscuro

   i. The realistic blending of light and shade to model forms.

   ii. Creates the illusion of volume.

   iii. Chiaroscuro and perspective enabled artists to create paintings in which real people seemed to occupy real space.

3. Pyramid configuration

   i. Byzantine and medieval art featured flat, rigid figures arranged in a horizontal line.

   ii. Renaissance artists used three-dimensional pyramid configurations to create symmetrical and balanced compositions.

4. Classical forms and Christian subjects

   i. Inspired by their study of Greek and Roman statues, Renaissance artists attempted to revive classical standards of beauty.

ii. It is important to remember that Renaissance artists did not abandon Christian themes and subjects. Rather, Renaissance art often combined classical forms with Christian subjects.

You do not need to memorize a long list of Renaissance artists and their works of art. Instead, focus on key masterpieces that illustrate Renaissance ideals and the impact of humanism. The five works described below are designed to provide you with a handy list of examples for multiple-choice and short-answer essay questions on the Italian Renaissance.

C. KEY EXAMPLES OF RENAISSANCE ART AND ARCHITECTURE

1. Filippo Brunelleschi, *The Dome of Florence Cathedral*
   i. Brunelleschi combined his knowledge of Roman engineering principles with innovative building techniques to construct a 100-foot-high dome that seemed to reach heavenward without any visible means of support.
   ii. The Dome became a visible and celebrated symbol of Florence's piety, power, and ingenuity.
2. Michelangelo, *David*
   i. *David's* contrapposto (stiff right leg and relaxed left leg) pose recalls statues from Greece and Rome.
   ii. Like many classical statues, *David* is a nude. However, unlike the serene classical statues, *David* defiantly faces Goliath. His muscular body is tense with gathering power as God's champion prepares for battle.
   iii. *David* can be viewed as a metaphor for Florence's victory over Milan. *David* symbolizes Florence while the unseen Goliath symbolizes Milan.
3. Raphael, *The School of Athens*
   i. *The School of Athens* depicts a gathering of ancient philosophers from various eras. The sages seem to move freely in a carefully designed three-dimensional space.
   ii. The toga-clad figures of Plato and Aristotle dominate the center of the painting.

iii. Raphael underscored the rising status of Renaissance artists by including portraits of his contemporaries among the ancient philosophers. For example, Plato is a portrait of Leonardo da Vinci. Raphael also included a portrait of himself on the far right, looking out at the viewer.

iv. *The School of Athens* brilliantly illustrates the Renaissance ideals of order, unity, and symmetry.

4. Piero della Francesca, *Federico de Montefeltro and Battista Sforza*

i. State portraits became popular in fifteenth-century Italy.

ii. Piero della Francesca (1439–1492) painted a double portrait of Duke Frederico de Montefeltro and his wife Battista Sforza.

iii. The portraits celebrate the power of the aristocratic elite. For example, Federico's hat and coat are rendered in the red color that had been conventional for portrait busts of Roman emperors.

5. Michelangelo, *Sistine Chapel Ceiling*

i. The 300 figures in the Sistine Chapel Ceiling represent a stunning fulfillment of the Renaissance goal of combining ancient Classical form with Christian subject matter.

ii. The *Creation of Adam* panel marks the culmination of a century of Renaissance research into the nature and possibilities of human anatomy. While Adam's body has the beauty of a Greek god, his face burns with an inner intensity inspired by his closeness to God.

iii. Both the Sistine Chapel Ceiling and St. Peter's Basilica provide visual symbols of the power of the Renaissance papacy.

VII. WOMEN DURING THE RENAISSANCE

A. THE DEBATE ABOUT WOMEN

1. The beginning of the Renaissance coincided with a "debate about women" (*querelle des femmes).*

2. Humanist scholars and others debated women's character, nature, and role in society.

B. CHRISTINE DE PIZAN (1364–1430), THE FIRST FEMINIST

1. Pizan was a prolific writer who became the first woman in European history to earn a living as an author.
2. Pizan wrote a history of famous women designed to refute "masculine myths" about women. She is now remembered as Europe's first feminist.

C. HUMANISM AND WOMEN

1. Renaissance humanism represented a real advance for aristocratic women.
2. Well-to-do girls received a humanistic education similar to boys. For example, young ladies studied the classics, played musical instruments, and corresponded with their families and friends.

D. CASTIGLIONE AND THE PERFECT COURT LADY

1. As mentioned earlier, Castiglione believed the perfect court lady should be attractive, well educated, and able to paint, dance, and play a musical instrument.
2. Although well educated, Castiglione's court lady was not expected to actively participate in political, artistic, or literary affairs. Instead, she should be a pleasing and attractive "ornament" for her upper-class husband.

E. ISABELLA D'ESTE (1475–1539), THE FIRST LADY OF THE RENAISSANCE

1. Isabella d'Este was the most famous Renaissance woman.
2. She was born into the ruling family of Ferrara and married the ruler of Mantua.
3. She was an art patron whose collection included works by many of the greatest Renaissance artists. Her life illustrates that becoming a patron of the arts was the most socially acceptable role for a well-educated Renaissance woman.
4. Isabella d'Este also provides an important example of how women often played an important role in smaller Renaissance courts.

F. LIMITATIONS ON WOMEN'S LIVES

1. Humanism only affected a relatively small number of Renaissance women.

2. The vast majority of Renaissance women did not experience any significant loosening in the restraints that traditionally restricted their lives. For example, women were excluded from guilds and denied basic civil rights.
3. Renaissance women continued to lead highly circumscribed lives. They were expected to participate in the endless labor required to provide food and clothing for their families. In addition, childbearing and child-raising severely restricted their freedom.

The role of women in the Italian Renaissance provides an excellent example of the processes of continuity and change. Although a few noteworthy women in the wealthiest class did experience significant gains in status, it is important to remember that humanism did not affect the lives of the majority of Renaissance women.

Chapter 4

The Northern Renaissance

I. THE NORTHERN RENAISSANCE

A. CONTACT WITH THE ITALIAN RENAISSANCE

1. During the late 1400s, students and artists from Northern Europe traveled to Italy where they became acquainted with the "new learning" and the new style of painting.
2. At the same time, merchants from the Low Countries, as well as France, Germany, and England, also visited Italy and learned about the advances of the Italian Renaissance.

B. CHRISTIAN HUMANISM

northern humanism = christian humanism

1. Northern humanists were often called Christian humanists. Like their Italian counterparts, the Christian humanists closely studied classical sources. However, they also sought to give humanism a specifically Christian context.
2. Christian humanists wanted to combine the classical ideals of calmness and stoical patience with the Christian virtues of piety, humility, and love. They believed that this fusion would create the best code of virtuous conduct.
3. Christian humanists were committed to moral and institutional reform.

It is important to understand the difference between Italian humanists and Northern humanists. While both studied classical texts, the Northern humanists also studied early Christian texts and were far more concerned with religious piety than their Italian counterparts.

northern cared abt christianism and wanted a merge of humanism

II. KEY FIGURES IN THE NORTHERN RENAISSANCE

A. DESIDERIUS ERASMUS (1466–1536)

1. Known as the "prince of the humanists," Erasmus was the most famous and influential humanist of the Northern Renaissance.
2. The greatest scholar of his age, Erasmus edited the works of the Church Fathers and produced Greek and Latin editions of the New Testament.
3. Erasmus is best known for writing *The Praise of Folly*, a witty satire that poked fun at greedy merchants, pompous priests, and quarrelsome scholars. Erasmus saved his most stinging barbs for the immorality and hypocrisy of church leaders, including Pope Julius II.
4. Erasmus was a devout Catholic committed to reforming the church from within. He called for the Church to return to simple, essential Christianity. Erasmus stressed that true religion was a matter of inward sincerity and pious devotion rather than outward observances such as pilgrimages or venerating relics.
5. Erasmus's hope for peaceful reform was shattered when Martin Luther nailed his Ninety-five Theses to the door of the Castle Church in Wittenberg.

B. THOMAS MORE (1478–1535)

1. More was the leading humanist scholar in England. A renowned author, lawyer, and statesman, More held many high public offices including lord chancellor under Henry VIII.
2. More is best known for writing *Utopia* (meaning "Nowhere"), a novel describing an imaginary society located somewhere off the mainland of the New World. The country of Utopia featured religious toleration, a humanist education for both men and women, and communal ownership of property.

C. MICHEL DE MONTAIGNE (1533–1592)

1. Montaigne was one of the most influential writers of the French Renaissance.
2. He is best known for popularizing the essay as a literary genre. Montaigne's writings feature numerous vivid anecdotes and a

skeptical tone best illustrated by his famous question, *Que sais-je?* ("What do I know?").

III. THE PRINTING REVOLUTION

A. JOHANNES GUTENBERG AND THE PRINTING PRESS

1. Johannes Gutenberg is credited with inventing the first printing press with movable type. In 1456, the first full work ever printed by movable type, the Mazarin Bible, was published.
2. Printing quickly spread across Europe. The Low Countries along with prosperous Italian and German cities became early centers of the printing revolution.
3. By 1500, presses in over 200 cities printed copies of about 40,000 books, pamphlets, and broadsides. Historians estimate that as many as 10 million items may have been printed, far more than the number of books produced in all of previous Western history.

B. IMPACT OF THE PRINTING PRESS

1. The ideas of Petrarch and other early Renaissance humanists spread slowly from person to person by a laborious process of hand copying. In contrast, the printing revolution enabled the ideas of Erasmus, Montaigne, and More to spread rapidly across Europe.
2. The diffusion of learning stimulated scholarship and exposed more people to fresh ideas.
3. The printing revolution promoted the growth of vernacular literature and national cultures.
4. Printing technology enhanced royal authority by enabling monarchs to print laws and spread propaganda.
5. At the same time, the printing revolution undermined the authority of the Church. For example, printing presses disseminated Luther's revolutionary ideas, thus helping to promote the Protestant Revolution.

The printing press had a revolutionary impact upon European life and thought. APEURO test writers often compose short-answer essay questions asking students to describe and analyze how the printing press altered European culture between 1450 and 1600. Like today's internet, the printing press promoted freedom of expression, disseminated information, and challenged the power of established authorities to control divergent views. At the same time, it is important to remember that the printing press also enabled monarchs to quickly spread their royal decrees.

IV. NORTHERN RENAISSANCE ART

A. CHARACTERISTICS

1. Northern Renaissance artists were the first to use and perfect oil painting.
2. The new oil paints enabled Renaissance artists to paint reality precisely as it appeared. Their works are renowned for meticulous details of everyday objects.
3. Many of the everyday objects in Northern Renaissance paintings are actually disguised symbols. For example, in *The Arnolfini Wedding,* the dog represents fidelity and the discarded shoes are a sign that a religious ceremony is taking place. At the time, people believed that touching the ground with bare feet ensured fertility.

B. KEY ARTISTS

1. Jan van Eyck (1390–1441)
   - i. Van Eyck was the most acclaimed Flemish artist of the fifteenth century.
   - ii. He was one of the pioneers in oil painting.
   - iii. Van Eyck is best known for the *Ghent Altarpiece* and *The Arnolfini Wedding.*

2. Albrecht Dürer (1471–1528)
   i. Dürer was the first Northern Renaissance artist to fully absorb the innovations of the Italian Renaissance.
   ii. He is best known for his woodcuts and self-portraits.
3. Hans Holbein the Younger (1497–1543)
   i. Like Dürer, Holbein blended the Northern Renaissance's love of precise realism with the Italian Renaissance's love of balanced proportion and perspective.
   ii. His best-known works are his realistic portraits of Henry VIII and Thomas More.
   iii. The portraits of Henry VIII are an excellent example of how portraits were used to visually express the rising power of the new monarchs.

The New Monarchs

I. THE RISE OF THE NEW MONARCHS

A. CHARACTERISTICS OF MEDIEVAL KINGS

1. Medieval kings received most of their income from their own estates and from grants of money from their vassals.
2. Medieval kings marched to war followed by an army of vassals who owed military service in exchange for land.
3. Medieval kings relied upon nobles for advice and counsel.
4. Powerful nobles waged war, taxed their peasants, and administered and enforced the law—all rights that were normally the prerogatives of a sovereign state.

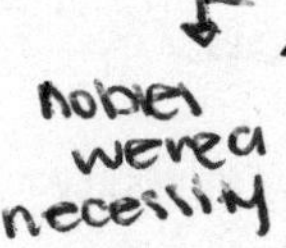

5. Medieval kings shared power with the Church and were often subordinate to the pope.

B. CHARACTERISTICS OF THE NEW MONARCHS

1. Between 1450 and 1550 strong rulers known as new monarchs unified France, England, and Spain.
2. The new monarchs retained their feudal income while also taxing towns, merchants, and peasants.
3. The new monarchs created professional armies that were paid from the royal treasury.
4. The new monarchs created a more centralized administrative bureaucracy that relied upon educated and loyal middle-class officials.
5. The new monarchs negotiated a new relationship with the Catholic Church.

C. FACTORS RESPONSIBLE FOR THE RISE OF THE NEW MONARCHS

1. Innovations in military weapons dramatically increased the power of the new monarchs. For example, cannonballs propelled by gunpowder enabled royal armies to breach the once impregnable stone walls of feudal castles. At the same time, soldiers equipped with new muzzle-loaded firearms could fire volleys that decimated the ranks of armored knights.

2. The growth of towns produced an increasingly prosperous middle class that prized peace and helped rulers establish and enforce predictable laws.

3. The development of a centralized administration gave the new monarchs greater control over commerce and trade.

II. NEW MONARCHS IN FRANCE, ENGLAND, AND SPAIN

A. FRANCE

1. Charles VII (reigned 1422–1461)

   i. Charles VII successfully concluded the Hundred Years' War by expelling the English from France.

   ii. He strengthened royal finances through such taxes as the taille (on land) and the gabelle (on salt). These two taxes were the main source of royal income for the next three centuries.

   iii. He combined cavalry and archers to form Europe's first permanent royal army. Charles VII completed 60 successful castle sieges in just one year.

   iv. He established a royal council, using middle-class merchants as his officials. Charles VII chose his advisors so wisely that he won the nickname "Charles the Well-Served."

2. Louis XI (reigned 1461–1483)

   i. Louis XI earned the nickname the "Spider King" because of his treacherous character and ruthless use of power. For example, he imprisoned a disloyal cardinal in a small cage for 11 excruciating years.

   ii. He encouraged economic growth by promoting new industries such as silk weaving.

3. Francis I (reigned 1515–1547)

   i. Francis I was the first French king to be called "Your Majesty."

   ii. He reached an agreement with Pope Leo X known as the Concordat of Bologna (1516), which authorized the king to nominate bishops, abbots, and other high officials of the Catholic Church in France. This agreement gave the French monarch administrative control over the Church.

B. ENGLAND

1. Henry VII (reigned 1485–1509)

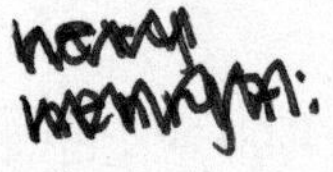

   i. Henry VII created a special court known as the Star Chamber as a political weapon to try prominent nobles. Court sessions were held in secret with no right of appeal, no juries, and no witnesses.

   ii. He used justices of the peace to extend royal authority into the local shires.

   iii. He encouraged the wool industry and expanded the English merchant marine.

2. Henry VIII (reigned 1509–1547)

   i. Henry VIII declared the king the supreme head of the Church of England, thus severing England's ties with the Catholic Church.

   ii. He dissolved the monasteries and confiscated their land and wealth.

C. SPAIN

1. The Iberian Peninsula in the mid-fifteenth century

   i. During this time, the Iberian Peninsula enjoyed a rich cultural diversity that included prominent Jewish and Muslim communities.

   ii. The kingdoms of Castile and Aragon dominated Navarre and Portugal. The Muslims held only the small kingdom of Granada.

2. Ferdinand (reigned 1479–1516) and Isabella (reigned 1474–1504)
   i. The marriage of Ferdinand of Aragon and Isabella of Castile (1469) created a dynastic union of the Iberian Peninsula's two most powerful royal houses.
   ii. Ferdinand and Isabella reduced the number of nobles on the royal council.
   iii. Ferdinand and Isabella completed the *Reconquista* by conquering Granada and incorporating it into the Spanish kingdom.
   iv. Isabella decreed that in a Christian state, there could be only "one king, one law, one faith." She and Ferdinand established the Inquisition to enforce religious conformity.
   v. In 1492, Ferdinand and Isabella issued an edict expelling all practicing Jews from Spain. Ten years later, they demanded that all Muslims adopt Christianity or leave Spain.

D. A COMPETITIVE STATE SYSTEM

1. By 1600, new monarchs in France, England, and Spain boasted standing armies, royal courts, and the financial support of increasingly prosperous merchants.
2. The emergence of powerful monarchs in France, England, and Spain marked the beginning of Europe's competitive state system.
3. The competitive state system promoted the practice of modern diplomacy. Rulers sent official representatives to rival nations in order to be informed about their plans and policies. The new diplomacy encouraged negotiation and prevented war.
4. The new diplomacy encouraged balance-of-power politics. Unrestrained by religious or legal limitations, sovereign rulers strove for power and wealth. When one nation posed a threat to neighboring states, they responded by forming a coalition to preserve the balance of power.

APEURO test writers often ask students to write short-answer essays describing the key features of the new monarchies in France, England, and Spain in the period between 1450 and 1550.

The Age of Exploration and the Commercial Revolution

I. FACTORS THAT ENCOURAGED EUROPEAN OVERSEAS EXPLORATION

A. THE RENAISSANCE SPIRIT OF INDIVIDUALISM

1. The explorers embodied the same spirit of individualism and curiosity that characterized Renaissance artists and humanist scholars.
2. The renewed interest in ancient writings that inspired Renaissance artists also gave the explorers new knowledge about mathematics, astronomy, and geography.

B. THE SEARCH FOR SPICES AND PROFITS

1. The Crusades helped stimulate a growing demand for Indian pepper, Chinese ginger, and Malukan cloves and nutmeg.
2. By the fourteenth century, European demand for Asian spices and luxury items far exceeded the supply. Muslims and Venetians controlled trade routes to the East.
3. The new monarchs in Spain and Portugal wanted direct access to the lucrative Asian markets.

C. THE DESIRE TO CULTIVATE CASH CROPS

1. A strong and growing demand for sugar motivated Europeans to look for lands suitable for cultivating this prized cash crop.
2. Europeans hoped to find lands where they could establish sugar plantations.

D. THE DESIRE TO SPREAD CHRISTIANITY

1. The Crusades left a legacy of hostility between Christians and Muslims.
2. Led by Spain and Portugal, Europeans hoped to reconquer northern Africa from the Muslims.
3. Europeans believed they had a duty to spread Christianity.

E. THE ABILITY TO USE NEW TECHNOLOGY

1. The newly designed caravel had square sails for running before the wind and triangular sails for tacking into the wind.
2. The magnetic compass and the astrolabe enabled mariners to determine their location at sea.

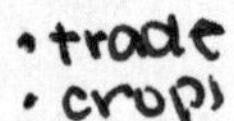

II. PORTUGAL: EAST BY SEA TO AN EMPIRE OF SPICES

A. PRINCE HENRY THE NAVIGATOR (1394–1460)

1. Prince Henry organized voyages along the west coast of Africa.
2. By the time of Prince Henry's death in 1460, the Portuguese had established a series of trading posts along the West African coast. These posts did a thriving business in gold and slaves.

B. THE PORTUGUESE TRADING-POST EMPIRE

1. Key explorers
   - i. Bartholomew Diaz rounded the Cape of Good Hope and returned to Portugal in 1488.
   - ii. Vasco da Gama reached the Malabar coast of India in 1498 and returned to Portugal with a cargo of pepper and cinnamon worth 60 times the cost of the expedition.
   - iii. Pedro Cabral accidentally discovered Brazil in 1500 while sailing to India. He returned to Portugal with 300,000 pounds of spices.
2. Commercial trading posts
   - i. The Portuguese did not attempt to conquer territories. Instead, they built fortified trading posts designed to control trade routes.

ii. The most important Portuguese trading posts were located at Goa on the Indian coast, at Malacca on the Malay peninsula, and at Macao on the southern coast of China.

C. CONSEQUENCES

1. The Portuguese ended the Venetian and Muslim monopoly of trade with Asia.
2. The center of European commerce shifted from the Mediterranean Sea to the Atlantic Ocean.
3. The new sea routes reduced the importance of the Baltic Sea, thus leading to the decline of the Hanseatic League.

III. SPAIN: WEST BY SEA TO A NEW WORLD

A. CHRISTOPHER COLUMBUS (1451–1506)

1. Although he believed he had reached Asia, Columbus had in fact discovered Caribbean islands that were part of a vast New World.
2. Columbus's voyages helped to propel Spain into the forefront of European exploration, conquest, and settlement.

B. THE SPANISH CONQUESTS

1. Hernando Cortes conquered the Aztec empire in Mexico (1519–1521).
2. Francisco Pizarro conquered the Inca empire in Peru (1532–1533).

C. SPANISH AMERICA

1. By the end of the sixteenth century, Spain possessed an American empire twenty times its own size.
2. The Aztecs and other indigenous peoples were converted to Christianity and became subjects of the Spanish king.
3. The king of Spain governed his American empire through a Council of the Indies in Spain and through viceroys in Mexico City and Lima, Peru.

IV. THE COLUMBIAN EXCHANGE

A. INTRODUCTION

1. The Age of Exploration—also called the Age of Discovery—involved more than just the search for gold, silver, and spices.
2. The new discoveries sparked an unprecedented global diffusion of agricultural products, animals, diseases, and human populations.

B. NEW WORLD TO OLD WORLD

1. Agricultural products: potatoes, maize, tomatoes, peanuts, tobacco, vanilla, and chocolate
2. Animals: turkeys
3. Diseases: possibly syphilis

C. OLD WORLD TO NEW WORLD

1. Agricultural products: coffee, cane sugar, wheat, and rice
2. Animals: cows, horses, pigs, sheep, goats, and chickens
3. Diseases: smallpox, measles, and diphtheria
4. Human populations: European colonists and African slaves

D. CONSEQUENCES OF THE COLUMBIAN EXCHANGE

1. For the New World
   - i. European diseases decimated indigenous populations. Approximately 90 percent of the indigenous peoples of the Americas perished between 1492 and 1600.
   - ii. The sudden collapse of entire New World communities enabled European colonists to more easily gain control over Native American lands.
2. For Europe
   - i. Nutritious New World crops revolutionized the European diet and fueled a surge in European population.
   - ii. The influx of gold and silver facilitated economic growth and contributed to the rising prosperity of the merchant class in Western Europe.

iii. The wealth generated by New World colonies facilitated Western Europe's historic shift from a stagnant feudal economy to a new and more energetic commercial capitalist economy.

3. For Africa

i. The Spanish quickly discovered that coffee and sugar flourished in New World soils and climates. These highly prized crops produced great profits but required a large labor force.

ii. The severe drop in the New World population forced the Spanish to look to Africa for a source of labor. Between the sixteenth and nineteenth centuries, European slave traders forcibly transported over 10 million Africans to the Americas. The African slave trade marked the largest involuntary migration of people in human history.

E. SUGAR AND SLAVERY

1. The history of slavery became intertwined with the cultivation of sugar.
2. Columbus introduced sugar cane to Hispaniola. Within a short time, a "white gold" rush began on sugar plantations and spread across the island.
3. Sugar quickly became the most valuable cash crop grown in the British Empire. For example, by 1700 the English West Indies produced 25,000 tons of sugar, worth four times the value of Chesapeake tobacco.
4. Sugar plantations required large fields, costly equipment, and a huge labor force working under strict supervision. The overwhelming majority worked on plantations in the Caribbean and Brazil.

V. THE COMMERCIAL REVOLUTION

A. CAUSES

1. New ocean trade routes

i. The trade in spices, sugar, and precious metals brought great wealth to the European trading nations.

ii. The wealth supported increased investment and a wide array of new economic ventures.

2. Growth of population

   i. The introduction of new foods played a key role in supporting population growth.

   ii. The population of Europe increased from 70 million in 1500 to 90 million in 1600.

   iii. The steady rise in population increased overall demand for goods and services.

3. Price revolution

   i. During the sixteenth century, the Western European economy experienced a steady inflation in prices.

   ii. The influx of gold and silver from the New World and the rising demand created by the growth of population contributed to the price revolution.

4. New nation-centered economic system

   i. Prior to 1500, the Western European economy was organized around towns and guilds. Both relied upon strict regulations to ensure their survival. As a result, there was very little innovation.

   ii. As commercial activity increased, a new nation-centered economic system began to replace the old town-and-guild framework.

B. KEY FEATURES

1. New entrepreneurs

   i. The expansion of commercial activity created large geographic markets. The new trading areas opened new opportunities while also requiring a new kind of economic leadership.

   ii. As the commercial revolution replaced the town-and-guild framework, merchants and bankers emerged as influential and successful entrepreneurs.

   iii. The Italian Medici family and the German Fuggers were prominent examples of the new economic entrepreneurs.

2. New industries
   i. The printing press created a national and even international market for books.
   ii. The new ocean trading routes sparked a rise in shipbuilding.
   iii. The emergence of nation-states supported the large-scale manufacture of cannons and muskets.
3. New domestic or putting-out system
   i. Strict guild regulations stifled competition and restricted production.
   ii. In order to avoid the restrictive guild system, entrepreneurs provided cloth, looms, and other equipment to rural families.
   iii. The putting-out or domestic system led to a significant increase in the production of cloth and other manufactured goods.
4. New joint-stock companies
   i. The new international trade required unprecedented amounts of capital. For example, merchants had to arm their ships, buy special privileges for local authorities, and build trading posts. Wars, storms, and rivals all threatened profits.
   ii. English and Dutch merchants formed joint-stock companies to maximize profits and limit risks.
   iii. Investors in a joint-stock company bought shares of ownership. If the company went bankrupt, its owners lost their investment. If the companies prospered, the investors' shares of ownership entitled them to collect a proportional share of the profits.

C. MERCANTILISM

1. The rulers of the new nation-states adopted a system of economic principles and policies called mercantilism.
2. Mercantilists wanted to build strong, self-sufficient economies.
3. According to mercantilist theory, colonies should export raw materials and import finished goods. This would create a favorable balance of trade and the resulting growth of national reserves of gold and silver.

Joint-stock companies and mercantilism are well-known economic terms that have generated a number of multiple-choice and short-answer essay questions. Given the emphasis on these terms, it is easy to overlook the putting-out system. Don't make this mistake. APEURO exams could include a set of multiple-choice questions designed to test your knowledge of the causes and consequences of the putting-out system.

D. CONSEQUENCES

1. Decline of early commercial centers
   i. During the 1400s, a confederacy of Baltic towns known as the Hanseatic League dominated northern European trade. As the center of European trade shifted to the rising nation-states in Western Europe, the Hanseatic League rapidly declined.
   ii. Led by Venice, Italian city-states had controlled the lucrative trade with India. The Portuguese broke this monopoly by pioneering a new sea route to Asia.
2. Rise of capitalism
   i. Capitalism is an economic system in which capital, or wealth, is invested to produce more capital.
   ii. Capitalism is based upon the private ownership of property such as land, raw materials, and equipment.
   iii. Capitalists are motivated by a desire to earn profits.
   iv. The Age of Discovery ushered in a new economic era dominated by commercial capitalism.
3. Rise of the bourgeoisie
   i. As commercial capitalism expanded so did the class of entrepreneurs. The new middle class became known as the bourgeoisie.
   ii. As commercial capitalism expanded, so did the wealth and power of the bourgeoisie.

UNIT 2 Age of Reformation

c. 1450 to c. 1648

Chapters 7–9

PREVIEW: UNIT 2 KEY CONCEPTS

- Religious pluralism challenged the concept of a unified Europe.
  - The Protestant and Catholic reformations fundamentally changed theology, religious institutions, culture, and attitudes toward wealth and prosperity.
  - Religious reform both increased state control of religious institutions and provided justifications for challenging state authority.
  - Conflicts among religious groups overlapped with political and economic competition within and among states.
- European society and the experiences of everyday life were increasingly shaped by commercial and agricultural capitalism, notwithstanding the continued existence of medieval social and economic structures.
  - Population shifts and growing commerce caused the expansion of cities, which often placed stress on their traditional political and social structures.
  - The family remained the primary social and economic institution of early modern Europe and took several forms, including the nuclear family.
  - Popular culture, leisure activities, and rituals reflecting the continued popularity of folk ideas reinforced and sometimes challenged communal ties and norms.
- The struggle for sovereignty within and among states resulted in varying degrees of political centralization.
  - The new concept of the sovereign state and secular systems of law played a central role in the creation of new political institutions.

The Protestant Reformation

I. LUTHERANISM

A. MARTIN LUTHER'S PERSONAL QUEST FOR SALVATION

1. Luther's early life was dominated by a private struggle to find the key to personal salvation.
2. The Catholic Church taught that salvation could be achieved by both good works and faith. For many long years, Luther struggled to follow this dual path to salvation. However, he was overwhelmed by a deep sense of personal guilt.
3. After many years of study, Luther began to examine St. Paul's Letter to the Romans. One evening, Luther read Paul's admonition that "the just shall be saved by faith."
4. Luther's arduous years of study prepared him for this fateful moment. At last he understood that salvation was a gift freely given by God.

B. NINETY-FIVE THESES

1. Luther's spiritual journey seemed to culminate in a personal revelation. But then historic events intersected with his life.
2. In 1517, Luther witnessed Johann Tetzel selling indulgences near Wittenberg. In Luther's time, an indulgence was a certificate granted by the pope in return for the payment of a fee to the church. The certificate stated that the soul of the dead relative or friend of the purchaser would have his time in purgatory reduced by many years or canceled altogether.
3. Part of the income from the indulgences sold by Tetzel was destined for Rome to help pay for the construction of the new St. Peter's Basilica.

4. Tetzel's aggressive marketing tactics appalled Luther. He believed that salvation could not be sold by the pope; it was a free gift given by God.
5. On October 31, 1517, Luther dramatically nailed his Ninety-five Theses to the door of the Castle Church in Wittenberg. Aided by the printing press, Luther's defiant challenge was soon disseminated across Europe. Within a short time, he became the most famous and controversial person in Europe.

C. LUTHER'S KEY BELIEFS

1. Salvation is achieved by faith alone.
   - i. The Catholic Church had long taught that salvation could be achieved by both faith and good works.
   - ii. Luther insisted that faith was the only path to salvation.
2. The Bible is the only valid authority for Christian life.
   - i. The Catholic Church taught that authority rests in both the Bible and the traditional teachings of the church.
   - ii. Luther insisted that all church teachings should be based on the Word of God as revealed in the Bible.
   - iii. Based upon his study of the Bible, Luther argued that Christ established just two sacraments: baptism and the Eucharist or Holy Communion. Luther thus rejected the Catholic teaching that there were seven sacraments.
3. The church consists of a priesthood of all believers.
   - i. The Roman Catholic Church was a hierarchical organization led by the pope.
   - ii. Luther insisted that because all Christians are spiritually equal, the church consists of the entire community of the Christian faithful.
4. All vocations have equal merit.
   - i. The Catholic Church taught that the monastic life was superior to the secular life.
   - ii. Luther rejected this belief, arguing that all honest work has equal merit. Each person should serve God in his or her own individual calling.
   - iii. Luther abolished monasteries and convents. He declared that the clergy should marry.

D. THE GERMAN PEASANTS' WAR, 1525

1. Causes
   i. German peasants originally supported Luther. They heard his message as one that promised freedom from oppression by the landlords and the clergy.
   ii. Complaints that nobles had seized village common lands and imposed exorbitant rents soon escalated to open attacks on monasteries, castles, and prosperous farms.
2. Luther's response
   i. The peasants believed Luther would support them. Luther, however, believed that Christians ought to obey their rulers—even unjust rulers—and that rebellion against the state was always wrong and must be crushed.
   ii. Horrified at the prospect of a bloody revolution, Luther urged the German nobility to crush the rebels.
3. Consequences
   i. The German Peasants' War of 1525 strengthened the authority of the German nobility.
   ii. Lutheranism became closely allied with the established political order controlled by the German nobility.

It is easy to focus on Luther's dramatic stand against indulgences while ignoring his response to the German Peasants' War. Don't make this mistake. The German Peasants' War can be used in short-answer essay questions as part of a discussion of the political and social consequences of the Protestant Reformation.

E. LUTHER AND THE ROLE OF CHRISTIAN WOMEN

1. The elimination of monasteries and convents was a key factor in changing the role of sixteenth-century women.
2. Luther believed that Christian women should strive to be models of obedience and Christian charity.

F. THE SPREAD OF LUTHERANISM

1. Lutheranism became the dominant religion in northern and eastern Germany. It is important to remember that most of southern Germany, Austria, and the Rhineland remained Roman Catholic.

2. Lutheranism became the predominant religion in Denmark, Norway, and Sweden.

G. THE PEACE OF AUGSBURG, 1555

1. Between 1546 and 1555, a religious civil war between Catholics led by Charles V and Protestants led by German princes tore Germany apart. It is important to note that the Catholic king of France supported the Protestant nobles. This is an example of the long-standing French policy of maintaining a divided Germany.

2. The Peace of Augsburg ended the civil war. The settlement gave each German prince the right to determine the religion of his state, either Roman Catholic or Lutheran. The Peace of Augsburg did not provide for the recognition of Calvinists and other religious minorities.

H. WAS LUTHER A REVOLUTIONARY OR A CONSERVATIVE?

1. Luther was a religious revolutionary.

   i. Luther's core beliefs went well beyond attempting to reform the Roman Catholic Church. His doctrines of justification by faith, priesthood of all believers, and the Bible as the sole authority marked a major departure from long-standing Catholic principles.

   ii. Luther's revolutionary actions included abolishing monasteries, reducing the number of sacraments, encouraging priests to marry, and repudiating the pope's authority to interpret the Bible.

   iii. Luther's belief that everyone should read the Bible led to the encouragement of education and the growth of literacy.

2. Luther was a political conservative.

   i. Luther insisted that Christians owed obedience to established authority. He maintained that religious reform should not affect the political status quo, except for its impact on the break with the papacy.

ii. Luther gave his support to the German nobility as they brutally suppressed the peasant rebellion.

II. CALVINISM

A. JOHN CALVIN'S KEY BELIEFS

1. Calvin's doctrines are clearly and systematically explained in his landmark book, *The Institutes of the Christian Religion*.
2. Calvin asserted that while God is just, perfect, and omnipotent, humans are corrupt, weak, and insignificant.
3. Since men and women are by nature sinful, they cannot actively work to achieve salvation. Because God is all-knowing, he has "determined, both whom he would admit to salvation and whom he would condemn to destruction." This "terrible decree" constitutes the theological principle called predestination.
4. By God's grace, a very few people will be saved from sin. Calvin called these people the "elect." → saved = elect
5. Calvin taught that the elect have a duty to rule society so as to glorify God. The ideal government should therefore be a theocracy in which church leaders dominate civil authorities.
6. Calvin and Luther agreed on many fundamental points of theology. However, they disagreed on the emphasis placed upon predestination and the relationship between church and civil authorities. While Luther believed that the church should be subordinated to the state, Calvin stressed that the elect have a duty to Christianize the state.

B. GENEVA, "CITY OF SAINTS"

1. In 1541, Protestants in Geneva, Switzerland, asked Calvin to transform their city into a model Christian community.
2. Calvin and his followers regulated all aspects of life in Geneva. They suppressed frivolous activities such as playing cards, dancing, and attending the theater. At the same time, they strictly enforced a high standard of morality that included regular church attendance.

C. THE SPREAD OF CALVINISM

1. Protestant reformers from France, England, and Scotland hailed Calvin's Geneva as "the most perfect school of Christ since the days of the Apostles." Geneva thus became both the center of Calvin's reformed church and a compelling model for other Protestant leaders.
2. In the late 1550s, John Knox brought Calvinism to Scotland. Within a decade, the Presbyterian Church founded by Knox and his followers became the basis for Scotland's established religion.
3. Calvinism soon spread to France where followers were called Huguenots. The new faith had particular appeal to French nobles and members of the middle class many of whom saw themselves as members of the elect.
4. Calvinists also founded Puritan churches in England and later in New England.

III. ANGLICANISM

A. HENRY VIII (REIGNED 1509–1547)

1. The "Defender of the Faith"
   - i. Henry VIII was a devout Catholic who detested Luther.
   - ii. Henry wrote a pamphlet calling Luther "a great limb of the Devil." Impressed by Henry's loyalty, the pope gave him a special title, "Defender of the Faith."
2. The problem of succession
   - i. Henry's political needs proved more important than his loyalty to the pope.
   - ii. Since Henry was only the second king of the Tudor dynasty, he was determined to have a male heir. When his wife, Catherine of Aragon, failed to give birth to a son, Henry asked Pope Clement VII to annul the marriage.
   - iii. The pope would normally have granted Henry's request. However, Catherine of Aragon was the aunt of the Holy Roman Emperor Charles V. At the time of Henry's request, Charles's armies controlled Rome. Caught between the plea of a distant English king and the immediate presence of a

powerful Holy Roman emperor, the pope delayed and finally refused to annul Henry's marriage.

3. The Act of Supremacy, 1534
   i. Thwarted by the pope, Henry turned to a radical solution to solve his marriage problem.
   ii. In 1533, Henry defied the pope, secretly married Anne Boleyn, and annulled his marriage to Catherine.
   iii. The following year, Parliament passed the Act of Supremacy. This landmark act declared the English king to be the "Protector and Only Supreme Head of the Church and Clergy of England."
   iv. Although Henry VIII rejected papal supremacy, he remained a devout Catholic. In 1539, Parliament approved the Six Articles defining the doctrine of the English Church. With the sole exception of papal supremacy, the Six Articles reaffirmed Catholic teachings while rejecting Protestant beliefs.
4. Dissolution of the monasteries
   i. Beginning in 1536, Parliament passed acts closing all English monasteries and seizing their lands.
   ii. Henry sold much of the land to nobles and to members of England's increasingly prosperous merchant class.
   iii. Enriched by the monastic lands, these groups became loyal supporters of the Tudor dynasty.

B. MAKING COMPARISONS: HENRY VIII AND MARTIN LUTHER

1. At first glance, Henry VIII and Martin Luther had very little in common. Henry rejected Luther's core doctrines, and the two exchanged derisive pamphlets filled with insults. Guided by his faith, Luther wanted to reform and then change the Catholic Church. Guided by his dynastic interests, Henry wanted a male heir in order to avoid a potentially bloody succession.
2. Henry VIII and Martin Luther had very different religious beliefs and motives. Nonetheless, they shared similar political attitudes. Both believed that the church should be subordinate to the state. Both Henry VIII and Martin Luther rejected papal authority. In addition, both followed policies intended to strengthen the nobility. As we have seen, Luther supported the nobility by encouraging them to suppress the rebellious peasants. Henry supported the nobility by allowing them to purchase monastic lands.

C. ELIZABETH I (REIGNED 1558–1603)

1. Religious issues

   i. Elizabeth I inherited a difficult religious problem. Since Henry VIII's break with Rome in 1534, royal religious policy had changed direction several times.

   ii. Protestants gained strength under Edward VI (reigned 1547–1553). Catholics experienced a renewal under Mary (reigned 1553–1558).

2. The Elizabethan Settlement

   i. Elizabeth was a politique who placed political necessities above her personal beliefs. She therefore strove to find a middle course that moderate Catholics and moderate Protestants would accept.

   ii. The Elizabethan Settlement restored the Church of England. Also known as the Anglican Church, the Church of England allowed priests to marry and to conduct sermons in English. However, the Church of England retained archbishops and bishops who wore elaborate robes and conducted services that remained formal and traditional.

   iii. Although Protestant in tone, the Church of England instituted dogmas that were deliberately broad and often ambiguous.

D. MAKING COMPARISONS: ISABELLA OF SPAIN AND ELIZABETH I OF ENGLAND

1. Both Queen Isabella of Spain and Queen Elizabeth I of England shared the goal of ruling over a united country. However, they followed dramatically different religious policies to achieve this goal.

2. Isabella was a devout Roman Catholic who decreed that in a Christian state, there could be only "one king, one law, one faith." She revived the Inquisition, conquered Muslim-controlled Grenada, and forced Jews and Muslims to become Christians or leave Spain. Her actions created religious unity, but at the price of harming Spain's economy.

3. Elizabeth was a politique. Although raised a Protestant, her religious views are largely unknown. What mattered most to Elizabeth was not the religious beliefs of her subjects, but their loyalty. She wanted to avoid destructive religious civil wars. It was not her intention, she said, "to pry windows into men's souls." Elizabeth's reign marked the beginning of a cultural golden age and a period of sustained economic growth and prosperity.

IV. ANABAPTISM

A. ANABAPTIST BELIEFS

1. Anabaptists, or rebaptizers, opposed infant baptism, insisting that only adult baptism conformed to Scripture.
2. Anabaptists advocated complete separation of church and state.
3. Anabaptists rejected secular agreements. For example, they refused to pay taxes, take civil oaths, hold public offices, or serve in the military.

B. ANABAPTIST LEADERS

1. Catholics, Lutherans, and Calvinists all condemned Anabaptist leaders as radicals.
2. Modern historians have labeled Thomas Münzer a "left wing" Anabaptist leader because he advocated the overthrow of the existing political and social order. Münzer was executed in 1525.
3. Luther's concept of the "priesthood of all believers" promoted an assertive spirit among Anabaptist women. For example, Elizabeth Dirks advocated gender equality, especially in the realm of church roles and the interpretation of Holy Scripture.

Most texts focus on comparing and contrasting the religious views of Luther and Calvin while devoting little attention to the Anabaptists. Don't neglect this small but influential Protestant sect. APEURO test writers often include them in short-answer essay questions.

V. THE IMPACT OF THE PROTESTANT REFORMATION ON THE ARTS

A. MARTIN LUTHER

1. Luther believed that painting and sculpture could play a role in spreading the word of God. He maintained that the visual arts could inspire and instruct illiterate worshippers who would find more meaning in paintings and sculpture than in long sermons.

2. Luther also favored incorporating music into church services. For example, he composed a number of hymns including "A Mighty Fortress Is Our God."

B. JOHN CALVIN

1. Calvin and his followers favored plain church architecture devoid of ornamentation and images.
2. Calvinists believed that ornamental architecture and paintings distracted worshippers, thus diminishing their religious experience.

C. POPULARITY OF WOODCUTS

1. Although Protestants discouraged using paintings, they did make full use of woodcuts to disseminate religious messages.
2. Albrecht Dürer's *Four Horsemen of the Apocalypse* is one of a series of fifteen famous woodcuts that vividly illustrate the terrors of the Apocalypse.

VI. THE IMPACT OF THE PROTESTANT REFORMATION ON WOMEN

A. WOMEN AND THE HOME

1. Protestants placed the family at the center of human life.
2. Protestants believed that marriage should promote a loving relationship between a man and his wife. The ideal Christian home thus became a place for love, tenderness, and other "gentler virtues." The relationship between Luther and his wife, Katherina von Bora, provides a good example of this new emphasis upon companionship.

B. WOMEN AND WORK

1. Luther taught that all vocations have equal merit in God's eyes.
2. This view gave greater dignity to wives performing routine domestic tasks.

C. WOMEN AND EDUCATION

1. Protestants placed great emphasis upon teaching people to read the Bible.

2. Mothers were often expected to teach their children how to read. This resulted in an increased emphasis on women's literacy.

D. WOMEN AND SOCIAL STATUS

1. It is important to remember that the Protestant Reformation did not challenge women's subordinate position in society. For example, women could not conduct legal transactions on their own.

The Catholic Reformation

Chapter 8

UNIT 2 | AGE OF REFORMATION

I. THE CATHOLIC REFORMATION

A. THE REFORMATION POPES

1. Renaissance popes, such as Julius II, concentrated their energies on commissioning art, building a new St. Peter's, and enhancing the power of their own families.
2. Beginning with Pope Paul III (1534–1549), a new generation of popes committed themselves to the following goals:
   - i. Defining and clarifying Church doctrine and practices
   - ii. Containing the Protestant challenge
   - iii. Reforming Church practices
   - iv. Enforcing strict moral standards
   - v. Reaffirming papal authority
   - vi. Reinvigorating the religious experience
   - vii. Creating new religious orders

B. THE COUNCIL OF TRENT

1. Reaffirmed Catholic doctrines
   - i. The Council of Trent rejected Luther's doctrine of justification by faith and reaffirmed that salvation is achieved by both faith and good works.
   - ii. The Council rejected the Protestant belief in the supremacy of the Bible and reaffirmed that equal weight should be given to Scripture and to traditional Catholic teachings.
   - iii. It rejected Luther's contention that there were just two sacraments and reaffirmed that there were seven sacraments.

↳ reaffirmed everything Luther went against

2. Reformed church abuses
   - i. The Council decreed that indulgences should no longer be sold in exchange for financial contributions.
   - ii. It forbade simony, the sale of church offices.
   - iii. The Council instructed bishops to live in the dioceses they served.
3. Reasserted traditional practices
   - i. The Council reaffirmed the veneration of relics and images as valid expressions of Christian piety.
   - ii. It confirmed the Vulgate as the authoritative Catholic edition of the Bible.
   - iii. It decreed that Latin continue to be the language of worship.
4. Resisted limiting papal authority
   - i. The Council ruled that no act of a council could be valid unless accepted by the Holy See.
   - ii. It preserved the papacy as the center of Catholic unity.

C. THE JESUITS

1. Ignatius Loyola (1491–1556)
   - i. Ignatius was an unknown Spanish soldier who suffered a severe injury while fighting the French.
   - ii. During his recovery, Ignatius experienced a religious conversion. He resolved to become a soldier of Christ and dedicate his life to fighting for the pope and the Catholic Church.
2. Society of Jesus
   - i. In 1540, Pope Paul III formally authorized the Society of Jesus. Those who joined were called Jesuits.
   - ii. Led by Ignatius, the Jesuits were a spiritual army that emphasized iron discipline and absolute obedience.
   - iii. Ignatius wrote *The Spiritual Exercises*, detailing a system of disciplined meditation, prayer, and study.

3. Activities of the Jesuits

    i. Catholic education: Jesuits founded hundreds of schools for middle- and upper-class boys. Jesuits were especially prominent as confessors and advisors to royal families.

    ii. Missionary work: Jesuit missionaries played a key role in preaching Christianity in the Americas and Asia.

    iii. Combating Protestantism: Jesuits spearheaded the revival of Catholicism in Bavaria, the southern Netherlands, and Poland.

II. BAROQUE ART

A. PURPOSE OF BAROQUE ART

1. The Protestant Reformation represented the greatest challenge to the Catholic Church since the Roman persecutions of the third century. Led by a series of reform popes, the Church launched a Catholic Counter-Reformation to halt the spread of Protestantism and reenergize the faithful.
2. The Council of Trent reaffirmed that works of art should be employed to stimulate piety and deepen the religious experience. Painters, sculptors, and architects tried to speak to the faithful by creating dramatic works of art that involved worshippers.

B. CHARACTERISTICS OF BAROQUE ART

1. Dramatic use of light and dark called tenebrism
2. Subject matter focused on dramatic moments and intense emotion
3. Portrayal of everyday people who are not idealized
4. Baroque buildings featuring grandiose scale and ornate decorations

C. KEY EXAMPLES OF ITALIAN BAROQUE ART

1. Gian Lorenzo Bernini, the *Ecstasy of Saint Teresa*: Highlights the moment when an angel pierces Saint Teresa's heart with a flaming golden arrow. Pain and pleasure merged as she felt as if God were "caressing her soul."
2. Michelangelo Merisi da Caravaggio, *The Calling of Saint Matthew*: Highlights the dramatic moment when Christ suddenly points a

beam of light on Matthew. Overwhelmed by Christ's presence, Matthew gives up his job as a tax collector and dedicates his life to Christ's service.

3. Artemisia Gentileschi, *Judith Slaying Holofernes*: Highlights the dramatic moment when Judith cuts off Holofernes' head, thus preventing the Assyrian general from destroying the land of Judah.

III. THE IMPACT OF THE CATHOLIC REFORMATION ON WOMEN

A. WOMEN AND RELIGIOUS ORDERS

1. Catholic women continued to take advantage of opportunities in religious orders sanctioned by the Church.
2. For example, the Ursuline Order of Nuns established an important order that provided religious education and training for young girls. The Ursulines used Christian education to combat heresy in France.

B. TERESA DE AVILA

1. A major Spanish leader in the reform movement for monasteries and convents. Immortalized in Bernini's famous sculpture the *Ecstasy of Saint Teresa.*
2. Preached that individuals could use prayer to establish a direct relationship with God.

Women's history is a very important strand in the AP® Euro course. It is important to understand how the Protestant Reformation (Chapter 7) and the Catholic Reformation affected the status of European women.

The Wars of Religion

I. THE WARS OF KING PHILIP II OF SPAIN

A. PHILIP'S EMPIRE

1. Emperor Charles V abdicated his many thrones in 1556. He left his territories in Austria, Bohemia, and Hungary to his brother Ferdinand.
2. Charles left his son Philip a vast empire that included Spain, Milan, Naples, the Netherlands, and the overseas empire in the Americas.

B. PHILIP'S GOALS

1. To advance Spanish power in Europe
2. To champion Catholicism in Europe
3. To defeat the Ottoman Turks in the eastern Mediterranean

C. BATTLE OF LEPANTO, 1571

1. A combined Spanish-Venetian fleet defeated the Turkish navy at Lepanto off the coast of Greece.
2. The victory enhanced Philip's prestige as a champion of Catholicism.

D. THE DEFEAT OF PHILIP: THE NETHERLANDS

1. When Philip succeeded to the throne, the Spanish Netherlands consisted of 17 largely Catholic provinces.
2. Philip threatened traditional liberties by imposing the Inquisition and dispatching troops to support it. Philip's ill-considered actions provoked riots against the Spanish authorities.

3. Philip responded to this challenge by sending 20,000 additional troops. Led by the ruthless Duke of Alva, the Spaniards levied new taxes and sentenced thousands to death.

4. Alva's brutal actions united the Netherlands against the Spanish. During the struggle, many showed their opposition to Spain by converting to Calvinism.

5. A new Spanish viceroy, the Duke of Parma, adopted more skillful tactics. By substituting diplomacy for force, Parma was able to induce the ten southern provinces to reaffirm their loyalty to Spain.

6. Led by the province of Holland, the Dutch in the seven northern provinces could not be won back. In 1581, they boldly declared their independence from Spain.

7. The war for control of the Netherlands continued until 1609. Under the terms of a truce, the 7 northern and now heavily Calvinist provinces gained their independence and were known as Dutch. The 10 Catholic southern provinces were known as the Spanish Netherlands.

E. THE DEFEAT OF PHILIP: ENGLAND

1. The English felt threatened by Philip's aggressive actions in the Netherlands.

2. Queen Elizabeth openly assisted the Dutch rebels with money and troops. She also encouraged English sea captains to raid Spanish treasure ships.

3. Outraged by Elizabeth's interference, Philip assembled a huge fleet known as the Spanish Armada to invade England. Philip hoped to depose Elizabeth and return England to Catholicism.

4. Harassed by fast English ships, the powerful but slow-moving Spanish Armada never reached England. Only 67 of the Armada's original 130 ships returned to Spain.

F. CONSEQUENCES OF PHILIP'S DEFEATS

1. Although still a formidable military power, Spain began a long period of political and economic decline.

2. Now independent, the Dutch began a golden age of commercial prosperity and artistic creativity.

3. As Spain's influence declined, England's power increased. The English were now free to develop their overseas trade and to colonize North America.

II. THE FRENCH WARS OF RELIGION

A. THE CATHOLICS

1. As we have seen (see Chapter 5), under the terms of the Concordat of Bologna (1516), Francis I recognized the supremacy of the papacy over a universal council. In return, French rulers gained the right to appoint all French bishops and abbots.
2. As a result of the Concordat of Bologna, the ruling Valois kings had no reason to support a revolt against Rome.

B. THE HUGUENOTS

1. Despite royal opposition, Calvinist ideas gained a strong foothold in France. By the 1560s, one-tenth of France's 18 million people had become Calvinists, also known as Huguenots.
2. Calvinism had special appeal to French nobles. By the 1560s, between two-fifths and one-half of the nobility had become Calvinists. For many nobles, Calvinism provided a means of expressing opposition to the Valois kings.

C. THE SAINT BARTHOLOMEW'S DAY MASSACRE, 1572

1. The growing strength of the Huguenots alarmed the French king Charles IX and his powerful mother Catherine de' Medici.
2. With Catherine's support, Catholics killed thousands of Huguenots who had gathered in Paris to celebrate the wedding of Margaret of Valois to the Huguenot leader Henry of Navarre. The violence quickly spread to the provinces, where as many as 20,000 Huguenots were killed.
3. The Saint Bartholomew's Day massacre ignited a bloody civil war between Catholics and Huguenots that continued for 15 years.

D. THE POLITIQUES

1. The civil war devastated French agriculture and commerce.

2. A small group of moderate Catholics and Huguenots realized that the disorder and destruction had to be stopped or France would collapse. Known as politiques, they supported a strong monarchy and official recognition of the Huguenots.
3. The death of Catherine de' Medici followed by the assassinations of the powerful Catholic Duke of Guise and King Henry III paved the way for the accession of Henry of Navarre, a leading politique who became Henry IV in 1589.

E. THE EDICT OF NANTES, 1598

1. Henry IV was the leader of the House of Bourbon and a Huguenot.
2. Many Catholics, including the people of Paris, still opposed Henry. Knowing that a majority of the French were Catholics, Henry chose to become a Catholic, saying, "Paris is worth a mass."
3. In 1598, Henry issued the Edict of Nantes proclaiming the toleration of Calvinism and recognizing the rights of French Protestants.
4. Henry's decision to convert and issue the Edict of Nantes saved France and prepared the way for the resurgence of royal power in the seventeenth century.

Be sure that you can identify the St. Bartholomew's Day massacre, define the term* politiques*, and explain the terms of the Edict of Nantes. One or more of these three key points have appeared on almost every APEURO exam.

THE THIRTY YEARS' WAR, 1618–1648

A. THE HOLY ROMAN EMPIRE IN 1600

1. The Holy Roman Empire included approximately 300 small principalities, duchies, and independent cities.
2. The Peace of Augsburg in 1555 (see Chapter 7) gave each German prince the right to determine the religion of his state, either Roman Catholic or Lutheran.

3. The Peace of Augsburg did not provide for the recognition of Calvinists. Nonetheless, a number of states, including the Palatinate, had adopted Calvinism.

B. CAUSES OF THE THIRTY YEARS' WAR

1. Unresolved conflicts
   - i. Unresolved religious hatreds, economic rivalries, and competing dynastic ambitions continued to divide European society.
   - ii. The spread of Calvinism introduced a new source of friction because Calvinists had been excluded from the Peace of Augsburg.
2. Religious divisions
   - i. In 1608, the Protestant states formed the Protestant Union to defend their interests.
   - ii. The following year the Catholic states formed the Catholic League to defend their interests.
   - iii. By 1609 two military alliances faced each other within the Holy Roman Empire. Each alliance was determined to prevent its rival from making any further gains.
3. Political divisions
   - i. The Austrian Habsburgs wanted to reverse the Protestant gains while building a stronger monarchy.
   - ii. The German principalities and independent cities were jealous of their rights and resisted any attempt at centralization.
4. International interference
   - i. France opposed any policy that would create a strong power in Germany. So, although France was a Catholic power, it allied itself with Protestant princes.
   - ii. The Lutheran kings of Denmark and Sweden were prepared to defend Protestant interests in the Holy Roman Empire.

C. THE FOUR PHASES OF THE THIRTY YEARS' WAR

1. The Bohemian Phase, 1618–1625
   - i. Bohemia was a small but flourishing kingdom in which Catholics, Lutherans, and Calvinists lived peaceably together under earlier Habsburg promises of toleration.

ii. However, their new ruler Ferdinand II was an Austrian Habsburg and a zealous Catholic who undermined religious toleration by closing the Protestant churches.

iii. The Thirty Years' War began as a religious civil war in Bohemia between the Catholic League led by Emperor Ferdinand II and the Protestant Union led by Frederick V.

iv. Emperor Ferdinand II's forces won a series of overwhelming victories that left the Habsburgs and Catholics in control of Bohemia.

2. The Danish Phase, 1625–1629

i. The fall of Bohemia alarmed Protestants. Supported by the Dutch and English, the Danish king, Christian IV, intervened to support the Protestants and to gain territory in northern Germany.

ii. Led by Albrecht von Wallenstein, the imperial armies crushed the Protestant forces.

iii. Flushed with victory, Emperor Ferdinand issued the Edict of Restitution restoring all Catholic properties lost to the Protestants since 1552.

3. The Swedish Phase, 1630–1635

i. Deeply unsettled by the Catholic victories, the Protestants, Dutch, and French turned for help to the Lutheran king of Sweden, Gustavus Adolphus.

ii. A charismatic ruler and brilliant military strategist, Gustavus Adolphus led a disciplined, well-equipped army. A sincere champion of Lutheranism, Gustavus hoped to create a federation of Protestant states in Germany under Swedish leadership.

iii. Gustavus defeated Wallenstein in a series of decisive battles. The Swedish victories prevented the Habsburgs from uniting the German states.

4. The French Phase, 1635–1648

i. The unexpected death of Gustavus Adolphus in 1632, forced Cardinal Richelieu of France to act. As a politique he was willing to disregard his religious beliefs in favor of pursuing French national interests. Although a Catholic nation, France intervened on the Protestant side to prevent a united Germany on its eastern border. The war thus became a power struggle between France and Sweden on one side and the Habsburg Empire and Spain on the other.

ii. The French, Dutch, and Swedish armies proved to be an irresistible force. They ravaged Germany and compelled the Catholic powers to begin serious negotiations.

D. THE PEACE OF WESTPHALIA, 1648

1. The setting

   i. Hundreds of diplomats representing the German states, France, Sweden, Spain, the Dutch, and the pope met in Westphalia. This marked the first war in modern history ended by a peace conference.

   ii. Although represented at Westphalia, the pope's objections were largely ignored, underscoring the degree of secularization taking place in Europe.

2. The provisions

   i. Each of the over 300 German states received the right to conduct diplomacy and make treaties.

   ii. Rulers were allowed to decide the religious faith in their territory. Calvinism was recognized as an acceptable faith.

   iii. The independence of the Dutch Republic and neutrality of Switzerland were formally recognized.

   iv. The French annexed portions of Alsace and Lorraine.

   v. Sweden received additional territory around the Baltic Sea.

E. CONSEQUENCES OF THE THIRTY YEARS' WAR

1. For Protestants and Catholics

   i. The Thirty Years' War reaffirmed and extended the principle of *cuius regio, eius religio* ("Whose the region, his the religion"). As a result, the European powers officially recognized Calvinism as a politically accepted faith.

   ii. The Thirty Years' War marked the decline of papal political influence. The European powers ignored the papal representative at the Westphalia negotiations. The pope never signed the treaties known together as the Peace of Westphalia.

   iii. The Thirty Years' War ended the wars of religion. The long war reduced religious differences as a source of conflict. The end of the Thirty Years' War thus marks the beginning of the rise of religious toleration in Europe.

2. For the German States
   i. The Thirty Years' War devastated the German economy and decimated its population. As many as one-third of the German-speaking people died from disease, famine, and combat.
   ii. Germany's long-term commercial growth suffered because the Treaty of Westphalia gave control of the mouth of the Rhine River to the Dutch.
   iii. The Thirty Years' War left Germany politically fragmented into more than 300 virtually sovereign states that had the right to ratify laws, collect taxes, and wage war. This fragmentation ended the Holy Roman Empire as an effective entity and delayed German unification for two centuries.

3. For France
   i. France achieved its primary goals of weakening the Habsburgs and keeping the Holy Roman Empire weak and divided.
   ii. France received portions of Alsace and Lorraine.
   iii. France emerged as the strongest power in Europe.

4. For Military Strategy
   i. The Thirty Years' War led to the formation of professional fighting forces that were not disbanded at the end of the fighting.
   ii. The size of national armies increased dramatically. For example, the French army doubled in size from 125,000 men to 250,000 men.
   iii. The dramatic growth in the size of national armies required more complex bureaucracies and an increase in taxes to fund the enlarged military establishments.

5. For Diplomacy

   i. The Peace of Westphalia established a new European balance of power that included fragmented German states, strengthened French power, and Dutch independence.

   ii. The Peace of Westphalia established the modern system of diplomatic relations among mutually recognized sovereign states.

The Thirty Years' War is both complex and important. Do not become bogged down trying to memorize the four phases of the war. Instead, focus on the long-term consequences of the Thirty Years' War for Germany and France. Pay special attention to the decline of the Holy Roman Empire and to the facts that prevented the development of a unified German state.

UNIT 3 Absolutism and Constitutionalism c. 1648 to c. 1815

PREVIEW: UNIT 3 KEY CONCEPTS

- The struggle for sovereignty within and among states resulted in varying degrees of political centralization.
  - The new concept of the sovereign state and secular systems of law played a central role in the creation of new political institutions.
  - The competition for power between monarchs and corporate and minority language groups produced different distributions of governmental authority in European states.
  - Monarchies seeking enhanced power faced challenges from nobles who wished to retain traditional forms of shared governance and regional autonomy.
  - Within states, minority local and regional identities based on language and culture led to resistance against the dominant national group.
- Different models of political sovereignty affected the relationship among states and between states and individuals.
  - In much of Europe, absolute monarchy was established over the course of the seventeenth and eighteenth centuries.
  - Challenges to absolutism resulted in alternative political systems.

The Dutch Golden Age
1600–1700

I. POLITICAL AND RELIGIOUS CHARACTERISTICS

A. POLITICAL INDEPENDENCE

1. During the late sixteenth century, the seven northern provinces of the Netherlands fought for and won their independence from Spain. The Peace of Westphalia formally recognized the Dutch Republic's independence.
2. Unlike the other continental nations, the Dutch were not governed by an absolute ruler.
3. Instead, political power passed into the hands of an oligarchy of wealthy merchants. However, strong assemblies in each province enabled elected delegates to give the people a voice in their local governments.

B. RELIGIOUS TOLERATION

1. Calvinism was the dominant faith in the Dutch Republic.
2. However, Catholics, Lutherans, Anabaptists, and Jews all enjoyed religious freedom.
3. The openness of Dutch society permitted a free exchange of ideas.
4. The Dutch placed economic prosperity ahead of religious uniformity. As a result, they created a cosmopolitan society that promoted commerce.

II. CAUSES OF DUTCH ECONOMIC PROSPERITY

A. "THE WHOLE WORLD STANDS AMAZED"

1. During the seventeenth century, Amsterdam emerged from relative obscurity to become the world's greatest center of trade.

2. Amsterdam's prosperity amazed European visitors. A contemporary Dutch historian proudly boasted, "The whole world stands amazed at its [Amsterdam] riches and from east and west, north and south they come to behold it."

B. SHIPPING AND COMMERCE

1. Shipbuilding played a key role in the Dutch economy. Amsterdam boasted the best shipbuilders in seventeenth-century Europe. Well-designed Dutch ships could be manned by fewer sailors than those of other countries thus reducing costs.
2. Over 2,000 Dutch merchant ships crisscrossed the world's oceans and seas. Their cargoes of spices, silks, cottons and other prized goods comprised over half of Europe's trade.

C. THE EAST AND WEST INDIES COMPANIES

1. Founded in 1602, the Dutch East Indies Company displaced the Portuguese and gained control of the lucrative East Indian spice trade. The East Indian Company became the forerunner of modern corporations.
2. Founded in 1621, the Dutch West India Company attempted to exploit the New World's rich array of resources. Dutch traders extracted fortunes in mahogany and sugar from the coasts of Brazil and Guiana and from the Caribbean islands. In addition, they founded New Amsterdam on the tip of Manhattan Island as a center for the lucrative trade in beaver and otter furs.

D. A CENTER OF FINANCE

1. Trading profits provided large quantities of capital for investment.
2. Amsterdam financiers founded the Amsterdam Exchange Bank in 1609. It quickly became the most efficient and reliable bank in Europe.
3. Amsterdam boasted the highest per capita income in Europe. The city's increasingly prosperous citizens formed the Amsterdam Stock Exchange as a center for trading in commodities.

E. CALVINISM AND COMMERCIAL CAPITALISM

1. The German sociologist Max Weber published his seminal work *The Protestant Ethic and the Spirit of Capitalism* in 1905. Weber argued that Protestantism in general and Calvinism in particular

promoted hard work, an unpretentious lifestyle, and the accumulation and reinvestment of wealth.

2. The Dutch demonstrated the close affinity between Protestantism and the development of commercial capitalism. They avoided ostentation and chose to live frugal lives that included wearing dark clothes and living in substantial but simply furnished homes.

3. A Dutch minister complained that merchants in Amsterdam devoted more time to reading business news than listening to sermons: "It would be better if on the Lord's Day, he gave some account of himself and, instead of reckoning his profits, reckoned up his sins."

III. THE GOLDEN AGE OF DUTCH ART

A. KEY CHARACTERISTICS

1. The Dutch Republic was a Protestant nation without an absolute ruler. This made Dutch art very different from the baroque art in Rome and Madrid. Baroque artists working in these cities created works of art designed to glorify the Catholic Church and inspire awe toward the ruling monarchs. In the Dutch Republic, private homes and public buildings replaced cathedrals and castles as the showplaces for works of art.

2. Lacking commissions from the Catholic Church and royal officials, Dutch artists turned to their nation's prosperous merchants. As self-made entrepreneurs they wanted to purchase paintings of themselves, their families, their possessions, and their country.

3. Dutch artists focused on painting individual and group portraits, landscapes, and genre scenes of everyday life.

B. DUTCH MASTERS

1. Rembrandt van Rijn established himself as Amsterdam's foremost portraitist. *The Night Watch* is Rembrandt's most famous painting. In a work of unprecedented vigor, Rembrandt portrayed the members of the Amsterdam Civic Guard assembling for Marie de' Medici's state visit. Captain Banning Cocq proudly gestures to his lieutenant, indicating that it is time for the company to march out. A golden natural light illuminates the lieutenant's lemon-yellow costume and the red sash across Captain Cocq's chest.

2. Frans Hals' portraits capture each person's characteristic expression. Few artists have depicted smiles and laughter so convincingly. His works form a portrait gallery of the men and women whose exuberant spirit turned the Dutch Republic into the most prosperous country in Europe.
3. Jan Vermeer's best-known paintings show interior rooms with one or two figures quietly absorbed in reading, writing, or playing music. His images of composed serenity sparkle with reflected light that pours through an inconspicuous window.
4. Rachel Ruysch's meticulous paintings of flowers expressed the Dutch love for their homeland's natural beauty. Her paintings are admired for their vivid colors and almost photographic depictions of flowers.

Dutch Baroque art and Catholic Baroque art served very different purposes and took very different forms. Make sure that you can compare and contrast the characteristics of these two artistic styles.

IV. THE DECLINE OF THE DUTCH REPUBLIC

A. COSTLY WARS

1. The Dutch enjoyed a golden age of commercial prosperity and artistic excellence unequalled in the rest of Europe. However, rivals in England and France coveted the Dutch markets and profits.
2. The Dutch and English fought a series of naval conflicts between 1652 and 1674. Although the Dutch won many battles, they could not fully recover from the crippling costs of these conflicts.
3. The Dutch were also threatened by France's growing power and territorial ambitions. In 1672, the French successfully occupied three of the seven Dutch provinces. The Dutch finally stopped the invasion by breaking their dikes and flooding vast areas of their country.

B. INCREASED ECONOMIC COMPETITION

1. In 1651, the English enacted the first of a series of Navigation Acts aimed at the Dutch. The acts mandated that all goods imported into England had to be carried by ships from the exporting countries. The Navigation Acts deliberately excluded Dutch merchants who often served as middlemen in trade exchanges.
2. The English and French also used tariffs to raise the prices of imported Dutch goods.
3. Dutch craftsmen found it increasingly difficult to compete with the newly revived French luxury industries. At the same time, England began to mass produce cheap textile products.
4. As the Dutch declined, England and France became the dominant European powers.

Chapter 11

England: The Emergence of a Parliamentary Monarch

1600–1688

UNIT 3 | ABSOLUTISM AND CONSTITUTIONALISM

I. ENGLISH SOCIETY IN THE SEVENTEENTH CENTURY

A. IMPACT OF THE COMMERCIAL REVOLUTION

1. As the commercial revolution gained momentum, the size of the English middle class increased.
2. With the exception of the Dutch Republic, the English middle class was proportionally larger than that of any country in Europe.
3. English entrepreneurs financed joint-stock companies that played a key role in promoting English colonies in North America.

B. GENTRY

1. The gentry included wealthy landowners who dominated the House of Commons.
2. It is very important to note that unlike France, the English gentry was willing to pay taxes. This had two significant consequences:
   - i. First, since the tax burden was more equitable in England, the peasantry was not overburdened with excessive taxes.
   - ii. Second, the gentry and thus the House of Commons demanded a role in determining national expenditures. This created an inevitable conflict with the Stuart kings.

C. RELIGION

1. By the end of the seventeenth century, Calvinists comprised the largest percentage of the English population.
2. Puritans continued to demand changes in the Anglican Church.

II. KEY ISSUES

A. THE ROLE OF THE MONARCH

1. The Stuart kings believed that their authority came from God.
2. The Stuart kings thus wanted a monarchy free from parliamentary restraints.

B. THE ROLE OF THE HOUSE OF COMMONS

1. The House of Commons was dominated by the gentry, merchants, and lawyers.
2. Members were determined to preserve traditional privileges such as freedom of open debate and immunity from arrest.
3. They demanded a stronger voice in political affairs.

C. ORGANIZATION OF THE ANGLICAN CHURCH

1. The Stuarts favored the established Episcopal form of church organization. In this hierarchical arrangement, the king, Archbishop of Canterbury, and bishops determined doctrine and practice.
2. The Puritans favored a Presbyterian form of church organization. This arrangement allowed church members a much greater voice in running the church and expressing dissenting views.

III. JAMES I (REIGNED 1603–1625)

A. DIVINE RIGHT OF KINGS

1. James believed that royal authority came directly from God.
2. James published a work called *The True Law of Free Monarchies* in which he asserted that "kings are not only God's lieutenants upon earth, and sit on God's throne, but even by God himself they are called gods."

B. QUARRELS WITH PARLIAMENT

1. Puritan members of Parliament urged James to "purify" the Church of England of "popish remnants" including the authority of bishops.

2. James was convinced that the Presbyterian system of church government would destroy royal control of the church and threaten the monarchy. He reportedly summed up his opposition by declaring, "No bishops, no king."

IV. CHARLES I (REIGNED 1625–1649) AND PARLIAMENT

A. LIKE FATHER, LIKE SON

1. Like his father, Charles I was a firm believer in the divine right of kings.
2. Like his father, Charles I was always in need of money.
3. And finally, like his father, Charles opposed the Puritans and supported the Anglican Church.

B. PETITION OF RIGHT, 1628

1. In return for grants of money, Charles I agreed to the Petition of Right.
2. The Petition of Right contained two key provisions:
   i. No one should be compelled to pay any tax or loan "without common consent by act of Parliament."
   ii. No one should be imprisoned without due process of law.

C. RELIGIOUS POLICIES

1. Religion was the single most explosive issue in England.
2. With Charles's encouragement, William Laud, Archbishop of Canterbury, attempted to transform the Church of England into a Catholic church without a pope.
3. In 1639, Laud foolishly attempted to impose the English Prayer Book on the Scottish Presbyterian Church.
4. Determined to defend their religion, the Scots formed an army and occupied northern England.

D. THE LONG PARLIAMENT, 1640–1648

1. Desperate for money to fight the Scots, Charles reluctantly recalled Parliament into session, thus precipitating a constitutional and religious crisis.

2. Determined to undo what they saw as royal tyranny, the Long Parliament executed Laud and passed a number of laws limiting royal power.

The period in England from 1640 to 1660 can be very confusing. Focus on the causes and consequences of the changing relationship between the monarchy and Parliament.

V. THE ENGLISH CIVIL WAR, 1642–1649

A. THE CAVALIERS

1. The Cavaliers were aristocrats, nobles, and church officials who remained loyal to the king.
2. Cavaliers favored a strong monarchy and an Anglican Church governed by bishops appointed by the crown.

B. THE ROUNDHEADS

1. The Roundheads included Puritans, townspeople, middle-class businessmen, and people from Presbyterian-dominated London.
2. Roundheads favored a Parliamentary monarchy and a Presbyterian church governed by elected "presbyters," or elders.

C. OLIVER CROMWELL

1. Led by Oliver Cromwell, a previously unknown country gentleman, the Roundheads defeated the Cavaliers.
2. Cromwell organized an army of zealous Protestants called the New Model Army.
3. In January 1649, Cromwell and his supporters executed King Charles I.

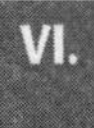

VI. THE INTERREGNUM UNDER OLIVER CROMWELL

A. THE COMMONWEALTH AND THE PROTECTORATE

1. With Charles I executed, Cromwell now held the reins of power.
2. The Commonwealth (1649–1653) abolished the monarchy and the House of Lords. Oliver Cromwell and a one-house Parliament exercised political power.
3. In late 1653, Cromwell took the title Lord Protector, establishing a one-man rule supported by the army.

B. FOREIGN POLICY

1. Cromwell brutally crushed a royalist uprising in Ireland. Protestant landlords replaced Catholic property owners. Nearly half of Ireland's population may have perished from famine and plague.
2. England passed the Navigation Act of 1651. The act barred Dutch ships from carrying goods between other countries and England. The act was also designed to give England greater control over its American colonies.
3. England waged a series of wars that weakened the Dutch.

C. DOMESTIC POLICY

1. The Puritans attempted to impose a strict moral code that censored the press, prohibited sports, and closed theaters.
2. Cromwell opposed radical groups such as the Levellers and the Quakers.
   - i. The Levellers advocated a more egalitarian society with nearly universal manhood suffrage and a written constitution guaranteeing equal rights to all.
   - ii. The Quakers rejected religious hierarchies and allowed women to preach at their meetings.

D. THE DEATH OF CROMWELL

1. Oliver Cromwell ruled until his death in 1658. His son Richard did not command the same respect as his father.
2. Parliament invited Prince Charles Stuart, the eldest son of Charles I, to return from exile.

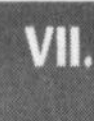

VII. THE RESTORATION

A. CHARLES II (REIGNED 1660–1685)

1. The Restoration restored the monarchy, the Church of England, and Parliament.
2. Nonetheless, the central issues concerning the relationship between the king and Parliament and the conflict over religion remained unresolved.

B. THE QUESTION OF THE SUCCESSION

1. Charles's second wife and his brother, the Duke of York, were Roman Catholic.
2. Since Charles had no legitimate children, his brother James was next in line to the throne.

C. TORIES AND WHIGS

1. The debate over James's successor divided Parliament into two groups:
   - i. The Whigs were deeply suspicious of Catholics and wanted to lawfully exclude James from the throne.
   - ii. The Tories felt a strong loyalty to the monarchy and supported James's right to the throne.
2. The Whigs and the Tories became the first political parties in the English-speaking world.

D. JAMES II (REIGNED 1685–1688)

1. Despite opposition from the Whigs, James II inherited the throne. He promptly adopted policies that antagonized both Whigs and Tories. Determined to return England to Catholicism, he appointed Catholics to influential positions of power.
2. James's second wife was a Catholic. In June 1688, she gave birth to a son who became the next heir to the throne.

VIII. THE GLORIOUS REVOLUTION

A. WILLIAM AND MARY

1. James's first wife had been a Protestant who raised their eldest daughter, Mary, as a Protestant. Mary was the wife of William of Orange, a powerful Dutch leader.
2. Civil war did not break out in 1688 as it had in 1642. Instead, Whigs and Tories invited William and Mary to overthrow James II for the sake of Protestantism.
3. Supported by an army of 25,000 men, William invaded England. He marched to London greeted by cheering crowds. Faced with united opposition, James II fled to France.

B. THE BILL OF RIGHTS, 1689

1. In 1689, Parliament required William and Mary to accept a Bill of Rights.
2. The Bill of Rights contained the following key provisions:
   i. The members of Parliament enjoyed the right to free debate.
   ii. Taxation required parliamentary consent.
   iii. Laws could be made only with the consent of Parliament.
   iv. The monarch could not be a Roman Catholic.
   v. Parliament would hold frequent sessions.
   vi. Parliament could be dissolved only by its own consent.
   vii. No subject could be arrested and detained without legal consent.

C. IMPORTANCE

1. The English rejected the theory of the divine right of kings.
2. The Glorious Revolution—as the overthrow of James II in favor of William and Mary came to be known—placed clear limits on the power of the English monarchy.
3. As power moved from the palace to Parliament, England became a constitutional monarchy controlled by an oligarchy of wealthy landed proprietors and merchants.

IX. MAKING COMPARISONS: HOBBES AND LOCKE

A. THOMAS HOBBES (1588–1679)

1. Background
   i. Hobbes published *Leviathan* in 1651, just two years after the execution of Charles I.
   ii. The horrors of the English civil war left a deep impression on Hobbes.
2. Beliefs on human nature
   i. Human beings are naturally self-centered and prone to violence.
   ii. Human beings are motivated to increase pleasure and minimize pain. They engage in a "perpetual and restless desire" for power.
3. Beliefs on the state of nature
   i. In a state of nature, people know neither peace nor security.
   ii. In a state of nature, life is "solitary, poor, nasty, brutish, and short."
4. Arguments for a strong government
   i. Without government, life would be intolerable and civilization impossible.
   ii. Government is the result of human necessity rather than divine ordination.
   iii. People give up their personal liberty to attain security and order.
   iv. Fearing the dangers of anarchy more than tyranny, Hobbes argued that rulers should have absolute and unlimited political authority.

B. JOHN LOCKE (1632–1704)

1. Background
   i. Locke published *Second Treatise of Government* in 1690.
   ii. Locke presented a compelling argument that justified the Glorious Revolution and later inspired Thomas Jefferson when he wrote the Declaration of Independence.

2. Beliefs on human nature

   i. Locke rejected the Hobbesian view that humans are innately brutish. People are instead the products of their training, education, and experience.

   ii. Locke viewed humans as creatures of reason and goodwill.

3. Locke's "law of nature"

   i. Locke formulated the theory of "natural rights."

   ii. He argued that people are born with basic rights to "life, liberty, and property."

   iii. These rights are derived from what Locke called the "law of nature," which existed before the creation of government.

4. Arguments for limited government

   i. People form governments to preserve their natural rights.

   ii. Government is a contract in which the rulers promise to safeguard the people's natural rights.

   iii. If rulers betray their trust, the governed have the right to replace them.

5. Influence

   i. Locke presented a cogent and compelling argument explaining the general principles underlying England's long struggle for a constitutional monarchy.

   ii. Inalienable rights, limited government, and the right of revolution became self-evident truths that Thomas Jefferson used to justify the American revolution.

Chapter 12

Absolutism in Western Europe: France and Spain 1589–1715

I. CHARACTERISTICS OF ABSOLUTISM IN WESTERN EUROPE

A. KEY CHARACTERISTICS

1. The monarch embodied the sovereignty of a country.
2. The monarch was not subordinate to a national assembly.
3. The monarch must exercise control over the nobility.
4. The monarch must exercise effective control over the Roman Catholic Church.
5. The monarch must command a large standing army.

B. KEY DIFFERENCES BETWEEN ABSOLUTE MONARCHS AND TWENTIETH-CENTURY DICTATORS

1. Absolute monarchs lacked the financial and technological resources commanded by twentieth-century dictators such as Stalin and Hitler.
2. Absolute monarchs did not attempt to mobilize mass support for their programs. For example, absolute monarchs did not have any program comparable to the Hitler Youth in Nazi Germany.
3. Absolute monarchs did commission art to create visual symbols of their power. However, they did not create propaganda campaigns comparable to those utilized by twentieth-century dictators.

II. THE RISE OF ABSOLUTISM IN FRANCE, 1589–1661

A. HENRY IV henry 4

1. The Edict of Nantes, 1598

   i. The edict granted religious toleration to the French Huguenots.

   ii. It established Henry IV as a politique who placed political expediency above religious principles.

2. The Duke de Sully and financial reform

   i. The French tax system was both inefficient and inequitable. Nobles were exempt from paying taxes. As a result, the burden fell most heavily upon the peasants.

   ii. Henry appointed the Duke de Sully as his chief minister. Sully could not make the tax system more just. But he did make it more efficient. His policies reduced the royal debt, built new roads and canals, revived industry and agriculture, and encouraged colonization in the New World.

3. The nobility of the robe

   i. The nobles posed the greatest threat to the extension of royal power. The influence of this "nobility of the sword" was based upon inherited privileges and a tradition of military service.

   ii. Henry IV and Sully began the process of raising revenue by selling government offices that conferred nobility. Known as robe nobles, these new nobles were members of the increasingly prosperous bourgeoisie.

B. LOUIS XIII AND CARDINAL RICHELIEU louis 13

1. The rise of Richelieu

   i. Henry IV was assassinated in 1610, leaving his nine-year-old son Louis XIII (reigned 1610–1643) as the second Bourbon monarch.

   ii. In 1624, Louis appointed Cardinal Richelieu to be his chief minister. Richelieu was the real ruler of France from 1624 until his death in 1642.

   iii. Richelieu worked tirelessly and successfully to enhance royal power. Like Henry IV, Richelieu was a politique who placed public order above religious zeal.

2. The intendant system
   i. Richelieu was determined to weaken the nobility.
   ii. At that time, France was divided into thirty-two administrative districts. Richelieu replaced nobles with royal officials called intendants. The intendants implemented royal orders.
   iii. The intendants were typically middle-class or minor nobles drawn from the nobility of the robe.
   iv. The intendant system played an important role in strengthening royal power.
   v. It is important to note that while the intendant system curbed the nobles' political power, it did not lessen their economic or social privileges.
3. International affairs
   i. Richelieu continued France's long-term policy of limiting Habsburg power.
   ii. Richelieu supported the Protestant powers during the Thirty Years' War. His skillful diplomacy and well-timed interventions helped defeat the Habsburgs and make France the leading European power.

C. THE FRONDE

1. The deaths of Richelieu in 1642 and Louis XIII the following year left the monarchy in the hands of the five-year-old Louis XIV and his chief minister, Cardinal Mazarin.
2. Sensing royal weakness, the nobles led a series of rebellions against royal authority. Known as the Fronde, these rebellions were intended to limit rather than overthrow the monarchy.
3. Increasing violence and instability forced the young king, Louis XIV, to flee Paris. Louis remembered this humiliation and vowed to control the nobility.

Both the intendant system and the Fronde generate a significant number of multiple-choice questions on the APEURO exam. The intendant system was designed to strengthen royal authority while the Fronde was intended to weaken the king's power. The Fronde played a key role in prompting Louis XIV to move to Versailles.

III. LOUIS XIV, THE SUN KING

A. BISHOP BOSSUET AND THE DIVINE RIGHT OF KINGS

1. Bishop Bossuet was a prominent French churchman, a renowned orator, and the principal theorist of the seventeenth-century doctrine of absolutism.
2. Bossuet argued that all power comes from God. The king inherited his position and authority from God.
3. Royal power was absolute. Subjects must obey their sovereign as the direct representative of God on earth.
4. While royal power was absolute, it was not arbitrary. Monarchs had to obey God's laws and were responsible to God for their conduct.

B. "I AM THE STATE"

1. Louis XIV was the most powerful monarch in French history. Unlike the English monarchs, Louis did not share his power with a parliament. In Louis's view, he and the nation were the same. He reportedly boasted, *"L'etat, c'est moi,"* meaning "I am the state."
2. Louis increased the powers of the intendants, refused to appoint a chief minister, and regularly attended meetings of his four great councils.
3. Louis continued Richelieu's policy of reducing the political power of the French nobility. He excluded nobles from key positions and instead appointed men from bourgeoisie and recently ennobled families.

C. THE VERSAILLES PALACE

1. As an absolute monarch, Louis XIV determined foreign policy, commanded the army, and supported the arts. His description of himself as the "Sun King" was accurate. In France, all aspects of political life and culture revolved around Louis XIV.
2. Louis XIV understood the power of art as propaganda and the value of visual imagery for cultivating a public image. The Versailles Palace was designed to be a visible symbol of Louis XIV's absolute power and greatness.

3. The Versailles Palace underscored France's cultural dominance. French art, philosophy, architecture, and fashions were envied and copied throughout the continent.

D. COLBERT AND MERCANTILISM

1. Louis XIV named Jean-Baptiste Colbert as controller general of finances. Colbert worked tirelessly to strengthen France's economy by implementing strict mercantilist policies.
2. Colbert expanded manufacturing by abolishing domestic tariffs that inhibited trade. At the same time, he protected French products by placing high tariffs on goods coming into the country.
3. Colbert recognized the importance of colonies as a source of raw materials and a market for manufactured goods. He encouraged people to emigrate to Canada where the lucrative fur trade promoted French commerce.
4. Colbert was able to raise royal revenues and promote economic growth. However, he was unable to make the tax system more equitable. Nobles continued to enjoy exemptions while peasants continued to bear a disproportionate tax burden.

E. REVOCATION OF THE EDICT OF NANTES

1. When Louis XIV's reign began, France's population of 19 million people included about a million Huguenots. The Huguenots continued to enjoy religious toleration and had remained loyal to the crown during the Fronde.
2. Louis's goal of having "one king, one law, one faith" precluded religious diversity. Supported by the French Catholic clergy and his Jesuit advisors, Louis revoked the Edict of Nantes in 1685. Royal officials closed Protestant churches and ordered all Protestant children baptized as Catholics.
3. Louis XIV paid a high price for his religious intolerance. To escape persecution, some 200,000 Huguenots fled to England, the Dutch Republic, Protestant German states, and the New World. As a result, France lost many skilled workers and business leaders.

IV. THE WARS OF LOUIS XIV

A. STRATEGIC GOALS

1. France was the most powerful and populous nation in Europe.
2. Louis XIV had two strategic goals:
   i. First, he wanted France to expand to its "natural frontiers" along the Rhine River and Switzerland.
   ii. Second, he wanted to make France a global power by inheriting the Spanish Habsburg possessions in the New World and in Europe.

B. THE BALANCE OF POWER

1. Louis XIV's powerful army and ambitious plans threatened to create a "universal monarchy" in which other nations would be subordinated to France's political will.
2. Alone, no European country was a match for France. However, by joining together, weaker countries could equal or even exceed French power. This defensive strategy is known as a balance of power. In such a balance, no one country can dominate the others.
3. Louis repeatedly sent French armies into the Netherlands in an attempt to extend his boundaries to the Rhine River. Each time, a coalition formed by the Dutch Republic thwarted him.

C. THE WAR OF THE SPANISH SUCCESSION, 1701–1713

1. In 1700, the balance of power was once again threatened when the childless king of Spain, Charles II, died. In his will, the dying king bequeathed the Spanish throne and its huge overseas empire to Louis's 17-year-old grandson, Philip of Anjou.
2. The nations of Europe feared that Louis could now create a universal monarchy that would upset the balance of power. Led by England, they formed a Grand Alliance that included Holland, Austria, Brandenburg, and the Italian duchy of Savoy.
3. The War of the Spanish Succession proved to be a costly struggle that left France battered and weakened. The war's huge debts played a key role in worsening financial and social tensions that would later erupt in the French Revolution.

D. THE TREATY OF UTRECHT, 1713

1. The Treaty of Utrecht created a new balance of power that preserved the peace for 30 years.
2. French gains
   i. Louis's grandson, Philip V, was allowed to remain king of Spain as long as the thrones of Spain and France were not united.
   ii. France was allowed to retain all of Alsace.
3. English gains
   i. England gained valuable Spanish naval bases at Gibraltar and in the Balearic Islands.
   ii. England gained the asiento (slave trade) from Spain.
   iii. England gained valuable French colonies in Nova Scotia and Newfoundland.
4. Austrian gains
   i. Austria gained the Spanish Netherlands (Belgium), which then became known as the Austrian Netherlands.
   ii. Austria obtained Naples, Milan, and Sardinia.
5. The Duke of Savoy
   i. As a reward for joining the Grand Alliance, the Duke of Savoy received Sicily and the title of king.
   ii. In 1720, Savoy ceded Sicily to Austria in exchange for Sardinia.
6. The Elector of Brandenburg
   i. As a reward for joining the Grand Alliance, the Elector of Brandenburg was recognized as king of Prussia.

Don't spend time studying Louis XIV's many wars. Instead, focus on the consequences of these wars and the provisions of the Treaty of Utrecht. It is important to note that the Spanish Netherlands (Belgium) became the Austrian Netherlands. Also note the emerging role of the rulers of Savoy and Brandenburg.

V. THE DECLINE OF SPANISH POWER

A. THE GOLDEN AGE OF SPAIN

1. Ferdinand and Isabella built the foundation of Spanish absolutism.
2. Spanish power reached its zenith during the reign of Philip II (reigned 1556–1598).
3. Spanish power and prestige began to steadily decline during the seventeenth century.

B. ECONOMIC DECLINE

1. The expulsion of Jews and converted Muslims, known as Moriscos, deprived Spain of prosperous merchants and skilled workers.
2. The flow of gold and silver from Mexico and Peru proved to be a mixed blessing. At first, the precious metals enriched the Spanish economy. However, the flood of imported silver also caused inflation, which increased the cost of Spanish textiles and other products. As a result, Spanish exports declined.
3. A series of costly wars with the Dutch Republic and France extended Spain's commitments beyond the nation's declining resources.
4. Spanish industry, commerce, agriculture, and population all declined.

C. POLITICAL DECLINE

1. Spain suffered from a series of weak and inept rulers who pursued misguided and ineffective policies.
2. Spanish rulers and aristocrats continued to lead extravagant lifestyles they could no longer afford.
3. Spanish armies suffered a series of disastrous defeats.

VI. MAKING COMPARISONS: THE ECONOMIC DECLINE OF THE DUTCH REPUBLIC AND SPAIN

A. GREATNESS AND PROSPERITY

1. In the sixteenth century, Spain conquered and then developed a world colonial empire. The sixteenth century was a period of Spanish greatness and prosperity.

2. In the seventeenth century, the Dutch Republic developed a commercial empire, becoming a center of international finance. The seventeenth century was a period of Dutch greatness and prosperity.

3. Nonetheless, by 1713, both Spain and the Dutch Republic were second-rate powers that were eclipsed by France and England.

B. FACTORS RESPONSIBLE FOR ECONOMIC DECLINE

1. The high costs of war

   i. A series of costly wars severely damaged Spain's economy. Spain fought lengthy wars with both the Dutch Republic and France.

   ii. The economy of the Dutch Republic also suffered from costly wars. In 1670, both France and England attacked the Dutch Republic. The French army occupied a substantial part of the country, forcing the Dutch to open their dikes to save Amsterdam. Led by William III, the Dutch played a key role in helping defeat France in the War of the Spanish Succession.

2. Economic competition

   i. Both the French and the English cast covetous eyes on Spain's New World possessions.

   ii. The enormous costs of fighting France for 40 years eroded the Dutch Republic's competitive edge. In addition, the Dutch faced increasing economic competition from England.

3. Small populations

   i. Spain's population shrank from approximately 7.5 million in 1550 to 5.5 million in 1660. A declining population reduced the domestic demand for Spanish goods.

   ii. The Dutch Republic's population increased from 1.5 million in 1600 to just under 2 million in 1700. Nonetheless, this population was too small to maintain and defend a global commercial empire.

Chapter 13

Absolutism in Eastern Europe 1600–1725

I. THREE DECLINING EMPIRES

A. EASTERN EUROPE IN 1648

1. The Holy Roman Empire, the Republic of Poland, and the Ottoman Empire occupied the area from the French border to Russia.
2. All three empires were declining. Each lacked a strong central authority and an efficient system of government.
3. Each of the declining empires contained diverse ethnic and language groups.

B. THE HOLY ROMAN EMPIRE

1. The Reformation left the Holy Roman Empire religiously divided between Catholics and Protestants.
2. The Thirty Years' War left the Holy Roman Empire politically divided into 300 independent states.
3. The empire had an elected emperor who had no imperial army, revenues, or centralized authority.
4. Led by the Habsburgs and the Hohenzollerns, Austria and Prussia gradually emerged as the leading German states.

C. THE REPUBLIC OF POLAND

1. On a map of Europe in 1660, Poland appears to be a large, united country. In reality, the king of Poland was elected by Polish nobles who severely restricted his power.
2. Poland did have a central legislative body known as a diet. However, action required the unanimous consent of each aristocratic member. Any member could break up or "explode" the diet by objecting to a policy or act.

3. Poland's lack of centralized power created a power vacuum that left it vulnerable to stronger and more aggressive nations.

D. THE OTTOMAN EMPIRE

1. Led by Suleiman the Magnificent (reigned 1520–1566), the Ottomans threatened Vienna.
2. In the middle of the seventeenth century, a series of ambitious rulers revitalized the Ottoman Empire. In 1683, a powerful Turkish army once again besieged Vienna.
3. Austrian forces reinforced by Poles and Germans successfully repelled the Turks. This marked the beginning of a steady decline in Ottoman power.

II. THE HABSBURGS

A. THE REVIVAL OF HABSBURG POWER

1. The Habsburgs were one of the oldest dynasties in Europe. Beginning in the early 1400s, most of the Holy Roman emperors were Habsburgs.
2. Habsburg power suffered a series of setbacks following the devastation of the Thirty Years' War and the extinction of the Habsburg line in Spain.
3. Despite these defeats, the Habsburg rulers successfully reaffirmed their power over Austria, Bohemia, and Hungary. In addition, the Treaty of Utrecht gave the Habsburgs control of Naples, Sardinia, and Milan in Italy and the Spanish Netherlands (subsequently renamed the Austrian Netherlands).
4. It is important to note that the Habsburg empire embraced a large number of ethnic groups who were unified only by their Catholic faith and their loyalty to the Habsburg dynasty.

B. CHARLES VI AND THE PRAGMATIC SANCTION

1. Emperor Charles VI (reigned 1711–1740) did not have a male heir.
2. Determined to insure a safe succession for his daughter, Maria Theresa, Charles drew up a document called the Pragmatic Sanction. It stated that the territories of the Habsburg empire were

indivisible and that Maria Theresa would inherit the throne and all Habsburg lands.

3. England and other foreign powers forced Charles to make a number of concessions before agreeing to the Pragmatic Sanction. Charles died believing he had guaranteed the peace and integrity of his realm.

III. THE RISE OF PRUSSIA

A. THE HOHENZOLLERNS OF BRANDENBURG-PRUSSIA

1. Brandenburg was a small state located between the Oder and Elbe rivers with its center in Berlin.
2. The ruler of Brandenburg was one of seven princes who elected the Holy Roman emperor.
3. The Hohenzollern family became the hereditary rulers of Brandenburg in 1417.
4. In the early seventeenth century, the Hohenzollerns inherited Cleves and some neighboring lands on the Rhine River and the duchy of Prussia on the Baltic coast to the northeast.
5. These diverse and geographically separated Hohenzollern possessions had no natural boundaries, few resources, and a population of just 1.5 million people.

B. FREDERICK WILLIAM, THE GREAT ELECTOR (REIGNED 1640–1688)

1. Although scattered and weak, the Hohenzollern possessions were the second-largest block of territory in the Holy Roman Empire. Only the Habsburgs could claim more land.
2. Known as the Great Elector, Frederick William began the process of forging the Hohenzollern territories into a strong power. He recognized that a well-equipped army would protect his territories and enable him to play a role in European balance-of-power politics.
3. Frederick William demanded and received the loyalty of the Junkers, the German landowners. In exchange, the Junkers received full power over the serfs who labored on their estates.

C. FREDERICK WILLIAM I (REIGNED 1713–1740)

1. Like the Great Elector, Frederick William I was determined to build a powerful army. During his reign, the Prussian military doubled to over 80,000 men. Although Prussia had Europe's thirteenth-largest population, it boasted the continent's third- or fourth-largest army.
2. Under the Hohenzollerns, military priorities and values dominated all aspects of Prussian life. Led by the Junkers, the officer corps became Prussia's most prestigious class. As noted by one foreign diplomat, "Prussia is not a state that possesses an army, but an army that possesses a state."

IV. RUSSIA BEFORE PETER THE GREAT

A. ISOLATION

1. Russia was geographically isolated from the rest of Europe. Sweden prevented Russia from reaching the Baltic Sea while the Ottoman Empire prevented Russia from reaching the Black Sea.
2. Russia was culturally isolated from the rest of Europe. The ideas of the Renaissance and Reformation and all the discoveries of the Age of Exploration and the Scientific Revolution scarcely affected Russia.

B. THE ROMANOV DYNASTY

1. Following the death of Ivan the Terrible in 1584, Russia experienced a period of weakness and disorder known as the Time of Troubles.
2. Hoping to restore order, an assembly of nobles elected Michael Romanov to be the next tsar. The Romanov Dynasty ruled Russia from 1613 to 1917.

V. PETER THE GREAT (REIGNED 1682–1725)

A. MODERNIZING RUSSIA

1. Peter the Great recognized that Russia had fallen behind Western Europe. Determined to learn from his rivals, Peter visited Holland and England, where he toured shipyards, examined new military equipment, and observed Western customs.

2. Peter returned to Moscow vowing to transform Russia into a great power. He began by creating a standing army trained by foreign officers. Peter then built a Russian navy originally trained by foreign officers.

3. Peter did not limit his changes to military organization and technology. He improved Russian agriculture by introducing the potato, strengthened the Russian economy by importing skilled workers, and liberated Russian women by allowing them to appear in public without veils. In a famous and much resented act, Peter forced nobles to shave off their traditional long beards.

B. DEFEATING SWEDEN

1. The Thirty Years' War left Sweden in control of the Baltic's entire eastern shore.

2. In 1700, Peter ordered his army to end Sweden's dominance of the Baltic. The Great Northern War between Sweden and Russia lasted from 1700 to 1721.

3. After suffering initial defeats at the hands of Sweden's king Charles XII, Peter ultimately won the war, thus gaining control over warm-water outlets on the Baltic shore.

4. The defeat contributed to Sweden's decline as a major European power. At the same time, Russia now became the dominant power on the Baltic Sea and a force in European politics.

C. BUILDING ST. PETERSBURG

1. Peter the Great began building St. Petersburg in 1703. Named after his patron saint, St. Petersburg would be "a great window for Russia to look out at Europe."

2. St. Petersburg quickly became a symbol of Peter the Great's new and more powerful Russia.

D. CONTROLLING THE BOYARS

1. The boyars were the old nobility who supported traditional Russian culture. Comprising about 7 percent of the population, this large noble class posed a threat to Peter's reform program.

2. Peter the Great did more than order the boyars to shave off their long beards and wear Western clothing. He also compelled them to construct costly townhouses in St. Petersburg and required every noble to serve in the army or in the civil administration.

E. EXPLOITING THE SERFS

1. Russia's peasants did not enjoy the benefits of Peter the Great's reforms. Instead, they were conscripted into Russia's army and forced to build St. Petersburg.
2. In central Europe, serfs were bound to the land. In contrast, Russian serfs could be sold apart from the land. This enabled nobles to force serfs to work in mines and factories.

F. EVALUATING PETER THE GREAT

1. Peter the Great provided a model of how an energetic and ruthless autocrat would change a nation. He successfully transformed Russia into a great power that would play an increasingly important role in European history.
2. Peter the Great's policies increased the disparities between the nobles and the peasants. Millions of exploited serfs formed an estranged class that did not share in Russian society.

Peter the Great's momentous reign has been the subject of numerous multiple-choice questions and free-response essays on the APEURO exam. Peter the Great's successes include his program of modernization, construction of St. Petersburg, and victory over Sweden in the Great Northern War. However, Russia's economy continued to rest on the exploitation of serfs.

Scientific, Philosophical, and Political Developments

c. 1648 to c. 1815

Chapters 14–17

PREVIEW: UNIT 4 KEY CONCEPTS

- The rediscovery of works from ancient Greece and Rome and observation of the natural world changed many Europeans' view of their world.
  - — New ideas in science based on observation, experimentation, and mathematics challenged classical views of the cosmos, nature, and the human body, although existing traditions of knowledge and the universe continued.
- The spread of Scientific Revolution concepts and practices and the Enlightenment's application of these concepts and practices to political, social, and ethical issues led to an increased but not unchallenged emphasis on reason in European culture.
  - — Enlightenment thought, which focused on concepts such as empiricism, skepticism, human reason, rationalism, and classical sources of knowledge, challenged the prevailing patterns of thought with respect to social order, institutions of government, and the role of faith.
  - — New public venues and print media popularized Enlightenment ideas.
  - — New political and economic theories challenged absolutism and mercantilism.
  - — During the Enlightenment, the rational analysis of religious practices led to natural religion and the demand for religious toleration.
- The experiences of everyday life were shaped by demographic, environmental, medical, and technological changes.
  - — By the eighteenth century, family and private life reflected new demographic patterns and the effects of the commercial revolution.

The Scientific Revolution

I. THE GEOCENTRIC VIEW OF THE UNIVERSE

A. OLD ASSUMPTIONS

1. Medieval philosophers accepted a geocentric view that held that the Earth was a motionless body located at the center of the universe. The sun, moon, and planets all moved around the Earth in perfectly circular paths. Common sense seemed to support this view, since the sun appeared to be moving around the Earth as it rose in the morning and set in the evening.
2. Medieval philosophers believed that different physical laws applied to the Earth and to the heavens. As a result, astrology, alchemy, and witchcraft were all accepted in a world where chance and miracles played important roles.

B. TRADITIONAL AUTHORITIES

1. The medieval view of the universe was supported by more than just common sense. Both the Greek philosopher Aristotle and the Alexandrian astronomer Ptolemy supported the geocentric theory.
2. The Church taught that God had deliberately placed the Earth at the center of the universe. Earth was thus a special place on which the great drama of life took place.

II. THE REVOLUTION IN ASTRONOMY

A. NICOLAUS COPERNICUS (1473–1543)

1. Copernicus was a Polish clergyman and astronomer. Published in 1543, his landmark book, *On the Revolutions of the Heavenly Bodies*, Copernicus directly challenged the geocentric view of the

universe. Copernicus presented his readers with a heliocentric view in which the Earth revolved around the sun, which was the center of the universe.

2. Copernicus's heliocentric theory represented the first new view of the universe in almost 2,000 years. His work alarmed both Protestant and Catholic leaders. They realized that the heliocentric theory would remove humans from their special place in the center of the universe. The impact of Copernicus's book was so far-reaching that its title gave rise to the use of the word *revolution* as meaning radical change.

B. JOHANNES KEPLER (1571–1630)

1. Copernicus's bold but controversial ideas were based on logic, not on direct observation. In the late 1500s, a Danish astronomer, Tycho Brahe, carefully recorded the movements of each known planet. When Brahe died in 1601, his assistant, Johannes Kepler, continued his work.

2 After carefully studying Brahe's data, Kepler formulated three laws of planetary motion:

   i. The planets revolve around the sun in elliptical orbits. This law refuted the old belief that planets moved in perfect circles. It placed the sun not at the center of a circle but as one focus of an ellipse.

   ii. Planets move more rapidly as their orbits approach the sun.

   iii. The time a planet takes to orbit the sun varies proportionately with its distance from the sun.

3. Kepler's three laws supported, clarified, and amended Copernicus's heliocentric system. They revealed the universe as a cosmos of order in which the same physical laws governed the motion of both the earth and the stars.

C. GALILEO GALILEI (1564–1642)

1. Galileo was an Italian scientist who used controlled experiments to observe and measure the motion of objects. Convinced that the "great book of the universe is written in the language of mathematics," Galileo formulated laws of motion and inertia that he expressed in mathematical formulas.

2. Galileo learned that a Dutch lens maker had built an instrument that could enlarge distant objects. Without seeing this device,

Galileo successfully built a telescope that made objects appear 30 times nearer and 1,000 times larger.

3. Galileo used his powerful new telescope to study the heavens. In 1610, he published *Starry Messenger* describing his astonishing discoveries. Galileo reported that the sun had spots, that Saturn had rings, that the moon had a rough and uneven surface, and that Jupiter had four moons.

4. Galileo's discoveries created a sensation. His description of the moon's surface shattered Aristotle's theory that the Earth was composed of impure materials, while the moon and stars were made of a pure, eternal substance that was smooth and perfect. Galileo's finding that moons orbited Jupiter supported the heliocentric theory, thus proving that everything in the cosmos does not revolve around Earth.

III. CONTROVERSY WITH THE CATHOLIC CHURCH

A. "A VERY DANGEROUS THING"

1. The Catholic Church viewed the new heliocentric model with deep suspicion. Led by Cardinal Bellarmine, Church officials believed that Copernican astronomy was clearly incompatible with Biblical references to the sun "rising" and the Earth "moving."

2. In a letter to one of Galileo's followers, Cardinal Bellarmine warned that the new view of the cosmos "is a very dangerous thing" because it threatened "to harm the Holy Faith by rendering Holy Scripture false."

B. THE INQUISITION

1. The Inquisition was a system of courts that investigated anyone who dared voice views that differed from orthodox Church views. In early 1616, the Inquisition directed Cardinal Bellarmine to summon Galileo to Rome and "admonish him to abandon" his heliocentric views.

2. Galileo understood the Inquisition's fearsome power. Like other astronomers, he remembered that in 1600 the Inquisition tried, convicted, and then burned Giordano Bruno at the stake for arguing that the Earth was a tiny part of an infinite universe.

3. Galileo appeared before Cardinal Bellarmine and prudently submitted to a papal edict declaring, "The view that the sun

stands motionless at the center of the universe is foolish, philosophically false, and utterly heretical, because [it is] contrary to Holy Scripture."

C. THE TRIAL OF GALILEO

1. Galileo could not remain silent. He pointedly argued, "I do not feel obliged to believe that the same God who has endowed us with senses, reason, and intellect has intended us to forgo their use."
2. In 1532, Galileo published *Dialogue Concerning the Two Chief World Systems*. Although ostensibly impartial, Galileo provided the Copernican adherents with the most persuasive arguments.
3. In 1533, the Inquisition charged Galileo with breaking his promise to obey the 1616 edict. On June 22, 1533, the Inquisition pronounced Galileo guilty of heresy and disobedience. The Court then forced the aging scientist to kneel before them and formally repudiate the Copernican theory.

D. GALILEO'S LEGACY

1. The 70-year-old Galileo appeared to be a broken and defeated man. He spent his remaining years living under house arrest, advocating a deductive method for the search for truth.
2. Although the Church had silenced Galileo, it could not stop the advance of science. The printing press spread Galileo's ideas and discoveries across Europe.

IV. THE SCIENTIFIC METHOD

A. SIR FRANCIS BACON (1561–1626) AND THE INDUCTIVE METHOD

1. Bacon contributed to scientific developments in the seventeenth century by advocating an inductive method for scientific experimentation.
2. The inductive method begins with direct observation of phenomena. This produces data that is systematically recorded and organized. The data leads to a tentative hypothesis that is retested in additional experiments.
3. Bacon argued that this process of controlled experimentation would lead to the formulation of universal principles and scientific laws.

B. RENÉ DESCARTES (1596–1650) AND THE DEVELOPMENT OF THE DEDUCTIVE METHOD

1. Descartes contributed to scientific developments in the seventeenth century by advocating a deductive method for the search for truth.
2. Descartes began by doubting all notions based on authority or custom. Instead, he started with a self-evident axiom known to be true. He then used logical reasoning to deduce various inferences.

C. CHARACTERISTICS OF THE SCIENTIFIC METHOD

1. Bacon's inductive method and Descartes's deductive method proved to be complementary parts of a systematic and logical way of seeking truth known as the scientific method.
2. The scientific method includes the following characteristics:
   - i. Belief in the existence of regular patterns in nature
   - ii. Use of controlled experiments to systematically record facts and verify hypotheses
   - iii. Search for mathematical formulas to describe natural phenomena

D. SCIENTIFIC SOCIETIES

1. Sponsored by governments and monarchs, scientists organized societies to promote research and spread scientific knowledge.
2. Founded in 1660, the Royal Society in England enjoyed international prestige. Other scientific societies were founded in Florence, Paris, and Berlin.
3. The scientific societies helped create an international scientific community.

V. SIR ISAAC NEWTON (1642–1727)

A. NEWTON AND THE LAW OF GRAVITATION

1. Newton published the *Principia* in 1687. This momentous work combined Kepler's laws of planetary motion, Galileo's laws of inertia and falling bodies, and Newton's own conception of gravitation into a single mathematical law of universal gravitation.

2. Newton's concise mathematical formula described all forms of celestial and terrestrial motion.

B. THE NEWTONIAN UNIVERSE

1. Newton demonstrated that the universe is governed by universal laws that can be expressed in mathematical formulas.
2. Newton viewed the universe as a vast machine, created by God but working according to universal laws that could be discovered, mastered, and utilized to improve human life.
3. Supernatural and miraculous forces played no role in Newton's universe.
4. Newton's mechanistic concept of the universe dominated Western thought until the discoveries of Albert Einstein in the early twentieth century.

The Scientific Revolution is one of the watershed events in European intellectual history. APEURO test writers do not expect you to memorize scientific laws or mathematical formulas. They do expect you to discuss how pivotal figures such as Galileo, Bacon, Descartes, and Newton adopted a new view of nature that challenged long-held views of the relationship between humanity and the universe.

VI. JOHN LOCKE (1632–1704)

A. *ESSAY CONCERNING HUMAN UNDERSTANDING* (1689)

1. Locke argued that at birth the human mind is a blank slate or "tabula rasa."
2. Since there are no innate ideas, all knowledge is derived from experience.
3. Human development is therefore shaped by educational and social institutions.

B. IMPLICATIONS OF THE BLANK SLATE THEORY

1. Locke's blank slate theory undermined the traditional Christian assertion that humankind was inherently sinful.
2. Instead, education is essential since humans have unlimited potential.
3. Locke's optimistic view of human potential influenced the philosophes' emphasis on the important role of education in shaping social progress.

Chapter 15

The Enlightenment

I. THE ENLIGHTENMENT

A. THE PHILOSOPHES

1. The philosophes were a group of thinkers and writers who espoused enlightened ideas. Taken together, they formed a grand "republic of letters."
2. The philosophes were not abstract philosophers. Instead, they dedicated themselves to exposing social problems and proposing reforms based upon implementing natural laws.
3. Although many leading philosophes were French, they were a cosmopolitan group who could be found in the American colonies and across Europe.

B. KEY IDEAS

1. Reason
   - i. To the philosophes, reason was the absence of intolerance, bigotry, and superstition. Reason meant informed thinking about social problems.
   - ii. Humans should rely on reason, not miracles, to improve society.
2. Nature and natural laws
   - i. The philosophes believed that natural laws regulate both the universe and human society.
   - ii. These natural laws can be discovered by human reason.
3. Happiness
   - i. Philosophes had little interest in the medieval belief that people should accept misery in this world to find salvation in the hereafter.

ii. Philosophes believed that happiness in this world was an inalienable human right.

4. Progress

   i. The philosophes were the first Europeans to believe in social progress.

   ii. The discovery of laws of economics and government would improve society and make progress inevitable.

5. Liberty

   i. The philosophes lived in societies that placed restrictions on speech, religion, and trade. They wanted to remove these limitations on human liberty.

   ii. The philosophes believed that intellectual freedom was a natural right. Without freedom of expression, there could be no progress.

6. Toleration

   i. The philosophes questioned institutional religious beliefs, arguing that they perpetuated superstition, intolerance, and bigotry.

   ii. The philosophes advocated full religious tolerance.

C. DEISM

1. Deists thought of God as a cosmic watchmaker who created the universe and then let it run according to immutable natural laws.
2. Much of the educated elite in Western Europe and America embraced deism. However, deism's reliance upon reason and its lack of emotion had little appeal for many people.
3. A new religious movement known as pietism stressed faith, emotion, and "the religion of the heart."

II. VOLTAIRE (1694–1778)

A. PRINCE OF THE PHILOSOPHES

1. Voltaire was the best known and most influential philosophe.
2. He was a prolific writer who popularized Newton's scientific discoveries, criticized France's rigid government, and denounced religious bigotry.

B. "CRUSH THE INFAMOUS THING"

1. Voltaire directed his most stinging barbs at the intolerance of organized Christianity, both Protestant and Catholic.
2. Voltaire championed religious tolerance. He often ended his letters with the passionate demand to *"ecrasez l'infame"* ("crush the infamous thing"). This ringing exclamation reminded his readers to continue the battle against the enemies of reason—bigotry, ignorance, and religious fanaticism.

III. DENIS DIDEROT (1713–1784) AND THE *ENCYCLOPEDIA*

A. PURPOSE

1. Diderot was a French philosophe who became the chief editor of the *Encyclopedia*.
2. Diderot's goal was to bring together all the most current and enlightened thinking about science, technology, mathematics, art, and government. "All things," Diderot explained, "must be examined, debated, investigated without exception and without regard for anyone's feelings."

B. IMPORTANCE

1. The *Encyclopedia* disseminated enlightened thinking across Europe and North America.
2. It undermined established authority by including articles about controversial political and religious subjects.

IV. BARON DE MONTESQUIEU (1689–1755)

A. *THE SPIRIT OF THE LAWS*

1. Montesquieu was a French nobleman and attorney who wanted to limit the abuses of royal absolutism.
2. *The Spirit of the Laws* represented an attempt to create a "social science" by applying the methods of the natural sciences to the study of government.

↳ applies science to the govt

B. SEPARATION OF POWERS

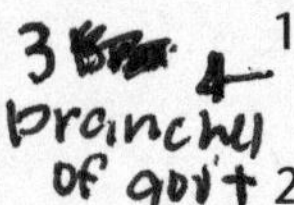

1. Montesquieu concluded that the ideal government separated powers among executive, legislative, and judicial branches.
2. This system of divided authority would protect the rights of individuals by preventing one branch of government from gaining unrestricted control over the entire society.
3. Montesquieu's ideas had a significant influence on the writers of the American Constitution.

V. JEAN-JACQUES ROUSSEAU (1712–1778)

A. NATURAL EDUCATION

1. Rousseau presented his ideas on education in the novel *Emile*.
2. Rousseau argued that a "natural education" should replace the rigid schooling typical of his time. The key principles of a natural education included the following:
   - i. Children are naturally good and entitled to an education that emphasizes freedom and happiness.
   - ii. People develop through various stages, and individuals vary within these stages. Education must therefore be individualized since "every mind has its own form."
   - iii. Children should be encouraged to draw their own conclusions from experience. This principle anticipated what is now called "discovery learning."

B. THE GENERAL WILL

1. *The Social Contract*, Rousseau's treatise on politics and government, is one of the most influential books on political theory in European history.
2. Thomas Hobbes and John Locke (see Chapter 11) argued that individuals entered a social contract with their rulers. In contrast, Rousseau argued that individuals entered into a social contract with one another. This created a community, or organized civil society.
3. The sovereign power in a state does not lie in a ruler. Instead, it resides in the general will of the community as a whole. The

general will or "public spirit" is defined as any action that is right and good for all.

4. Rulers are servants of the community. If they fail to carry out the people's will, they should be removed.

5. Rousseau's concept of the general will and the sovereignty of the people influenced leaders of both the French and American revolutions. It is also important to note that twentieth-century dictators justified their rule by claiming to embody their nation's general will.

C. ROUSSEAU AND THE ENLIGHTENMENT

1. Like other philosophes, Rousseau was committed to defending individual freedom and changing the existing social order.

2. However, Rousseau distrusted reason and science. He trusted emotions and spontaneous feeling more than cold logic. As a result, Rousseau foreshadowed the romantic reaction to the Enlightenment.

Textbooks contain long lists devoted to discussing the contributions of leading philosophes. Voltaire and Rousseau generate by far the most questions on the APEURO exam. Be sure you know that Voltaire supported religious toleration and opposed superstition and ignorance. Test items on Rousseau stress his concept of the general will and his views of education as presented in the novel **Emile.**

VI. THE NEW ECONOMICS

A. THE FRENCH PHYSIOCRATS

1. French economic reformers called physiocrats were the first to question mercantilist principles.

2. Led by François Quesnay, the physiocrats argued that economic activities should be freed from artificial restrictions. Governments should follow a laissez-faire policy of noninterference with the economy.

↳ no gov't interference in economy

B. ADAM SMITH (1723–1790)

1. Adam Smith was the most influential advocate of laissez-faire economics.
2. Like Newton, Smith combined the thought of his predecessors into a single system based upon the study and application of natural laws.
3. Published in 1776, *The Wealth of Nations* is a landmark book that gave birth to classical economic thought.

C. KEY IDEAS IN *THE WEALTH OF NATIONS*

1. The role of government
   - i. Governments must not interfere with the free functioning of the market.
   - ii. Governments should limit their role to defending the state against foreign invasion, protecting property, and enforcing contracts.
2. Free markets
   - i. In a free market, the economic laws of supply and demand will create a self-regulating economic system.
   - ii. Regulations such as tariffs hinder free trade and should be abolished.
3. Self-interest and the "invisible hand"
   - i. Smith maintained that every individual is motivated by self-interest.
   - ii. Competition and self-interest are socially beneficial: "Self-interest drives people to action and the Invisible Hand of competition acts as an automatic regulator so that the market will generate wealth for a nation."

D. MAKING COMPARISONS: THE ECONOMIC POLICIES OF JEAN-BAPTISTE COLBERT AND ADAM SMITH

1. Colbert
   - i. Believed that mercantilist policies offered the best way to increase French power and wealth
   - ii. Followed economic policies designed to give France a favorable balance of trade. Colbert promoted Caribbean

sugar plantations, established slaving stations in Africa, and encouraged colonies in Canada.

iii. Subsidized French industry by granting monopolies and enforcing high tariffs

2. Adam Smith

   i. Urged governments to abandon regulatory policies such as tariffs, trading monopolies, and navigation acts

   ii. Advocated a policy of free trade and minimal government interference in the economy

   iii. Believed that self-interested individuals working in a free market would increase production and wealth

VII. ENLIGHTENMENT VIEWS OF THE ROLE OF WOMEN

A. THE INCLUSIVE VIEW

1. Most leading philosophes believed that the principles of liberty and equality should be extended to women.
2. These philosophes therefore argued that women should have greater access to education and to intellectual life.
3. Some philosophes supported granting women a degree of political equality. They pointed out the contradiction between advocating freedom from arbitrary governments while at the same time maintaining unrestrained control over women.

B. THE DOMESTIC VIEW

1. **Some Enlightened thinkers made a distinction between a public sphere dominated by men and a private sphere dominated by women.**
2. **They argued that there are "natural" differences between men and women.**
3. **Women should concentrate their natural talents on the domestic sphere where their roles as wives and mothers had preeminent importance.**

Peace, War, and Enlightened Despots 1715–1789

I. CHARACTERISTICS OF THE EIGHTEENTH CENTURY

A. POLITICAL

1. Monarchy remained the most prevalent form of government.
2. Divine-right monarchy evolved into enlightened despotism in Eastern Europe.
3. Aristocrats regained much influence. Powerful nobles and wealthy merchants influenced and sometimes dominated inept monarchs.

B. INTERNATIONAL RELATIONS

1. The great powers of Europe included Britain, France, Austria, Prussia, and Russia. Spain, Holland, Poland, Sweden, and the Ottoman Empire were no longer considered great powers.
2. The great powers fought limited wars:
   - i. Professional armies fought wars based on maneuver and strategy rather than bloody mass combat.
   - ii. Rulers fought wars for specific territorial and economic objectives.
   - iii. There were no religious wars among the great powers.

C. THREE DISTINCT PERIODS

1. A period of peace and prosperity from 1715 to 1740
2. A period of warfare from 1740 to 1763
3. A period of enlightened despotism from 1763 to 1789

II. PEACE AND PROSPERITY, 1715–1740

A. GROWING PROSPERITY

1. Great Britain emerged as Europe's leading commercial nation.
2. The upper classes benefited the most from the rising tide of commercial prosperity.
3. The labor of African slaves and Eastern European serfs supported key commodities:
   i. African slaves labored on immensely profitable Caribbean sugar plantations.
   ii. Serfs labored in the rich grain-producing regions of Eastern Europe.

B. ENGLAND UNDER WALPOLE

1. The first two Hanoverian monarchs spoke little English and exercised little real power.
2. A ruling aristocracy of landed gentry and wealthy merchants dominated Parliament.
3. Robert Walpole emerged as England's first prime minister. Walpole led the Whig party in Parliament and was the government's leading minister.

C. FRANCE UNDER LOUIS XV

1. Louis XV (reigned 1715–1774) was a weak leader who was dominated by his royal mistresses and court favorites.
2. The nobles regained much of the power and privileges they lost during the reign of Louis XIV.
3. Although France was a prosperous and potentially powerful country, government debts continued to mount.

III. WARFARE, 1740–1763

A. GREAT POWER RIVALRIES

1. The Hohenzollerns of Prussia and the Habsburgs of Austria vied for power in central Europe.
2. The British and the French vied for trade in North America, the West Indies, and India.

B. THE WAR OF THE AUSTRIAN SUCCESSION, 1740–1748

1. The Austrian-Prussian rivalry
   - i. The Pragmatic Sanction guaranteed Maria Theresa's (reigned 1740–1780) right to inherit the Habsburg throne and territories.
   - ii. Frederick the Great ignored the Pragmatic Sanction and seized Silesia. Located on the northeastern frontier of Bohemia, Silesia boasted a million people, a prosperous linen industry, and rich deposits of iron ore.
   - iii. Supported by France, Frederick's army successfully captured Silesia.
2. The Anglo-French rivalry
   - i. In Europe, the French supported Prussia and the English supported Austria.
   - ii. In Canada, American colonists captured the French fortress of Louisbourg.
   - iii. In India, the French seized Madras from the British.
3. The Treaty of Aix-la-Chapelle
   - i. Frederick retained control of Silesia, thus confirming Prussia's status as a great power and chief rival of Austria in German affairs.
   - ii. The English restored Louisbourg to France, and the French gave Madras back to England.

C. THE DIPLOMATIC REVOLUTION

1. The Austrian chancellor, Count Kaunitz, vowed to recover Silesia.
2. Kaunitz successfully formed a coalition that included France, Austria, and Russia. One consequence of this new alliance was the marriage of Marie Antoinette, daughter of Maria Theresa, to the future Louis XVI of France.
3. England then formed an alliance with Prussia to implement its policy of maintaining a balance of power on the continent.
4. Note that this diplomatic revolution did not change the basic rivalries between England and France, and Austria and Prussia.

D. THE SEVEN YEARS' WAR, 1756–1763

1. The colonial war
   - i. In Canada, the British defeated the French and gained control of Quebec.
   - ii. In the West Indies, the British gained control of major French sugar islands.
   - iii. In India, the British gained control over key French trading posts.
2. The war on the Continent
   - i. The anti-Prussian alliance achieved a series of victories that threatened to crush Prussia.
   - ii. Prussia was saved from defeat when Russia's new tsar, Peter III (reigned 1762), who admired Frederick the Great, dropped out of the war.

E. THE TREATY OF PARIS, 1763

1. The British acquired French Canada and the land between the Appalachian Mountains and the Mississippi River.
2. France retained her Caribbean sugar islands and a few commercial installations in India.
3. Prussia retained possession of Silesia.

The great power rivalries and wars that took place between 1740 and 1763 can be confusing. It is important to remember that Prussia kept Silesia and that the British strengthened their global empire.

IV. ENLIGHTENED DESPOTISM, 1763–1789

A. THE CONCEPT OF ENLIGHTENED DESPOTISM

1. The philosophes urged Europe's absolute rulers to use their power for the good of the people.
2. Enlightened despots would combat ignorance and superstition by eliminating irrational customs, promoting religious toleration, reforming legal codes, and supporting education.
3. It is important to note that the philosophes did not support democracy. Like Thomas Hobbes (see Chapter 11), they believed that the people could not be trusted with self-government.
4. George III of England (reigned 1760–1820) and Louis XV of France (reigned 1715–1774) had little or no interest in either the philosophes or the concept of enlightened despotism. Catherine the Great of Russia, Frederick the Great of Prussia, and Joseph II of Austria were Europe's best-known enlightened despots.

B. CATHERINE THE GREAT (REIGNED 1762–1796)

1. Enlightened reforms
   - i. Corresponded with Voltaire and invited Denis Diderot to visit her court
   - ii. Supported Russia's first private printing presses
   - iii. Provided formal education for the daughters of the nobility
   - iv. Restricted the practice of torture
   - v. Allowed limited religious toleration to Jews
   - vi. Convened a legislative commission to draft a new enlightened law code. However, the nobles refused to concede any of their privileges and very little was accomplished.

2. Pugachev's Rebellion
   - i. From 1773 to 1775, a Cossack soldier named Emelian Pugachev led a dangerous uprising of serfs living along the Volga River. The rebellion finally ended when Pugachev was captured, tortured, and executed.
   - ii. Pugachev's Rebellion marked the end of Catherine's program of enlightened reforms.
   - iii. Determined to prevent any future rebellions, Catherine gave the nobles additional privileges and absolute power over their estates and serfs.
3. Territorial expansion
   - i. Catherine ignored the philosophes' arguments against war. During her reign, Russia gained territory at the expense of the Ottoman Empire and Poland.
   - ii. Catherine's armies defeated the Ottomans and gained control over the Crimean Peninsula and most of the northern shore of the Black Sea.
   - iii. Catherine, along with Prussia and Austria, annexed Polish territory in a series of partitions that took place in 1772, 1793, and 1795. As a result of these partitions, Poland disappeared as an independent nation.
4. Overall evaluation
   - i. Catherine attempted to strengthen Russia by streamlining state bureaucracies, reforming local governments, and promoting measures to encourage economic growth.
   - ii. Catherine enjoyed the favorable publicity she received from her contacts with leading philosophes. However, she was not prepared to risk radical reform.
   - iii. Catherine reacted negatively to the French Revolution. For example, she banned books by the philosophes and exiled critics to Siberia.

C. FREDERICK THE GREAT (REIGNED 1740–1786)

1. Enlightened reforms
   - i. Called himself "the first servant of the state"
   - ii. Invited Voltaire to live in his palace at Potsdam

iii. Supported scientific agriculture

iv. Prepared a unified national code of law

v. Abolished the use of torture except for treason and murder

vi. Encouraged Huguenots from France and Jews from Poland to immigrate to Prussia

2. The Junkers and serfs

i. A firm believer in social order, Frederick strengthened the Junkers' privileges.

ii. The Junkers retained full control over their serfs.

D. MAKING COMPARISONS: PETER THE GREAT AND FREDERICK THE GREAT

1. Goals

i. Both Peter the Great (see Chapter 10) and Frederick the Great were determined to transform their countries into great powers.

ii. Both Peter the Great and Frederick the Great imported Western ideas to accelerate the pace of change.

2. Policies

i. Both rulers waged wars to conquer strategic territory.

ii. Peter's victory over Sweden enabled Russia to take over warm-water outlets and become the leading Baltic power. Frederick's victory over Austria enabled Prussia to take control over Silesia and become a leading German power.

iii. Both rulers imported Western ideas. Peter took the unprecedented step of visiting Western Europe. His program of westernization opened Russia to new ideas, crops, and technologies. Frederick took the unprecedented step of inviting Voltaire to live in Prussia. His program of enlightened despotism opened Prussia to religious toleration, scientific agriculture, and a new code of laws.

iv. Both rulers instituted changes that affected only the top layers of their societies. The serfs in both Russia and Prussia remained tied to the land and completely dominated by nobles.

E. **JOSEPH II (REIGNED 1780–1790)**

1. Enlightened reforms

   i. Abolished serfdom and feudal dues

   ii. Abolished the system of forced labor known as the robot

   iii. Proclaimed religious toleration for all Christians and Jews

   iv. Reduced the influence of the church

   v. Reformed the judicial system

   vi. Abolished torture and ended the death penalty

2. Protest and reaction

   i. The nobles bitterly opposed Joseph's program of reforms.

   ii. Following Joseph's death, the new emperor, Leopold II, placated the nobles by repealing many of Joseph's reforms.

   iii. Serfdom and the robot remained in effect until 1848.

The enlightened despots have generated a significant number of both multiple-choice and short-answer essay questions on the APEURO exam. You should be able to discuss the extent to which Catherine the Great, Frederick the Great, and Joseph II succeeded and failed as enlightened despots.

Life and Culture in Eighteenth-Century Europe

I. THE AGRICULTURAL REVOLUTION

A. TRADITIONAL AGRICULTURAL PRODUCTION

1. In the early 1700s, peasants living in village communities farmed much of the land in Western Europe.
2. Peasant farmers used an open-field system that included these characteristics:
    i. Animals grazed on the common or open lands.
    ii. Villagers divided the remaining land into long, narrow strips. Fences and hedges did not divide this open land.
    iii. Peasants traditionally used a two- or three-field system of crop rotation. This system was intended to restore exhausted soil. In practice, it meant that one-third to one-half of the land was allowed to lie fallow on any given year.

B. INNOVATIONS IN THE LOW COUNTRIES

1. Reasons for Low Country leadership in farming
    i. The Low Countries were the most densely populated region in Europe. Dutch farmers were thus forced to seek maximum yields from their lands.
    ii. The Low Countries contained a growing urban population that created demand for farm products.
2. New innovations in the Low Countries
    i. Enclosed fields.
    ii. Continuous crop rotation.
    iii. Use of manure as fertilizer.

iv. Planting of a variety of crops.

v. Use of drainage to reclaim marshes.

C. ENGLISH AGRICULTURE

1. Agricultural innovators

   i. Charles "Turnip" Townshend advocated continuous crop rotation using turnips, wheat, barley, and clover.

   ii. Jethro Tull invented a seed drill that allowed for sowing crops in a straight row.

   iii. Robert Bakewell pioneered selective breeding of livestock.

2. The enclosure movement

   i. English landowners consolidated previously scattered pasturelands into compact fields enclosed by fences and hedges.

   ii. The new enclosed farmland enabled landowners to rapidly implement agricultural innovations. This encouraged the development of market-oriented agricultural production.

   iii. The enclosure movement forced many poor rural people to move to cities and work in factories.

The enclosure movement has generated a number of multiple-choice questions on the APEURO exam. It is important to remember that during most of the eighteenth century, the enclosure of common land primarily took place in the Low Countries and England. Peasants in France and Germany successfully resisted the enclosure of their open fields.

II. THE POPULATION EXPLOSION

A. FACTORS LIMITING POPULATION GROWTH

1. Periodic crop failures caused widespread famine.

2. Epidemic diseases such as bubonic plague decimated Europe's population.

3. Frequent wars destroyed crops and spread contagious diseases. For example, the Thirty Years' War reduced the population of the German states by at least one-third.

B. FACTORS PROMOTING POPULATION GROWTH

1. The agricultural revolution produced a more abundant food supply.
2. The potato became a key food staple during the eighteenth century. A single acre of potatoes could feed a family for a year.
3. Advances in transportation reduced the impact of local crop failures.
4. Eighteenth-century wars were fought by professional armies with specific geographic and economic objectives. As a result, eighteenth-century wars were less destructive than the seventeenth-century religious wars.
5. Although still in its embryonic stage, medical care did begin to improve. For example, Edward Jenner's inoculation reduced deaths caused by smallpox.
6. Commercial capitalism led to increased prosperity and thus the ability to afford more children.
7. Powerful monarchs suppressed civil wars, thereby allowing population to increase.

C. POPULATION STATISTICS

1. Europe's population increased from 120 million in 1700 to 190 million in 1800.
2. The population of England rose from 6 million in 1750 to more than 10 million in 1800.
3. The population of France increased from 18 million in 1715 to 26 million in 1789.
4. The population of Spain increased from 7.6 million in 1700 to 10.5 million in 1800.

LIFE IN THE EIGHTEENTH CENTURY

A. MARRIAGE AND THE FAMILY BEFORE 1750

1. Most young married European couples lived in nuclear families. Large multigenerational households were not the norm.
2. Most couples postponed marriage until they were in their mid- to late twenties.
3. Couples delayed marriage in order to acquire land or learn a trade.
4. A combination of parental authority and strict laws exercised tight control over marriage.

B. PATTERNS OF MARRIAGE AND THE FAMILY AFTER 1750

1. The growth of the cottage industry increased income and helped young people become financially independent.
2. As income rose, arranged marriages declined.
3. Increased mobility reduced parental and village controls.
4. Young peasant women increasingly left home to work as domestic servants.

C. CHILD REARING

1. Because of the high mortality rate among infants, parents were reluctant to become emotionally attached to their children.
2. Jean-Jacques Rousseau (see Chapter 15) encouraged parents to provide a warm and nurturing environment for their children.
3. Upper-middle-class parents began to place a greater emphasis on child rearing.

D. INCREASED LIFE EXPECTANCY

1. During the eighteenth century, the life spans of Europeans increased from 25 to 35 years.
2. New foods, such as the potato, combined with better farming techniques improved the diet of the poor.
3. Improved sanitation and the beginning of the science of immunology reduced death rates. Edward Jenner performed the first smallpox vaccination in 1796. The conquest of smallpox was the greatest medical triumph of the eighteenth century.

IV. THE RISE AND FALL OF WITCHCRAFT

A. WITCHCRAFT PERSECUTIONS

1. During the sixteenth and seventeenth centuries, between 100,000 and 200,000 people were officially tried for witchcraft.
2. Between 40,000 and 60,000 people were executed for witchcraft.
3. Elderly, widowed women were the most likely to be accused of witchcraft.

B. REASONS FOR THE GROWTH OF EUROPEAN WITCH HUNTS

1. Religious reformers stressed the great powers of the Devil. The Devil's diabolical activities reinforced the widespread belief in witchcraft.
2. Women were believed to be weak and thus susceptible to the Devil's temptations.
3. Religious wars and economic uncertainty caused great social and economic stress. Older, widowed women usually lacked power and thus became convenient scapegoats.

C. REASONS FOR THE DECLINE OF WITCHCRAFT

1. Religious wars finally came to an end, thus restoring social stability.
2. Protestants emphasized the concept of a supreme God, thus making the Devil seem less threatening.
3. The Scientific Revolution and the Enlightenment emphasized reason and uniform laws of nature. Support for superstition and witchcraft declined as educated Europeans turned to rational explanations of natural events.

APEURO test writers have devoted a number of multiple-choice and free-response questions to witchcraft. Remember that witchcraft trials and executions most often affected elderly widows. Make sure that you study the reasons for both the growth and the decline of witchcraft.

V. MAJOR ARTISTIC STYLES

A. ROCOCO

1. Basic characteristics

   i. The Rococo style reached its peak of popularity during the reign of Louis XV (1715–1774).

   ii. Artists depicted lighthearted and often frivolous scenes of "nobles at play."

   iii. Paintings featured light-colored pastels.

   iv. Architecture featured highly decorated interior ceilings.

2. Leading artists and works

   i. Antoine Watteau, *Pilgrimage to Cythera* – depicts a group of amorous couples who have spent a day at a magical island dedicated to Venus.

   ii. François Boucher, *Cupid a Captive* – depicts a "captive" Cupid bound with flowers enjoying the company of a group of charming captors.

   iii. Jean-Honoré Fragonard, *The Swing* – commissioned by a baron to depict his mistress on a swing with himself as an amorous observer.

B. NEOCLASSICAL ART

1. Basic characteristics

   i. Neoclassical style supplanted Rococo during the 1780s.

   ii. Key figures were depicted as classical heroes.

   iii. Works portrayed the classical virtues of self-sacrifice and devotion to the state.

   iv. Compositions emphasized the Greek ideals of restraint, simplicity, and symmetry.

2. Leading artists and works

   i. Jacques-Louis David, *Oath of the Horatii* – uses an event from Roman history to extol the republican virtues of honor and self-sacrifice.

ii. Jean-Antoine Houdon, *Voltaire Seated* – dressed the revered writer in classical robes to emphasize his wisdom and republican virtues.

iii. Thomas Jefferson, Monticello – uses a dome and symmetrical portico to create a new republican architecture.

Conflict, Crisis, and Reaction in the Late Eighteenth Century

c. 1648 to c. 1815

Chapters 18–20

PREVIEW: UNIT 5 KEY CONCEPTS

- Different models of political sovereignty affected the relationship among states and between states and individuals.
  - The French Revolution posed a fundamental challenge to Europe's existing political and social order.
  - Claiming to defend the ideals of the French Revolution, Napoleon Bonaparte imposed French control over much of the European continent, which eventually provoked a nationalistic reaction.
- The expansion of European commerce accelerated the growth of a worldwide economic network.
  - Commercial rivalries influenced diplomacy and warfare among European states in the early modern era.
- The spread of Scientific Revolution concepts and practices and the Enlightenment's application of these concepts and practices to political, social, and ethical issues led to an increased but not unchallenged emphasis on reason in European culture.
  - While Enlightenment values dominated the world of European ideas and culture, they were challenged by the revival of public expression of emotions and feeling.
  - Revolution, war and rebellion demonstrated the emotional power of mass politics and nationalism.

The French Revolution and Napoleon

1789–1799

I. TENSIONS IN THE OLD REGIME

A. PEASANT DISTRESS

1. Peasants comprised over four-fifths of France's 26 million people.
2. Peasants lost half their income to taxes. They paid feudal dues to nobles, tithes to the church, and royal taxes to the king's agents. In addition, they paid a land tax called the taille and performed forced labor called the corvée. Although they paid most of the taxes, the peasants received few services in return.
3. Overburdened peasants lived at the edge of destitution. Grain shortages led to sharp increases in the price of bread. The rising cost of bread was a major cause of discontent.

B. ARISTOCRATIC PRIVILEGE

1. French nobles enjoyed a position of unrivaled privilege. For example, nobles were except from paying taxes. Every bishop in France was of noble birth and only nobles could receive commissions in the army.
2. The nobles refused to consider making sacrifices of any kind. They were determined to maintain and even increase their political power and economic privileges.

C. ROYAL INEPTITUDE

1. Louis XV (reigned 1715–1774) was a weak and indecisive ruler.
2. Louis XVI (reigned 1774–1792) became king when he was just 20 years old. He was a good man but a very poor king. Louis XVI was an excellent locksmith and preferred hunting to ruling. His Austrian-born wife Marie Antoinette correctly described him as a timid person who was "afraid to command."

D. BOURGEOISE DISCONTENT

1. France's foreign trade increased by 500 percent between 1713 and 1789.
2. The steady growth in commerce brought bourgeoise merchants rising profits. However, their growing wealth did not translate into either political power or social status. Discontented bourgeoise began to view the privileged nobles as "parasites" who contributed little to the French economy while erecting barriers to social mobility.
3. Discontented members of the French bourgeoise wanted a more efficient government, a larger voice in political affairs, and a more open society.

E. PHILOSOPHE CRITICISM

1. The French philosophes believed that human reason would inevitably lead to social progress.
2. Philosophes argued that France's rigid social structure violated every rule of reason by maintaining an outdated status quo that protected the privileges of a favored few.
3. The philosophes advanced a message of liberty and equality that undermined the legitimacy of French monarchs, who ruled by divine right.

II. THE ESTATES GENERAL

A. CALLING THE ESTATES GENERAL

1. Both Louis XV and Louis XVI enjoyed extravagant lifestyles that created a massive public debt.
2. The cost of fighting the Seven Years' War and financing the American War for Independence dramatically worsened the financial crisis.
3. By the spring of 1789, the imminent threat of bankruptcy confronted Louis XVI with a grave crisis. His finance ministers hoped to avoid bankruptcy by taxing the nobles. However, the nobles refused to pay taxes unless the king called a meeting of the Estates General, which had not met since 1614. Louis reluctantly summoned representatives of the three estates to meet at Versailles on May 5, 1789.

↳ first meeting of the estates general in 150+ years

B. THE THREE ESTATES

1. The First Estate: the clergy
   - i. The Catholic Church held about 20 percent of the land.
   - ii. The French clergy paid no direct taxes. Instead, they gave the government a "free gift" of about 2 percent of their income.
2. The Second Estate: the nobility
   - i. Nobles comprised 2 to 4 percent of the population.
   - ii. Nobles owned about 25 percent of the land.
3. The Third Estate: everyone else
   - i. The Third Estate comprised 95 percent of the population.
   - ii. It included a diverse group of peasant farmers, urban workers, middle-class shopkeepers, wealthy merchants, and successful lawyers.
   - iii. Those in this group resented aristocratic privileges.

C. THE TENNIS COURT OATH, JUNE 1789

1. Members of the First and Second Estates assumed that each estate would receive one vote. This traditional would enable them to impose their will on the Third Estate.
2. This dispute represented more than a struggle over procedure. It marked a struggle for power between those who wanted to preserve their privileges and those who wanted a more equal and open society.
3. Abbé Sieyès, a previously unknown clergyman, became the Third Estate's leading spokesman. In a bold pamphlet, he asked "What is the Third Estate? Everything. What has it been until now in the political order? Nothing. What does it want to be? Something." Sieyès' pointed questions and forceful answers emboldened members of the Third Estate and energized the push for reform at the Estates General.
4. Faced with continued royal resistance, the Third Estate defied the king by declaring itself the National Assembly of France. Locked out of their official meeting place, the Third Estate deputies gathered in an indoor tennis court where they took an oath "never to separate, and to meet wherever circumstances might require, until a constitution should be firmly established."

5. The Tennis Court Oath marked the beginning of the French Revolution. In effect, the Third Estate deputies proclaimed an end to absolute monarchy and the beginning of representative government.

III. THE NATIONAL ASSEMBLY, 1789–1791

A. THE STORMING OF THE BASTILLE

1. Determined to reassert royal authority, Louis XVI ordered a mercenary army of Swiss guards to march toward Paris and Versailles.
2. In Paris, angry mobs were already protesting the soaring price of bread. As tensions rose, a mob stormed the Bastille, a royal fortress and prison. The mob freed a handful of prisoners and seized the Bastille's supply of gunpowder and weapons.
3. The fall of the Bastille marked an important symbolic act against royal despotism. It also pushed Paris to the forefront of the ongoing revolution.

B. THE DECLARATION OF THE RIGHTS OF MAN AND CITIZEN, AUGUST 1789

1. The National Assembly adopted the *Declaration of the Rights of Man and the Citizen* on August 26, 1789. Written primarily by Abbé Sieyès and the Marquis de Lafayette (in consultation with Thomas Jefferson who was in Paris at the time), the Declaration embodied the Enlightenment principles of natural rights, limited government, and religious toleration.
2. The Declaration began by forthrightly declaring, "Men are born free and remain free and equal in rights." These rights included "liberty, property, security, and resistance to oppression."
3. The Declaration provided for freedom of religion, freedom from arbitrary arrest, freedom of speech and the press, and the right to petition the government.
4. The Declaration further established the principle that laws could be made and taxes levied only by the citizens or their representatives. The nation, not the king, was sovereign.
5. The Declaration was a landmark in the fight against privilege and despotism.

C. THE RIGHTS OF WOMEN

1. French laws excluding women from voting and holding office contradicted the soaring ideals announced in the *Declaration of the Rights of Man and of the Citizen.*
2. Politically active women published pamphlets, organized clubs, and petitioned the National Assembly to demand more rights and a greater voice in public affairs.
3. In 1791, Olympe de Gouges composed a *Declaration of the Rights of Women* in which she declared, "Woman is born free and lives equal to men in her rights." She further insisted that "male and female citizens being equal in the eyes of the law, must be equally admitted to all honors, positions, and public employment."
4. In 1792, Mary Wollstonecraft published *A Vindication of the Rights of Women.* She argued that women are not naturally inferior to men. The appearance of inferiority is created by a lack of education.
5. French women did gain increased rights to inherit property and to divorce. However, male revolutionaries reacted disdainfully to the idea of female political participation. As a result, women did not gain the right to vote or to hold office.

women could divorce + inherit but NOT ✓ vote

D. THE WOMEN'S MARCH TO VERSAILLES, OCTOBER 1789

1. Food shortages in Paris sparked yet another popular explosion. On October 5, 1789, a crowd of several thousand hungry, angry, and desperate women marched 12 miles from Paris to Versailles.
2. The *poissardes*, or Parisian market women demanded cheap bread and insisted that the royal family move to Paris.
3. Fearing for his safety, Louis XVI quickly capitulated. On October 6, 1789, the royal family left Versailles accompanied by a triumphant crowd of shouting poissardes. The royal family established themselves in a palace located at the center of Paris. A few days later, the deputies of the National Assembly moved to Paris.
4. Like the fall of the Bastille, the women's march to Versailles demonstrated the newfound power of ordinary people to influence the course of historic events.

E. THE CIVIL CONSTITUTION OF THE CLERGY, AUGUST 1790

1. This act, passed by the National Assembly, did the following:
   - i. Confiscated the lands owned by the Roman Catholic Church
   - ii. Decreed that bishops and priests would be elected by the people and paid by the state
   - iii. Required the clergy to take a loyalty oath to support the new government
2. It is important to note that Pope Pius VI condemned the act and that over half of the clergy refused to take the oath of allegiance. Alienated Catholics proved to be persistent opponents of the French Revolution.

F. REFORMS OF THE NATIONAL ASSEMBLY

1. The National Assembly
   - i. created a constitutional monarchy
   - ii. divided France into 83 departments governed by elected officials
   - iii. established the metric system of measurement
   - iv. abolished internal tariffs
   - v. abolished guilds
2. The National Assembly did *not*
   - i. abolish private property
   - ii. give women the right to vote

IV. THE LEGISLATIVE ASSEMBLY, 1791–1792

A. FACTIONS IN THE LEGISLATIVE ASSEMBLY

1. Members of the Legislative Assembly sat together in separate sections of the meeting hall. The political terms *right*, *center*, and *left* are derived from this seating arrangement.
2. Conservatives who favored a constitutional monarchy made up the Right.
3. Moderates comprised a large group in the Center.

4. Radicals who distrusted the king and wanted the Revolution to continue sat to the Left. The Left was divided into two groups:
   i. The Jacobins wanted to overthrow the monarchy and create a republic. Key Jacobin leaders included Jean-Paul Marat, Georges-Jacques Danton, and Maximilien de Robespierre. Note that the Marquis de Lafayette was not a Jacobin.
   ii. The Girondists wanted to involve France in a war that would discredit the monarchy and extend France's revolutionary ideals across Europe.

Make sure that you can identify both the Jacobins and the Girondists. It is important to remember that Lafayette was not a Jacobin. Also keep in mind that the Girondists favored using war to spread French revolutionary ideals.

B. FRANCE VERSUS AUSTRIA AND PRUSSIA

1. Leopold II of Austria and Frederick William II of Prussia issued the Declaration of Pillnitz (August 1791) declaring that the restoration of absolutism in France was of "common interest to all sovereigns of Europe."
2. The Legislative Assembly declared war against Austria and Prussia in April 1792, thus beginning the War of the First Coalition.
3. The war began badly for the poorly equipped French armies. By the summer of 1792, Austrian and Prussian armies were advancing toward Paris.

C. THE SECOND FRENCH REVOLUTION

1. Faced with defeat, recruits rushed to Paris singing the *Marseillaise*, a stirring appeal to save France from tyranny. The rejuvenated French forces stopped the Austro-Prussian army, thus saving the Revolution.
2. During the summer of 1792, radicals called sans-culottes (literally "without breeches") took control of the Paris Commune (city government). The revolutionary Paris Commune intimidated the Legislative Assembly into deposing Louis XVI and issuing a call for the election of a national convention. This new body would then form a more democratic government.

3. Violence once again exploded in Paris. Convinced that royalists would betray the Revolution, mobs of sans-culottes executed over a thousand priests, bourgeoisie, and aristocrats. These "September massacres" marked the beginning of a second French Revolution dominated by radicals.

V. THE NATIONAL CONVENTION, 1792–1795

A. THE EXECUTION OF LOUIS XVI

1. The newly elected National Convention abolished the monarchy and declared that France was now a republic in which every adult citizen had the right to vote and hold office. Women could not vote, however, despite the important role they had already played in the Revolution.
2. The National Convention then had to decide Louis XVI's fate. The Girondists favored imprisonment while the Jacobins demanded that he be executed as a tyrant and a traitor.
3. After a contentious debate, the National Convention passed a resolution condemning Louis XVI to death. The resolution passed by one vote.
4. Supported by the sans-culottes, the Jacobins branded the Girondins as counterrevolutionaries and ousted them from the National Convention.

B. EUROPEAN REACTION

1. At first, European liberals supported the French Revolution and applauded the fall of the Old Regime.
2. The English statesman Edmund Burke offered a conservative critique of the French Revolution. Burke warned that mob rule would lead to anarchy and ultimately military dictatorship. To many moderate Europeans, the September massacres and the execution of Louis XVI vindicated Burke's dire predictions.

C. FOREIGN AND DOMESTIC THREATS

1. England, Spain, Holland, and Sardinia joined with Prussia and Austria. In the spring of 1793, First Coalition armies converged on France.

2. Internal strife also threatened the National Convention. Girondists and royalist Catholics rebelled against the tyranny of radical Jacobins.

D. THE REIGN OF TERROR

1. The execution of Louis XVI did not solve the National Convention's problems. Foreign armies still threatened France's borders. The Jacobins also had thousands of enemies within France itself—peasants horrified by the beheading of the king, priests who refused to accept government controls, and rival leaders who stirred up rebellion outside of Paris.
2. Faced with foreign invaders and the threat of domestic rebellion, the National Convention established the Committee of Public Safety to defend France and safeguard the Revolution.
3. Led by Robespierre, the Committee of Public Safety exercised dictatorial power as it carried out a Reign of Terror.
4. The guillotine quickly became the supreme symbol of the Terror. In the name of creating a Republic of Virtue, Robespierre executed the queen, his chief rivals, and thousands of "dangerous" class enemies including Olympe de Gouges.

E. THE REPUBLIC OF VIRTUE

1. Robespierre and his supporters launched a cultural revolution designed to create a "Republic of Virtue." Their campaign to "republicanize everything" affected all aspects of French life. For example, the figure of Liberty appeared on coins, bills, and letterheads. Decks of cards no longer had kings, queens, and jacks. Instead, they had cards called liberties, equalities, and fraternities.
2. As believers in reason, the Jacobins wanted to make their calendar scientific. They divided the year into 12 months of 30 days and gave each month a new, "reasonable" name. For example, October was renamed Brumaire of Fog Month. The new calendar had no Sundays because the radicals considered religion a bastion of superstition.
3. The elimination of Sunday was part of a campaign of de-Christianization that included both Catholic and Protestant churches. Zealous Jacobins dismantled church bells and beheaded medieval statues of kings on the façade of Notre Dame cathedral.

F. THE "NATION IN ARMS"

1. While the Terror crushed domestic dissent, Robespierre turned to the danger posed by the First Coalition. In 1793, the Committee of Public Safety proclaimed a "levée en masse" decreeing compulsory military service for all able-bodied men aged 18 to 25.
2. The levée en masse created a national military based upon mass participation. This marked the first example of the complete mobilization of a country for war.
3. Motivated by patriotism and led by a corps of talented young officers that included Napoleon Bonaparte, France's citizen-soldiers defeated the First Coalition's professional armies.
4. The French forces posed as liberators who abolished feudal dues as they spread their revolutionary message of liberty and equality.

G. THE THERMIDORIAN REACTION

1. The Committee of Public Safety successfully crushed internal dissent and defeated the First Coalition. Despite these victories, Robespierre continued to pursue his fanatical dream of creating a Republic of Virtue.
2. Fearing for their lives and yearning for stability, the National Convention reasserted its authority by executing Robespierre.
3. Robespierre's death ended the radical phase of the French Revolution. On the new revolutionary calendar, July was called *Thermidor* from the French word for "heat." Hence, the revolt against Robespierre is called the Thermidorian reaction.

VI. THE DIRECTORY, 1795–1799

A. BOURGEOISIE MISRULE

1. The government consisted of a two-house legislature and an executive body of five men known as the Directory.
2. Dominated by rich bourgeoisie, the Directory proved to be corrupt and unpopular.

B. THE FALL OF THE DIRECTORY

1. Public discontent mounted as the Directory failed to deal with inflation, food shortages, and corruption.

2. On November 9, 1799, an ambitious and talented young general named Napoleon Bonaparte overthrew the Directory and seized power.

VII. MAJOR EFFECTS OF THE FRENCH REVOLUTION, 1789–1799

A. FRANCE

1. The French Revolution replaced the Bourbon monarchy with a republic. *The Declaration of the Rights of Man and of the Citizen* became a foundational document for the cause of liberty and human rights. France became the first nation to grant universal male suffrage.
2. The French Revolution played a key role in the rise of modern nationalism. French citizens no longer identified themselves as members of an estate. Instead, they pledged allegiance to their nation above other individual or group interests.

B. WESTERN EUROPE

1. France's rejuvenated army conquered the Austrian Netherlands, the Dutch Republic, areas of Germany on the left bank of the Rhine River, Switzerland, and most of Italy. They promptly abolished feudal privileges and taxes.
2. The people living in France's "sister republics" originally greeted the French as welcome liberators. However, as France's rule became more and more oppressive, people began to resent the French and become more aware of their own national identity.

C. THE UNITED STATES

1. America's founders hoped that the new republic would avoid developing permanent political parties. However, Alexander Hamilton's financial program stimulated the formation of two political factions—Hamilton's Federalists and Thomas Jefferson's Democratic-Republicans.
2. The outbreak of the French Revolution further deepened these divisions. Hamilton and his supporters were outspoken supporters of Great Britain and opponents of France. In contrast, Jefferson and his supporters were openly pro-French. These differences played a key role in the formation of America's two-party system.

D. HAITI

1. Haiti was a French colony called Saint-Domingue (later named Haiti). The island's lucrative sugar plantations made it the most profitable French colony in the world.

2. When the French Revolution began, the population of Saint-Domingue included 30,000 whites, 28,000 people of color, and 465,000 slaves.

3 The soaring ideals of the French Revolution inspired the island's slaves and free people of color to demand their freedom. Toussaint L'Ouverture emerged as a charismatic leader who played a key role in helping Haitians win their independence.

4. The successful slave uprising led to the founding of an independent state that was both free from slavery and ruled by non-whites and former captives.

↳ haiti gained independence from the french

The Rise and Fall of Napoleon

I. THE RISE OF NAPOLEON

A. NEW OPPORTUNITIES

1. Napoleon was born in 1769 in an obscure town in Corsica, a French island off the Italian coast. He won a scholarship to study at a French military school where he distinguished himself as an eager student of military history.

2. Napoleon originally found his advancement blocked because he lacked noble birth. However, the French Revolution removed these barriers and provided opportunities for an ambitious and talented young officer.

↳ not from an important family

B. CONQUERING HERO

1. Napoleon steadily rose through the ranks of the republican army. By seizing opportunities presented by the Revolution, he became a general at the age of 24.

2. In 1796, Napoleon received command of the French forces in northern Italy. His combination of decisive actions and tactical genius enabled the French to win a series of stunning victories. Napoleon triumphantly returned to France as a conquering hero.

C. COUP D'ÉTAT, 1799

1. Ambitious politicians inside the Directory hoped to use Napoleon's popularity and his loyal troops to overthrow the government.

2. The plotters staged a successful coup d'état on November 9, 1799. The new government vested executive power in the hands of three consuls. As First Consul, Napoleon exercised undisputed authority.

↳ Napoleon "unfairly" gained power

D. NAPOLEON IN CONTROL

1. Although the Consulate maintained a republican façade, Napoleon controlled the new government's entire executive powers.
2. In 1802, Napoleon ordered a plebiscite, or popular vote to approve his position as Consul for Life. France's male electorate gave Napoleon 99.9 percent of their votes. Two years later, voters once again registered their near unanimous approval when Napoleon crowned himself Emperor of the French.
3. The Revolutionary era began with an attempt to limit the power of an arbitrary royal government. Napoleon successfully used the democratic process to undermine democracy. As Emperor, he wielded unchecked power over France's domestic and foreign policies.

II. NAPOLEON AND DOMESTIC REFORM, 1801–1805

A. THE CONCORDAT OF 1801

1. Napoleon understood the importance of ending the strained relationship between the French government and the Catholic Church.
2. The Concordat of 1801 granted the Catholic Church special status as the religion of "the majority of Frenchmen." The pope regained the right to confirm church dignitaries appointed by the French government, depose French bishops, and reopen religious seminaries. Napoleon also agreed to abandon the confusing ten-day revolutionary calendar and reestablish Sundays and religious holidays.
3. In return, the pope recognized the French government and accepted the loss of church properties confiscated during the Revolution.
4. The Concordat of 1801 enabled Napoleon to regain the loyalty of French Catholics. Although the government recognized Catholicism as the "preferred" religion of France, the agreement protected freedom of worship for other faiths.

B. THE NAPOLEONIC CODE

1. Napoleon's legal experts replaced centuries of confusing and outdated feudal laws with a uniform legal code that is still the basis of French law.

2. The new code guaranteed many achievements of the French Revolution, including equality before the law, freedom of religion, the abolition of privilege, and the protection of property rights.
3. Revolutionary legislation had emancipated women and children by establishing their civil liberties. Napoleon undid most of this progress by restoring the father's absolute authority in the family. Women and children were once again legally dependent on their husband or father. For example, women could not buy or sell property or begin a business without the consent of their husbands. Any income she earned would pass to his descendants, not hers.

↳ a step-back for women

C. A CENTRALIZED BUREAUCRACY

1. The National Assembly replaced France's traditional provinces with 83 departments. Self-governing assemblies enjoyed local autonomy. Napoleon kept the departments but appointed prefects who directly supervised local affairs.
2. Napoleon charted a privately owned national bank to provide a depository for government funds and a source of credit for French businessmen.
3. Napoleon created elite secondary schools or lycées. National curriculum standards became the hallmark of a rigidly centralized academic system.

D. LIBERTY OR DESPOTISM?

1. Napoleon claimed that he preserved the gains of the French Revolution. His supporters argued that he fulfilled the philosophes' dream of an enlightened despot by preserving the principle of equality before the law, guaranteeing religious toleration, and opening careers to all men of talent.
2. His critics pointed out that these gains came with a steep price. The more power Napoleon accumulated, the more he wanted. Napoleon severely limited political expression. He enacted laws designed to censor plays, books, and newspapers. For example, before the coup, Paris had 73 newspapers. By 1811, the city just had four newspapers, all following the official government line.

III. THE NAPOLEONIC EMPIRE, 1804–1815

A. "EUROPE WAS AT MY FEET"

1. Napoleon's insatiable ambition and the continuing enmity of England made war inevitable.
2. Great Britain persuaded Austria, Prussia, and Russia that they must act together to restore the balance of power and resist the spread of French influence.
3. Between 1805 and 1807, Napoleon defeated Austrian, Prussian, and Russian forces in a series of brilliant military victories. Napoleon accurately boasted, "Europe was at my feet." Only Great Britain stood between Napoleon and his dream of achieving French hegemony over all of Europe.
4. Napoleon hoped to invade England. However, at the Battle of Trafalgar in October 1805, Admiral Horatio Nelson attacked and defeated a French fleet off the southern coast of Spain. The victory thwarted goals of controlling the seas and mounting an invasion of England.

B. THE REORGANIZATION OF GERMANY

1. Napoleon's victories enabled him to dissolve the Holy Roman Empire. He consolidated previously independent German states into a French-dominated Confederation of the Rhine.
2. Posing as a champion of the Revolution, Napoleon abolished feudalism and granted peasants freedom from manorial duties.
3. It is important to note that Napoleon unwittingly sparked a wave of German nationalism that fueled resistance to his rule. People who at first welcomed the French as liberators now felt they were being exploited by foreign invaders. Napoleon thus inadvertently accelerated the cause of German unification.

C. THE CONTINENTAL SYSTEM

1. Napoleon turned to economic warfare to weaken the English economy. In 1806, he ordered the beginning of a Continental System by imposing heavy penalties on anyone trading with England. Napoleon imposed a heavy strain on continental economies by forbidding the importation of English goods.

↳ trade w/ england = more expensive

2. Napoleon hoped that the Continental System would damage Great Britain by disrupting its export-driven economy and causing labor unrest. But these goals did not materialize. Great Britain responded by dramatically increasing its trade with Latin America. At the same time, smugglers successfully evaded Napoleon's agents by importing finished goods and New World sugar and tobacco.

IV. NATIONAL RESISTANCE IN SPAIN

A. NATIONALISM

1. Nationalism enabled French governments to raise highly motivated mass armies.
2. As Napoleon spread the principles of the French Revolution across the continent, he inadvertently aroused nationalist feelings across Europe. Nationalism in Germany and Spain became closely linked with opposition to French domination.
3. Napoleon underestimated the growing power of nationalism to inspire opposition to French rule. One contemporary critic understood this vulnerability when she observed: "He never reckoned with the one power that no arms could overcome—the enthusiasm of a whole people."

B. THE BEGINNING OF SPANISH RESISTANCE

1. In 1808, Napoleon awakened Spanish nationalism by replacing the country's ruling dynasty with his brother Joseph Bonaparte.
2. Faced with the arbitrary removal of their royal family, the Spanish people rose in rebellion. Angry crowds rioted against French troops stationed in Madrid. The French responded by executing hundreds of rebels and innocent bystanders. The riots and executions marked the beginning of a bloody conflict known as the Peninsular War.
3. Francisco de Goya depicted the atrocities in Madrid in his epic painting *The Third of May 1808*. Goya's memorable image dramatically juxtaposed an anonymous French firing squad with the haunting faces of their victims.

C. THE "SPANISH ULCER"

1. Napoleon's highly trained army outnumbered the Spanish and their British allies. However, bands of highly mobile Spanish guerrilla fighters ambushed the French and then disappeared into the countryside. Both sides committed atrocities that contributed to a prolonged and bitter conflict.

2. The guerrillas and a British expeditionary force pinned down a French army of about 300,000 men. Faced with mounting losses, Napoleon referred to the conflict as his "Spanish ulcer." The Peninsular War damaged the aura of French invincibility and inspired other nationalists to view the Spanish as unwanted invaders rather than as liberators.

V. THE FALL OF NAPOLEON

A. MAKING COMPARISONS: NAPOLEON AND TSAR ALEXANDER I

1. Napoleon believed he could replace Europe's crumbling state system with a supernational empire ruled from Paris. He further believed that the era of balance of power politics was over and that nationalist strivings would not stand in his way.

2. In contrast, Tsar Alexander I persuaded traditional Russian foreign policy objectives. He wanted to retain a Russian sphere of influence in Eastern Europe and in the Baltic region. Alexander opposed Napoleon's Continental System and reopened Russia's ports to British and neutral vessels.

3. Napoleon concluded that he could no longer tolerate Alexander's interference with his imperial goals. He mobilized a Grand Army of 600,000 men to invade Russia. The campaign began on June 23, 1812.

B. THE RUSSIAN DEBACLE

1. The Russian campaign proved to be a debacle. Instead of directly attacking the Grand Army, the Russian generals retreated toward Moscow. As they withdrew, the Russians carried out a scorched-earth policy of burning homes, destroying crops, and slaughtering livestock.

2. Napoleon reached Moscow on September 14, 1812. The next day, fires probably set by Russian troops, destroyed almost three-fourths of the city.

3. Alexander refused to surrender forcing the frustrated Napoleon to order a belated retreat. The retreat soon became a rout. A combination of bitterly cold weather, disease, and merciless Russian attacks decimated the once Grand Army. Less than 100,000 of Napoleon's troops survived the ordeal.

C. NAPOLEON'S FINAL BATTLES

1. Napoleon's enemies quickly took advantage of his weakness. Great Britain, Russia, Prussia, and Austria formed a Grand Alliance that defeated Napoleon at the Battle of Nations in October 1813.
2. The allied armies entered Paris in March 1814. Napoleon abdicated his throne and was exiled to Elba, a tiny island 9 miles off the Tuscan coast.
3. In March 1815, Napoleon escaped from Elba and formed a new army. Led by Great Britain and Prussia, the Grand Alliance defeated Napoleon at the Battle of Waterloo in June 1815.
4. Napoleon abdicated a second time and was shipped to St. Helena, a remote island in the South Atlantic. Once the master of Europe, Napoleon now lived in lonely exile writing his memoirs. He died in 1821.

Napoleon's battles have fascinated generations of military historians—but APEURO test writers are not military historians. You should know that the Battle of Austerlitz solidified Napoleon's reputation as a military genius. Otherwise, focus your study time on the impact Napoleon's conquests had in spreading nationalism and in dissolving the Holy Roman Empire.

VI. NAPOLEON'S LEGACY

A. IMPACT ON FRANCE

1. Napoleon's defeat temporarily ended the Revolutionary era in France. But the restored Bourbon King Louis XVIII could not restore the Old Regime.
2. The great ideals of the Revolution—liberty, equality, and nationalism—lived on. The concept of revolution as a legitimate

means of achieving social and political goals continued to justify revolutionary political changes.

3. Napoleon's domestic program created France's centralized bureaucracy, its unified secondary educational system, and its legal code.

B. IMPACT ON THE EUROPEAN BALANCE OF POWER

1. Napoleon permanently altered the European political landscape. He eliminated the petty German states. At the same time, Russia began to exercise an important voice in the affairs of Western Europe.

2. For the first time in two centuries, France lost its status as the richest and strongest state in Europe.

Chapter 20

Restoration and Romanticism 1815–1848

I. THE SEARCH FOR STABILITY

A. FORCES OF THE PAST

1. Traditional institutions of power
   i. Monarchy
   ii. Aristocracy
   iii. Church
   iv. Patriarchal family
2. Conservatism
   i. Believed that national, historic, and religious traditions are the essential foundations of any society.
   ii. Maintained that all change should be gradual.
   iii. Appealed to those who were frightened by the social disorder, violence, and terror fomented by the French Revolution.

B. FORCES OF THE FUTURE

1. Industrialization
   i. Began in Great Britain in the late eighteenth century.
   ii. Strengthened the size and significance of business leaders, merchants, and the middle class.
   iii. Created a new class of urban workers.
2. Liberalism
   i. Believed in natural rights that governments must protect.
   ii. Supported civil liberties, including freedom from arbitrary arrest and imprisonment and guarantees for freedom of speech, the press, assembly, and religion.

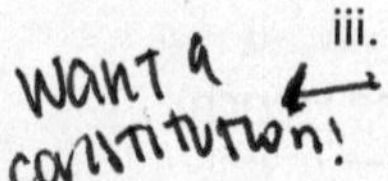

iii. Believed that individual rights are best protected by a written constitution that creates a limited government with carefully defined powers.

iv. Admired the British system of constitutional monarchy.

v. Favored representative government.

vi. Opposed full democracy.

vii. Advocated economic individualism and opposed government intervention in the economy.

viii. Expressed little concern for the plight of urban workers.

ix. Inspired revolts in France in 1830 and 1848 and key reforms in Great Britain.

3. Nationalism

i. Believed that a nation consists of a group of people who share similar traditions, history, language, and sense of political identity.

ii. Argued that every nation should be sovereign and include all members of a nationality.

iii. Insisted that a person's greatest loyalty should be to a nation-state.

iv. Stirred powerful forces for change.

II. RESTORING THE OLD ORDER: THE CONGRESS OF VIENNA

A. ELABORATE POMP

1. The crowned heads of Austria, Prussia, Russia, and dozens of lesser states along with the ministers of nearly every European government assembled in Vienna, Austria, in the fall of 1814.
2. The Austrians entertained their guests with elegant balls, lavish dinners, festive fireworks, and concerts by Beethoven.

B. SERIOUS DELIBERATIONS

1. Led by Prince Klemens von Metternich, the Austrian Minister of Foreign Affairs, the great powers conducted serious negotiations to redraw the map of Europe and attempt to create a durable peace.

2. Like the other aristocratic dignitaries, Metternich opposed the forces of liberalism and nationalism unleashed by the French Revolution and Napoleon. He believed in the value of maintaining the status quo. "The first and greatest concern for the immense majority of every nation," Metternich insisted, "is the stability of laws—never their change."

C. THE PRINCIPLE OF LEGITIMACY

1. Legitimacy meant restoring ruling families that had been deposed by the French Revolution and Napoleon.
2. As the younger brother of Louis XVI, Louis XVIII returned as the legitimate Bourbon ruler of France.
3. Bourbon rulers were also returned to their thrones in Spain and Naples.
4. The Congress restored the House of Orange in Holland and the House of Savoy in Sardinia-Piedmont.

D. THE BALANCE OF POWER

1. The leaders at Vienna wanted to weaken France so that it would no longer be able to wage wars of aggression and threaten the balance of power.
2. At the same time, the victorious powers did not want to impose a punitive treaty that would humiliate and antagonize France.
3. France was forced to return to its 1790 borders and to pay an indemnity of 700 million francs. However, France was allowed to keep most of its overseas possessions, its army, and an independent government.
4. To keep France from renewing its drive for power, the Congress encircled France with strengthened powers:
   i. The Austrian Netherlands was united with the Dutch Republic to form a single kingdom of the Netherlands.
   ii. A group of 39 German states were loosely joined into a newly created German Confederation, dominated by Austria.
   iii. The Congress recognized Switzerland as an independent and neutral nation.
   iv. The Kingdom of Sardinia in Italy was strengthened by the addition of Piedmont and Savoy.

E. TERRITORIAL SETTLEMENTS

1. Russia acquired more Polish territory.
2. Sweden retained Norway.
3. Prussia acquired two-fifths of Saxony and territory in the Rhineland along the border of France.
4. Austria acquired the northern Italian provinces of Lombardy and Venetia as compensation for its loss of Belgium.
5. Britain gained valuable territories for its overseas empire, including Malta, the Cape of Good Hope, Trinidad, and Tobago.

F. EVALUATION

1. The Congress of Vienna negotiated the most extensive European settlements since the agreements at Westphalia in 1648. The decisions proved to be acceptable to both the victors and to France.
2. It created a framework for peace that prevented a war among the great powers for forty years. No wars of worldwide dimensions occurred for a full century.
3. It created a balance of power that lasted until the unification of Germany in 1871.
4. It represented a temporary triumph for the conservative order. The leaders of the Congress of Vienna could not contain the forces of liberalism and nationalism unleashed by the French Revolution.

III. ROMANTICISM

A. THE ROMANTIC MOVEMENT

1. Swept across Europe during the first half of the nineteenth century.
2. Influenced religion, art, music, and philosophy.
3. Inspired a desire for freedom of thought, feeling, and action.

B. KEY CHARACTERISTICS

1. The primacy of emotion
   i. The Enlightenment stressed reason as a way to understand nature.

ii. Romantics rejected reason, and instead stressed emotion, intuition, and subjective feelings. The German novelist Johann Wolfgang von Goethe emphasized the importance of feeling over thinking when he wrote, "What I know, anyone can know, but my heart is my own, peculiar to itself."

2. A different past

i. Neoclassical artists looked to Greece and Rome for models of order and clarity.

ii. Romantics looked to the medieval period for models of chivalrous heroes, miraculous events, and unsolved mysteries. The deeds of legendary kings and knights seemed more worthy of song and story than those of contemporary factory owners and railway engineers.

3. A new view of nature

i. Enlightened thinkers relied on the scientific method to study and understand nature. They viewed nature as a well-ordered machine.

ii. Romantics preferred to contemplate the beauty of nature. They were inspired by raging rivers, gathering storms, and majestic mountains veiled in mist. These natural wonders were a source of spiritual inspiration that evoked feelings of awe and wonder.

4. Heroic individuals

i. Enlightened thinkers and artists depicted disciplined heroes who relied on reason and exhibited self-restraint.

ii. Romantic artists celebrated heroic rebels who acted spontaneously and overcame the constraints place on them by governments, religions, and societal conventions. For example, the British poet Lord Byron became a Romantic hero when he rushed off to fight and die in the Greek war for independence from the Turks.

C. MAKING COMPARISONS: ENLIGHTENED AND ROMANTIC VIEWS OF RELIGION

1. The Enlightenment embraced a mechanical view of human nature and the physical world. Enlightened thinkers rejected faith and instead relied on a rational, scientific approach to understand the relationship between human beings and the natural world. The Enlightenment favored the deist view that a distant God created

the natural world and, like a "divine watchmaker," stepped back from his creation and humanity's daily concerns.

2. The Romantics believed in a loving, personal God. They stressed emotions, inner faith, and religious inspiration. Romantics embraced the wonders and mysteries of nature as a way to feel the divine presence.

D. KEY ROMANTIC WRITERS, ARTISTS, AND COMPOSERS

1. Writers
   - i. William Wordsworth and Samuel Taylor Coleridge, *Lyrical Ballads*—a collection of poems that mark the beginning of the English Romantic movement in poetry.
   - ii. Friedrich Schiller, "Ode to Joy"—celebrates the unity of all humankind.
   - iii. Jacob and Wilhelm Grimm, *Grimm's Fairy Tales*—a collection of over 200 German folk stories that illustrate the fusion of nationalism and romanticism.
2. Artists
   - i. Caspar David Friedrich, *The Wanderer Above the Mists*—depicts a lonely but captivating traveler standing on a mountain peak contemplating a mysterious and awesome vista that can be dimly seen through the surrounding mist.
   - ii. Eugène Delacroix, *Liberty Leading the People*—depicts working and middle-class citizens united by their common yearning for liberty.
   - iii. John Constable, *The Hay Wain*—portrays a farmer and his hay wagon as integral and harmonious parts of the natural landscape.
3. Composers
   - i. Ludwig van Beethoven, Ninth Symphony—incorporates Schiller's "Ode to Joy" into a soaring presentation of human emotions.
   - ii. Richard Wagner, "The Ring of the Nibelung"—fuses music and drama by reshaping ancient Germanic myths into a story of how unselfish love finally triumphs over the obsessive pursuit of money and power.

E. ROMANTICISM AND NATIONALISM

1. Romantic authors believed in revolutionary movements that would give people more freedom and control over their lives. By studying the past, writers helped make people aware of their common heritage. The resurgence of national feeling sparked nationalist movements across Europe.
2. German authors placed special emphasis on the common historic. Cultural, and linguistic ties that bound together the "Volk" or living "national community." For example, the Grimm brothers published a large collection of fairy tales they believed expressed the authentic spirt of German culture.

The Romantic movement is one of the most frequently tested APEURO topics. Multiple-choice questions focus on the romantic emphasis on emotion. Free-response questions focus on comparison between the Enlightenment and romantic views of nature.

UNIT 6 Industrialization and Its Effects

c. 1815 to c. 1914

Chapters 21–23

PREVIEW: UNIT 6 KEY CONCEPTS

- The Industrial Revolution spread from Great Britain to the continent, where the state played a greater role in promoting industry.
  - — Great Britain established its industrial dominance through the mechanization of textile production, iron and steel production, and new transportation systems in conjunction with uniquely favorable political and social climates.
  - — Following the British example, industrialization took root in continental Europe, sometimes with state sponsorship.
- The experiences of everyday life were shaped by industrialization, depending on the level of industrial development in a particular location.
  - — Industrialization promoted the development of new classes in the industrial regions of Europe.
  - — Europe experienced rapid population growth and urbanization, leading to social dislocations.
  - — Over time, the Industrial Revolution altered the family structure and relations for bourgeois and working-class families.
- Political revolutions and the complications resulting from industrialization triggered a range of ideological, governmental, and collective responses.
  - — Ideologies developed and took root throughout society as a response to industrial and political revolutions.
  - — Governments, at times based on the pressure of political or social organizations, responded to problems created or exacerbated by industrialization.

Chapter 21

The Industrial Revolution in Great Britain

I. INTRODUCTION

A. GENERAL OVERVIEW

1. The Industrial Revolution refers to the process by which economic production shifted from the use of hand tools to the use of power machinery, first fueled by coal and steam.
2. The Industrial Revolution began in Great Britain in the 1750s.
3. The Napoleonic Wars delayed industrial growth in Western Europe.
4. Continental Europe began to industrialize after 1815. The Industrial Revolution spread from Western Europe to Eastern Europe.

B. HISTORIC IMPACT

1. The Industrial Revolution caused a process of modernization that dominated life in the nineteenth century.
2. The Industrial Revolution concentrated factories and workers in industrial centers. This promoted a process of urbanization that led to the growth of urban centers across Europe. Between 1800 and 1850, the number of European cities with a population of more than 100,000 inhabitants rose from 22 to 47.
3. The Industrial Revolution led to the formation of a new self-conscious social class, the working class, or proletariat.
4. The Industrial Revolution also led to the formation of a new and expanding middle class, or bourgeoisie.
5. The Industrial Revolution and urbanization had a dramatic effect upon families, including the role of women and childhood experiences.

6. The Industrial Revolution improved the standard of living by providing more consumer products, improved medical care, and new leisure activities.
7. The benefits of industrialization solidified Britain's position as one of the dominant European powers.

II. REASONS FOR BRITISH LEADERSHIP

A. THE ENCLOSURE MOVEMENT

1. This movement, which privatized land formerly available to all for grazing and farming, concentrated land ownership in fewer hands.
2. With no land to work, small farmers were displaced, thus forming a pool of cheap labor.

B. THE AGRICULTURAL REVOLUTION

1. Crop rotation replaced the open-field system.
2. Landowners experimented with new crops such as turnips and new inventions such as the seed drill.
3. The revolution in agriculture made it possible for fewer farmers to feed more people.

C. THE POPULATION EXPLOSION

1. New farming methods produced more food.
2. Medical advances such as Edward Jenner's discovery of a smallpox vaccine reduced death rates.
3. The combined population of Great Britain and Ireland increased from 10 million in 1750 to 30 million in 1850.
4. This dramatic increase in population created a growing market that stimulated production.

D. THE COMMERCIAL REVOLUTION

1. Successful British merchants had large amounts of wealth accumulated from global trade.
2. Great Britain had a stable, well-developed banking system that funded industrial development.

E. GEOGRAPHIC ADVANTAGES

1. Britain had abundant supplies of coal and iron ore. Coal replaced wood as a key source of energy, while iron was used to manufacture tools and construct buildings.
2. Britain was geographically compact. No place in Britain was more than 70 miles from the sea or more than 30 miles from a navigable river. As a result, Britain formed a national market.
3. Britain had many rivers and ports, which facilitated trade and shipping.

F. STABLE AND SUPPORTIVE GOVERNMENT

1. Political stability encouraged economic growth and innovation.
2. Britain had no internal tariffs or trade barriers.

G. THE ENLIGHTENMENT

1. Founded in London in 1660, the Royal Society became a world-famous organization for the exchange of ideas and practical inventions.
2. British society encouraged and rewarded inventors and entrepreneurs.

III. THE TEXTILE INDUSTRY

A. THE INCENTIVE

1. The global demand for cotton cloth was enormous.
2. Prompted by huge potential profits, British entrepreneurs financed new ways of spinning and weaving cotton.

B. THE INVENTIONS

1. In 1733, John Kay invented the flying shuttle, enabling a single weaver to work twice as fast.
2. In the mid-1760s, James Hargreaves invented the spinning jenny, a spinning machine that made it possible for a single weaver to work six to eight threads at a time.

3. In 1769, Richard Arkwright invented a water frame that used water power from fast-moving streams to drive spinning machines.
4. In 1779, Samuel Crompton invented a spinning machine called the mule that combined the best features of the spinning jenny and the water frame to produce thread that was stronger, finer, and more uniform than earlier spinning machines.
5. In 1785, Edmund Cartwright invented a power loom that used water power to dramatically speed up weaving.
6. In 1793, Eli Whitney invented the cotton gin, making it possible to efficiently remove seeds from the cotton fiber.
7. As a result of these continuous technological improvements, the output of cotton fiber from British textile factories rose from 40 million yards in 1785 to more than 2 billion yards in 1850.

APEURO test writers do not focus on the sequence of inventions that revolutionized the textile industry. Instead, you should know that these inventions marked a shift from human and animal power to mechanical power. The mechanization of the spinning and weaving process in the textile industry ushered in the Industrial Revolution.

C. THE STEAM ENGINE

1. James Watt patented the first steam engine in 1769.
2. The steam engine rapidly replaced water power in British textile factories.
3. Steam power played a key role in boosting iron production.

D. THE RAILROAD

1. Steam power enabled inventors to build railroad locomotives.
2. English entrepreneurs wanted a railroad line to connect the port of Liverpool with the inland city of Manchester, the heart of the spinning and weaving industry. The Liverpool-Manchester Railway opened in 1830.
3. By 1850, Britain had over 6,000 miles of railroad track. Each mile of newly laid track required 300 tons of iron.

4. Railroads revolutionized the technology of overland travel. For centuries, a team of four horses pulled uncomfortable stagecoaches on long and tedious trips. Railroads provided a faster, cheaper, and more comfortable means of transportation.

5. Railroads improved diet by providing access to perishable food. Trains carried fresh fish inland from the coasts and fresh vegetables from rural farms to city markets.

6. Railroads promoted leisure travel by making it possible for urban residents to spend a weekend at coastal resorts.

7. The railroads successful combination of steam, coal, and iron became the supreme symbol of the new age of industrial progress.

APEURO test writers place great emphasis upon the significance of railroads as a turning point in European history. You should be able to identify specific historic examples that illustrate the importance of railroads. You should also be able to identify limitations of nineteenth-century railroads. For example, railroads were not widespread in Eastern Europe and rail travel was limited to the middle and upper classes until late in the nineteenth century.

IV. WORKING-CLASS PROTEST IN GREAT BRITAIN

A. THE LUDDITES

1. The new textile technologies threatened the jobs of Britain's 250,000 hand-loom weavers. Named after Ned Ludd, frustrated English weavers known as Luddites broke into early textile factories and smashed the machinery.

2. These acts of despair could not stop the Industrial Revolution. Parliament quickly responded by passing a law making the destruction of machines a capital offense. By 1850, there were less than 50,000 weavers.

3. Workers gradually came to realize that destroying machines would not improve their lives. Instead, they had to form labor unions to fight for higher wages and better working conditions.

B. EARLY LABOR UNIONS

1. The Combination Acts of 1799 and 1800 prohibited British workers from organizing to improve their condition.
2. Under pressure from labor and middle-class reformers, Parliament repealed the Combination Acts in 1824.
3. In 1875, British trade unions won full legal status, including the right to strike.

V. GREAT BRITAIN'S INDUSTRIAL DOMINANCE

A. STATISTICAL MEASURES OF BRITISH PROSPERITY, 1850

1. Manufactured one-half of the world's cotton.
2. Mined two-thirds of the world's coal.
3. Mined more than one-half of the world's iron.
4. Controlled one-third of the world's international trade.
5. Possessed more railroad lines than France, Russia, Austria, Belgium, and all the Italian states combined.

B. THE GREAT EXHIBITION, 1851

1. The exhibition was held to celebrate Britain's undisputed economic and technological dominance.
2. Britain's Hall of Machinery featured the locomotive engines, hydraulic presses, and power looms that had powered the Industrial Revolution.
3. European visitors marveled at the wonders of "the British miracle" and used the exhibition as a way to measure their own countries' technological progress.

C. MAKING COMPARISONS: THE CRYSTAL PALACE AND THE ARC DE TRIOMPHE

1. The Crystal Palace in London
   - i. Commissioned to celebrate British leadership in the industrial age.
   - ii. Enclosed 18 acres and almost 1 million square feet of exhibition space.

iii. Featured prefabricated glass panels and cast-iron columns.

iv. Demonstrated the possibilities of mass production.

2. The Arc de Triomphe in Paris

   i. Commissioned to celebrate French victories during the Revolution and the Age of Napoleon.

   ii. Based on the triumphal arches of ancient Rome.

   iii. Combined a Neoclassical arch with romantic relief sculptures.

   iv. Reached a height of 164 feet, making it the largest arch ever built.

Chapter 22

The Second Wave of Industrialization

I. THE SECOND INDUSTRIAL REVOLUTION

A. NEW INDUSTRIES

1. The Bessemer process increased steel production while reducing costs. By 1900, steel had replaced iron in machinery, ships, railroad tracks, and building construction. For example, steel girders replaced stone and iron as the supports for buildings. Steel frames enabled architects to build the first "cloud scrapers."
2. Led by Germany, the chemical industry grew rapidly. New products included soaps, dyes, fertilizers, and explosives.

B. NEW SOURCES OF POWER

1. Coal and steam gave way to electricity, oil, and gasoline in powering even more intricate machinery.
2. Electricity proved to be especially versatile. It lit homes and powered everything from industrial machinery to the new streetcars.

C. NEW FORMS OF COMMUNICATION AND TRANSPORTATION

1. First demonstrated by Alexander Graham Bell in 1876, the telephone quickly became an essential part of modern life. The telephone linked families and friends while also playing a key role in speeding business transactions.
2. The invention of the internal combustion engine enabled mechanics to build gasoline-powered automobiles.

D. NEW FORMS OF INDUSTRIAL ORGANIZATION

1. Business enterprises became larger and more powerful.

2. Business leaders formed trusts in the United States, amalgamations in Great Britain, and cartels in Germany to control production, distribution, and price levels.

3. Capitalists such as Andrew Carnegie, John D. Rockefeller, Alfred Krupp, and Alfred Nobel wielded enormous economic power and political influence.

E. NEW INDUSTRIAL POWERS

1. Worldwide industrial production more than tripled between 1870 and 1914. Great Britain, Germany, and the United States dominated the world economy. In 1913, these three nations produced two-thirds of the world's manufactured goods.

2. Although Great Britain continued to be a major industrial power, its rate of growth slowed. Germany and the United States emerged as new and formidable industrial rivals.

3. Germany's emergence as Europe's leading industrial power altered the European balance of power, posing a challenge to Great Britain's political and economic leadership.

II. POPULATION GROWTH AND URBANIZATION

A. POPULATION GROWTH

1. As a result of falling death rates and improved agricultural and industrial production, Europe's population rose from 193 million in 1800 to 423 million in 1900.

2. In 1900, Europeans comprised 24 percent of the world's population. The figure today is just 12 percent.

B. URBANIZATION

1. Large-scale urbanization had been virtually unknown in Europe before the early nineteenth century.

2. The factory system transformed many small towns into crowded cities. For example, between 1760 and 1850, the population of Manchester, England, surged from 45,000 to 300,000.

3. The sudden influx of people created slums where entire families lived in a single dark room.

4. In 1914, the urban population reached 80 percent in Britain, 60 percent in Germany, and 45 percent in France.

III. SOCIAL EFFECTS OF INDUSTRIALIZATION

A. THE FACTORY SYSTEM

1. The factory was a place where large numbers of workers used machines to manufacture goods.
2. As the factory system spread, the putting-out system disappeared.
3. The factory system created two self-conscious social classes, the working class or proletariat and the middle class or bourgeoisie.

B. WORKING-CLASS MISERY

1. The Industrial Revolution brought misery and poverty to the growing urban working class.
2. Factory workers often labored on dangerous machines for 14 hours a day.
3. The demand for cheap labor led to the widespread employment of women and young children.
4. Workers had no health insurance and little job security.
5. The plight of the working class, including child labor and gender exploitation, dominated social and political issues during the nineteenth century.

C. MIDDLE-CLASS PROSPERITY

1. The middle classes, or bourgeoisie, enjoyed unprecedented prosperity, political power, and leisure time.
2. The *haute bourgeoisie* included wealthy bankers, merchants, and industrialists.
3. The *petite bourgeoisie* included shopkeepers, skilled artisans, professional men, and the clergy.

IV. NEW IDEOLOGIES: LIBERALISM

A. POLITICAL LIBERALISM

1. Liberals believed in freedom of thought, religion, and trade. They also stressed freedom from restrictions and injustices of the Old Regime.
2. In his seminal essay *On Liberty*, the British social philosopher John Stuart Mill supported only the most necessary interference by the government in the affairs of the individual.
3. Liberals favored a limited democracy with property qualifications for voting and holding office.

B. ECONOMIC LIBERALISM

1. Liberals accepted the laissez-faire economic policies advocated in Adam Smith's *Wealth of Nations* (See Chapter 15).
2. Liberals insisted that the laws of supply and demand would act as an "invisible hand" so that selfish individual acts would ultimately benefit the whole society by increasing productivity and thus overall prosperity.
3. Liberals opposed legislation designed to improve wages and hours as unnecessary interference with the competitive free market.
4. Liberals believed that government policies should be limited to enforcing contracts, protecting private property, and ensuring national defense.
5. Liberals exhibited general indifference toward the plight of the working class. They prided themselves on being tough and ruthless men who survived economic downturns, overcame destructive wars, and replaced obsolete machinery with expensive new technologies.

V. NEW IDEOLOGIES: SOCIALISM

A. SHARED BELIEFS

1. The existing distribution of wealth is unjust. The "haves" possess more than they need while the "have-nots" possess barely enough to survive.

2. The resources and means of production should be owned by the community.
3. The profits of human labor should be equitably distributed.

B. UTOPIAN SOCIALISM

1. Charles Fourier, Louis Blanc, and Robert Owen were the most prominent Utopian Socialists.
2. They advocated social and economic planning to create societies based on cooperation rather than competition. For example, Owen built a model factory in New Lanark, Scotland. He constructed houses near the factory and rented them to his employees at reasonable rents. Owen increased wages and shortened working hours. He eliminated child labor, providing his workers' children with free school instead. Both productivity and profits increased, supporting Owen's contention that satisfied workers where also better workers.
3. Owen was less successful with a project he attempted in the United States. Founded in 1825 as a model communal village, New Harmony, Indiana, attracted an unworkable mix of hard-working idealists, contentious radicals, and selfish scoundrels. As a result, the community dissolved within four years.

C. SCIENTIFIC SOCIALISM

1. Karl Marx and Friedrich Engels challenged the moderate approach of early socialists like Owen as the work of misguided dreamers or utopian socialists. In contrast, Marx and Engels described their ideas as scientific socialism because they were based on a scientific study of historic forces.
2. Friedrich Engels was the German-born manager of a cotton business in Manchester. The working conditions of factory laborers appalled Engels. In his book *The Condition of the Working Class in England*, Engels denounced the capitalist middle class for using economic liberalism as a convenient rationalization to justify their ruthless exploitation of the working class.
3. Engels met and befriended a fellow German, Karl Marx. Engels persuaded Marx to move to England where he subsidized Marx's research and writing.
4. Marx and Engels published the *Communist Manifesto* in 1848. They boldly asserted that "the history of all hitherto existing societies is the history of class struggles."

5. Historians before Marx emphasized the role of ideas in causing events. Marx took a very different approach. He argued that economic forces played the dominant role in shaping the social, political, and religious institutions.
6. Marx argued that human societies have always been divided into two classes—the haves and the have-nots. The haves control the means of producing goods and thus possess great wealth and power. The have-nots perform backbreaking labor but receive low wages and endure poor working conditions.
7. Marx contended that the history of class conflict is best understood through the dialectical process of thesis, antithesis, and synthesis. The thesis is the dominant state of affairs. It inevitably gives rise to a conflicting or contradictory force called the antithesis. The resulting clash between the thesis and the antithesis produces a new state of affairs called the synthesis.
8. Marx argued that nineteenth-century society had split "into two great classes directly facing each other: bourgeoisie and proletariat." As the owners of the means of production, the bourgeoisie were the thesis. The proletariat or workers were the antithesis.
9. Marx contended that a class struggle between the bourgeoisie and the proletariat would lead "to the dictatorship of the proletariat."
10. The "dictatorship of the proletariat" would be a transitional phase leading "to the abolition of all classes and to a classless society" in which there would be no private ownership of the means of production.
11. Marx and Engels argued that women were exploited by both men and capitalists.
12. Modern historians criticize Marx by pointing out that the European wars since the seventeenth century were not fought between the "oppressed" and their "oppressors," but between rival religions and competing nations.

Marxism is one of the most frequently tested topics on the APEURO exam. Test writers expect you to use Marxian concepts such as class struggle to analyze events such as the French Revolution and the Russian Revolution.

D. EVOLUTIONARY SOCIALISM

1. Marx predicted that as workers became more exploited they would unite to overthrow the bourgeoisie. Instead, as capitalism matured, working conditions improved.
2. Led by Eduard Bernstein, "evolutionary" socialists began to revise Marxian doctrine to adjust to the new economic realities.
3. Bernstein rejected Marx's concept of class struggle and instead sought to achieve socialist goals by a process of gradual reform.

Chapter 23

Restoration and Revolution

I. MAINTAINING THE OLD ORDER: THE CONCERT OF EUROPE

A. THE CONGRESS SYSTEM

1. England, Austria, Prussia, and Russia formed a Quadruple Alliance committing them to preserve the conservative order.
2. The great powers also agreed to hold periodic meetings or congresses to prevent crises from escalating into wider wars.
3. The effort to achieve consensus on foreign policy issues was known as the Concert of Europe. It marks the first significant experiment in collective security.

B. REVOLT AND REPRESSION

1. The Congress of Vienna disappointed liberals and nationalists across Europe. Discontentment led to revolts that tested Metternich and the Concert of Europe.
2. Uprisings in Spain and Italy
   i. The repressive policies of the restored Spanish Bourbon King Ferdinand VII provoked demands for a more representative government. Acting with the consent of the other great powers, the French forces intervened, enabling Ferdinand to regain absolute power.
   ii. Repressive monarchs in Naples and Sardinia-Piedmont also sparked rebellions. Metternich promptly responded by sending in Austrian forces who defeated the rebels.
3. Repression in Germany
   i. Young Germans continued to hope for liberal reforms and a united Germany. Disillusioned by the Congress of Vienna, they formed student associations to discuss their concerns.

ii. Alarmed by these student activists, Metternich persuaded the major German states to issue the Carlsbad Decrees. The decrees dissolved the student associations, censored books and newspapers, and used secret police to harass dissidents.

4. The Decembrist Revolt in Russia

i. When Tsar Alexander I died in December 1825, a group of army officers rebelled, calling for constitutional reform.

ii. Alexander's successor, Nicholas I (reigned 1825–1855) ruthlessly suppressed the Decembrists.

iii. Under Nicholas I's oppressive regime, Russia became Europe's most powerful reactionary stronghold.

iv. Nicholas I turned Russia into a police state. The tsar was a ruthless autocrat who forbade representative assemblies, monitored university curricula, and censored all dissenting viewpoints.

II. LIBERAL REFORM IN ENGLAND

A. THE REFORM BILL OF 1832

1. The House of Commons was less representative of the British people than at any time in its 500-year history.
2. Many boroughs (electoral districts) were sparsely populated, and a few had no people at all. Meanwhile, new industrial cities such as Manchester had no representatives.
3. After a decade of pressure from factory owners and merchants, Parliament passed the Reform Bill of 1832. It created a number of new districts representing heavily urban areas. It also doubled the number of voters to include most middle-class men. And finally, the Reform Bill of 1832 resulted in the supremacy of the House of Commons over the House of Lords.
4. Under the Reform Bill of 1832, only about one in five adult males could vote. Workers, women, and the poor were all disenfranchised.

B. THE REPEAL OF THE CORN LAWS

1. The Corn Laws placed a high tariff on imported corn, wheat, and other grains. The tariff benefited large landowners by providing them with a protected market for their crops.

2. Prominent industrialists formed the Anti-Corn Law League. They advocated a free-trade policy that would lower the price of food and increase the profits of industry.
3. Wealthy landowners stubbornly resisted all reform proposals. However, the Irish potato famine dramatically strengthened support for cheaper imported grains.
4. Parliament finally voted to repeal the Corn Laws in 1846. This marked a victory for Britain's urban population and for the proponents of free trade.

C. THE CHARTIST MOVEMENT

1. Britain's disenfranchised workers demanded more sweeping reforms.
2. In 1838, working-class leaders drew up a People's Charter that demanded universal manhood suffrage, a secret ballot, equal electoral districts, and the abolition of property requirements for membership in the House of Commons.
3. Despite widespread public support, Parliament adamantly refused to consider the Chartists' proposals. It is important to note that most of the Chartist reforms would be ultimately adopted.

D. CONSEQUENCES

1. The British people saw that reform was possible without a violent revolution.
2. England experienced much less internal unrest than the other countries in Europe.

III. THE REVOLUTIONS OF 1830

A. THE FRENCH REVOLUTION OF 1830

1. In 1824, Charles X (reigned 1824–1830) succeeded his brother, Louis XVIII. A dedicated reactionary, Charles X vigorously opposed republicanism, liberalism, and constitutionalism.
2. Charles X's reactionary policies infuriated both his liberal and working-class opponents.
3. Discontent with Charles X's arbitrary policies ignited three days of rioting in July 1830. Eugène Delacroix captured the spirit of the uprising in his famous painting, *Liberty Leading the People*.

4. Delacroix's tribute to liberty portrayed a unified people dedicated to overthrowing tyranny. The unity proved to be brief. While the workers wanted a republic, the bourgeoisie wanted a constitutional monarchy.

5. The bourgeoisie prevailed. With their support, Louis Philippe, Duke of Orleans, became "king of the French." Louis Philippe prided himself on being a "citizen king" who supported France's business interests.

B. REVOLUTION IN BELGIUM

1. The July Revolution in France helped spark discontent in Belgium.

2. The Congress of Vienna united the Austrian Netherlands (Belgium) with Holland to form a single kingdom of the Netherlands.

3. Catholic Belgium and Protestant Holland had very little in common. In 1830, riots in Belgium quickly turned into a widespread demand for independence.

4. Both Great Britain and France opposed intervention. In 1830, the great powers recognized Belgium as a neutral state.

C. ITALIAN NATIONALISM

1. Austria dominated northern Italy.

2. Italian nationalists formed a secret society called the Carbonari ("charcoal burners"). The Carbonari hoped to drive out the Austrians and unify Italy.

3. Inspired by the events in France and Belgium, the Carbonari rebelled. However, Metternich promptly sent in Austrian troops to restore order.

4. The Carbonari's failure left Giuseppe Mazzini as Italy's foremost nationalist leader.

IV. THE REVOLUTIONS OF 1848

A. CAUSES

1. Conservative leaders steadfastly refused to respond to the problems and social tensions created by industrialization and urbanization.

2. Working-class radicals and middle-class liberals were convinced that the repressive Metternich system had outlived its usefulness.
3. Nationalists in Italy and Germany yearned for unification. At the same time, national minorities in the Austrian Empire demanded independence.
4. Widespread crop failures, rising prices of food, and growing unemployment helped fuel popular unrest and calls for change.

B. REVOLUTION IN FRANCE

1. Affluent bourgeoisie dominated France during the reign of Louis Philippe (reigned 1830–1848). A leading minister rejected demands for extending the franchise to the working class by proclaiming, "Enrich yourself and you will have the vote."
2. Unable to withstand public pressure, Louis Philippe's government collapsed in February 1848.
3. As tension and unrest gripped Paris, liberals, socialists, and Bonapartists all vied for power.
4. Following a bloody confrontation between workers and the capitalist-backed government, French voters overwhelmingly elected Louis Napoleon as president of the Second French Republic. The nephew of Napoleon Bonaparte, Louis promised to restore order at home and glory abroad.

C. DEFEAT IN ITALY

1. Led by Giuseppe Mazzini, the "Young Italy" movement sought to establish a liberal republic embracing all Italy.
2. The Austrians once again proved to be too strong while the Italians once again proved to be too divided.

D. HOPE AND FAILURE IN GERMANY

1. A growing number of German nationalists hoped for a more liberal German state.
2. In 1834, all the major German states except Austria formed the Zollverein, an economic union that eliminated internal tariffs. The Zollverein facilitated commerce and set a precedent for greater union.

3. Riots broke out in Berlin in 1848. Frederick William IV (reigned 1840–1861) responded by issuing a series of reforms, including calling a Prussian assembly to draft a new constitution.
4. Meanwhile, another assembly met in Frankfurt to draft a constitution for all Germany.
5. The hopes of German reformers were soon crushed. Supported by the army, Frederick William dissolved the Prussian assembly. He then rejected the Frankfurt assembly's plan for a constitutional monarchy declaring that he would refuse to "pick up a crown from the gutter."
6. The failure of the German reform movement had fateful consequences for Germany and the future of Europe.

E. REVOLUTIONS IN THE AUSTRIAN EMPIRE

1. Austria was a huge dynastic state in which a dominant German-speaking nation ruled a large number of subject nationalities and ethnic groups.
2. Revolutionary fervor quickly spread from Paris to Vienna. As tensions mounted, Metternich resigned and fled to England.
3. An Austrian constituent assembly abolished the robot, or forced labor, thus removing a major source of peasant discontent.
4. Revolution quickly spread from Vienna to Hungary, where Louis Kossuth demanded self-government.
5. Despite initial setbacks, the Austrian government regained control. Only Hungary remained defiant. The new Austrian emperor, Francis Joseph (reigned 1848–1916), accepted the offer of Tsar Nicholas I to help defeat the Hungarians. A joint invasion by Russian and Austrian forces crushed Hungarian resistance.

F. KEY POINTS

1. The revolutions of 1848 failed because of internal divisions, a lack of popular support outside the cities, and the continued strength of conservative forces.
2. Although temporarily frustrated, the basic liberal principle of government by consent continued to gain influence as the middle class grew in size, wealth, and influence.

3. Peaceful reforms enabled England to avoid violent revolts.
4. Repressive policies stifled reform in Russia.
5. The ideas of nationalism and national unification continued to grow and gain support.
6. The era's idealistic romantic spirit now yielded to a new age of political realism.

The revolutions of 1848 form a particularly complex sequence of events. Do not spend time memorizing the chronology of what happened. Instead, focus on the causes and consequences of the various revolutions.

Nineteenth-Century Perspectives and Political Developments

c. 1815 to c. 1914

Chapters 24–26

PREVIEW: UNIT 7 KEY CONCEPTS

- European states struggled to maintain international stability in an age of nationalism and revolutions.
  - — The breakdown of the Concert of Europe opened the door for movements of national unification in Italy and Germany as well as liberal reforms elsewhere.
  - — The unification of Italy and Germany transformed the European balance of power and led to efforts to construct a new diplomatic order.
- A variety of motives and methods led to the intensification of European global control and increased tensions among the Great Powers.
  - — Industrial and technological developments (e.g., the second industrial revolution) facilitated European control of global empires.
- European ideas and culture expressed a tension between objectivity and scientific realism on one hand, and subjectivity and individual expression on the other.
  - — Following the revolutions of 1848, Europe turned toward a realist and materialist worldview.

Chapter 24

Nationalism, Realpolitik, and Realism 1850–1871

I. INTRODUCTION

A. THE IMPORTANCE OF NATIONALISM

1. Nationalism dominated European politics between 1848 and 1870.
2. Nationalism held that all people derive their identities from their nations. A nation is a group of people who share a common culture, sense of identity, and aspiration to achieve political independence.
3. Nationalist aspirations led to the unification of Italy and Germany, thus ending the Concert of Europe created by the Congress of Vienna.
4. Nationalist aspirations led to the breakup of the Ottoman Empire and the transformation of the Austrian Empire.

B. THE POLITICS OF REALPOLITIK

1. A new generation of European statesmen abandoned the politics of idealism in favor of a pragmatic tough-minded use of shrewd diplomacy and military force known as Realpolitik.
2. The most skillful practitioners of Realpolitik included the French Emperor Napoleon III, the Italian prime minister Camillo di Cavour, and the Prussian prime minister Otto von Bismarck.

C. THE REALISTS AND SOCIAL REALITIES

1. Realism emerged as a new literary and artistic style that reflected a growing disenchantment with romanticism.
2. Like the Realpolitik political leaders, Realist authors and artists applied a detached eye to objectively describe social realities.

II. NAPOLEON III (REIGNED 1852–1870)

A. ESTABLISHMENT OF THE SECOND EMPIRE

1. In 1848, French voters elected Louis Napoleon Bonaparte (nephew of Napoleon I) the new president of the Second French Republic.
2. Just four years later, Louis Napoleon proclaimed France an empire and declared himself Emperor Napoleon III. A vast majority of the French people endorsed these proclamations.

B. ECONOMIC PROGRESS

1. Napoleon III understood the importance of modern industrialization. His economic policies included the following achievements:
   - i. Railroad mileage increased by more than fivefold.
   - ii. Moderate free-trade policies doubled exports.
   - iii. Industrial production doubled, enriching the middle class.
2. Napoleon did not ignore the working class. He legalized trade unions and improved public housing.

C. REBUILDING PARIS

1. Napoleon named Baron Georges Haussmann to oversee a vast project to redesign Paris.
2. Haussmann replaced narrow streets and congested working-class neighborhoods with wide avenues, impressive public monuments, and expansive parks.
3. The rebuilding project accomplished several objectives:
   - i. It transformed Paris into a symbol of France's prosperity and greatness.
   - ii. It made it much harder for rioters to blockade streets.

D. QUEST FOR GLORY

1. Napoleon believed that the Concert of Europe (see Chapter 23) limited France's foreign policy.
2. Napoleon was determined to follow a foreign policy calculated to undermine the Concert of Europe and win international glory for himself and for France.

III. THE CRIMEAN WAR, 1853–1856

A. THE CAUSES

1. A squabble over jurisdiction within the holy places in Turkish-ruled Jerusalem brought France (the protector of the Catholics) and Russia (the protector of the Orthodox clergy) into diplomatic controversy, with Turkey in the middle.
2. Tsar Nicholas I saw an opportunity to dominate Turkey and secure entrance into the Mediterranean through the Turkish Straits.
3. Austria felt threatened by Russia's expansion into the Balkans.
4. France and Britain opposed any change in the regional balance of power.

B. THE WAR

1. The war was named after the Crimean peninsula, part of the Russian Empire that juts out into the Black Sea.
2. The major action of the Crimean War was a year-long siege of Sevastopol on the Crimean Peninsula.
3. The Crimean War lined up most of the European powers against Russia. France, Britain, Turkey, and a contingent of 18,000 men from Piedmont-Sardinia captured the strongly defended Russian fortress at Sevastopol.
4. Austria did not participate in the actual fighting. Russia resented Austria's "ingratitude" for the aid Nicholas I had given the Austrians during the Hungarian uprising in 1849.
5. The new Russian tsar, Alexander II, sued for peace after the fall of Sevastopol in 1855.
6. The war claimed over 500,000 lives, most caused by disease and inadequate medical care.

C. CONSEQUENCES

1. The Crimean War marked the first great power conflict since the Congress of Vienna in 1815 (see Chapter 20).
2. The Crimean War left a legacy of unresolved international tensions.
3. Napoleon III achieved his objective of breaking the alliance between Russia and Austria. The coalition between these two

conservative powers had blocked France's ambitions for greater influence since 1815.

4. Napoleon III emerged as a leading figure in European affairs. This new prestige encouraged him to play a greater role in Italy.
5. By entering the war on the side of France and Britain, Piedmont-Sardinia hoped to gain allies in its drive for Italian unification.
6. Russia's humiliating defeat forced Alexander II to launch an ambitious program of reforms.
7. The Crimean War left Austria isolated from its two traditional allies, Russia and Prussia. This exposed a now vulnerable Austria to Italian and German nationalism.
8. The English nurse Florence Nightingale organized a battlefield nursing service to care for the British sick and wounded. She played an important role in professionalizing nursing for women.

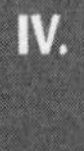

IV. RUSSIA: REACTION AND REFORM

A. TSARIST RUSSIA IN THE 1850s

1. Tsar Alexander II was an autocrat whose will was law.
2. Russia's aristocracy continued to own almost all the land and be exempt from taxes.
3. Russia had a very small middle class. Ninety-five percent of the people were peasants, most of whom were serfs.

B. ALEXANDER'S REFORMS

1. The emancipation of the serfs, 1861
   i. In 1861, Alexander II issued an Emancipation Edict freeing the serfs.
   ii. Although they were free, the peasants still did not own the land.
2. The creation of zemstvos
   i. In 1864, Alexander introduced a system of local and regional self-government through elected assemblies called zemstvos.

ii. Although the zemstvos did provide some opportunity for public discussion, they did not lead to the creation of a national assembly.

C. ALEXANDER'S DEATH

1. Alexander II's reforms only partially succeeded in developing the administrative, economic, and civic institutions that strengthened nation-states elsewhere in Europe.
2. The more changes Alexander II introduced, the more hopes he aroused. When it became apparent that the tsar continued to maintain a tight grip on power, disillusioned intellectuals began to refer to themselves as "nihilists" or believers in nothing.
3. At first nihilists expounded radical ideas and disregarded conventional manners. For example, rebellious daughters of the nobility cut their hair short and used phony marriages to escape parental control.
4. During the late 1870s, some nihilists formed a secret society, "The People's Will," whose aim was to overthrow the government.
5. Faced with mounting dissent, Alexander II wavered between renewed reaction and new reform policies.
6. On March 13, 1881, a member of the People's Will hurled a bomb at Alexander's carriage as he rode through Saint Petersburg. The gravely wounded tsar died later that day.
7. Alexander II's death triggered a major suppression of civil liberties, thus ending hopes for peaceful reforms in Russia.

V. THE UNIFICATION OF ITALY

A. THE SITUATION IN 1850

1. Repeated failures

   i. The Carbonari (see Chapter 23) had failed to incite a successful revolution.

   ii. Giuseppe Mazzini and the Young Italy Movement had failed to rally support for a republic.

2. Continued obstacles
   - i. Austria continued to control Lombardy and Venetia while also dominating other small Italian states.
   - ii. A reactionary Bourbon regime continued to control the kingdom of the Two Sicilies.
   - iii. Pope Pius IX opposed the cause of Italian nationalism.
3. Piedmont leadership
   - i. Italian nationalists looked to the kingdom of Piedmont-Sardinia for leadership. It was the only Italian state ruled by an Italian dynasty.
   - ii. In 1852, Piedmont's King Victor Emmanuel II named Count Camillo di Cavour his prime minister.

B. CAVOUR AND THE PRACTICE OF REALPOLITIK

1. Realpolitik
   - i. Early Italian nationalists such as Mazzini had been inspired by romantic ideals of nationalism.
   - ii. Cavour was a realist guided by the dictates of political power. He believed that shrewd diplomacy and well-chosen alliances were more useful than grand proclamations and romantic rebellions.
   - iii. Cavour's successful combination of power politics and secret diplomacy is called Realpolitik, "the politics of reality."
2. Strengthening Piedmont
   - i. Cavour launched an ambitious economic program that included building railroads and expanding commerce.
   - ii. Cavour modernized Piedmont's army.
3. The Franco-Piedmont alliance
   - i. Cavour understood that Austria was the greatest obstacle to Italian unity.
   - ii. Cavour formed an alliance with Napoleon III to drive Austria out of northern Italy.

C. WAR WITH AUSTRIA, 1859

1. The combined French and Piedmont armies defeated the Austrians. Meanwhile, Italian nationalists staged revolts across northern Italy.
2. Sardinia annexed all of northern Italy except Venetia.

D. GIUSEPPE GARIBALDI AND THE RED SHIRTS

1. The pragmatic Cavour and the romantic Garibaldi agreed that Italy should be freed from foreign control.
2. While Cavour was uniting the north, he also secretly supported Garibaldi in the south.
3. In May 1860, Garibaldi and his small but zealous force of so-called Red Shirts successfully invaded and liberated the kingdom of the Two Sicilies.
4. Garibaldi agreed to step aside and let Victor Emmanuel rule the areas he had conquered.

E. PERSISTENT PROBLEMS

1. In March 1861, an Italian parliament formally proclaimed the Kingdom of Italy with Victor Emmanuel II as king "by the grace of God and the will of the nation." Tragically, Cavour died just two months later.
2. The newly unified Kingdom of Italy faced a number of persistent problems:
   - i. Unification was still not complete. Venetia remained under Austrian control and the papacy led by Pius IX remained hostile to the new Italian state.
   - ii. Northern Italy was urban, sophisticated, and increasingly industrialized. Southern Italy remained rural, backward, and poor.
   - iii. The new government was burdened by a heavy debt.

Cavour and Garibaldi are compelling historic figures who command interest and APEURO questions. However, don't forget to study the often overlooked but still important problems that plagued the newly founded Kingdom of Italy.

VI. THE UNIFICATION OF GERMANY

A. THE SITUATION IN 1860

1. Obstacles to unity
   i. Germany remained politically divided into a number of small states that jealously guarded their independence.
   ii. The German Confederation remained a loose grouping of 39 states dominated by Austria.
   iii. French foreign policy continued to support German rivalries while opposing Germany unity.
2. Prussia's growing strength
   i. Prussia's population increased from 11 million in 1815 to more than 18 million in 1850.
   ii. Led by Prussia, the Zollverein (see Chapter 23) promoted German economic growth while demonstrating the advantages of unity.

B. OTTO VON BISMARCK, MASTER OF REALPOLITIK

1. In 1862, William I chose as his prime minister a Junker and staunch conservative named Otto von Bismarck.
2. A master of Realpolitik, Bismarck set out to strengthen Prussia.
3. Bismarck enlarged and reequipped the Prussian army so that he could take advantage of opportunities for further territorial expansion.
4. Disavowing liberalism as frivolous and misguided, Bismarck firmly declared, "The great questions of our day cannot be solved by speeches and majority votes—that was the great error of 1848 and 1849—but by blood and iron."

C. WAR WITH DENMARK, 1864

1. Bismarck led Prussia into war with Denmark to win two border provinces, Schleswig and Holstein.
2. The victory combined with shrewd diplomacy enabled Bismarck to begin the process of eliminating Austria from German affairs.

It has been said that only three people truly understood the controversy over Schleswig and Holstein. APEURO test writers do not expect you to be the fourth person to master this topic. As you study Bismarck and the wars with Denmark, Austria, and France, avoid getting bogged down in the details. Instead, focus on the consequences of each war.

D. WAR WITH AUSTRIA, 1866

1. The Seven Weeks' War
   - i. In 1866, Bismarck provoked Austria into declaring war on Prussia.
   - ii. Prussia's revitalized army easily crushed the Austrians in a brief conflict known as the Seven Weeks' War.
2. Consequences
   - i. Austria agreed to the dissolution of the German Confederation.
   - ii. With Austria excluded from German affairs, Bismarck organized a North German Confederation dominated by Prussia.
   - iii. As Prussia's ally, Italy annexed Venetia.

E. WAR WITH FRANCE, 1870

1. The causes
   - i. France feared the sudden emergence of a strong and aggressive Prussia. It is important to note that France had opposed German unity for centuries.
   - ii. Bismarck adroitly exploited a minor dispute between France and Prussia over the search for a new Spanish monarch. By skillfully editing the Ems Dispatch, Bismarck inflamed relations between France and Prussia.
   - iii. Napoleon III declared war on Prussia on July 19, 1870.
2. The war
   - i. The Prussians successfully invaded France and forced Napoleon III to surrender on September 2, 1870.

ii. On January 18, 1871, King William I was proclaimed German emperor in the Hall of Mirrors at the Palace of Versailles.

3. The consequences

    i. Bismarck imposed a harsh settlement. He forced France to pay a huge indemnity and cede Alsace and most of Lorraine to the German empire.

    ii. The loss of rich deposits of coal and iron ore was a severe blow to France's economy. The loss of these provinces was an even greater blow to French national pride.

    iii. The unification of Germany created a new European balance of power. As the German empire rapidly industrialized, it became the strongest state on the continent of Europe and a formidable rival to Great Britain. As a new great power, Germany played a key role in every major international crisis from 1871 to 1945.

F. MAKING COMPARISONS: CAVOUR AND BISMARCK

1. Similarities

    i. Both Cavour and Bismarck were shrewd masters of Realpolitik. For example, Cavour participated in the Crimean War in order to gain allied support for Piedmont-Sardinia's leadership in the drive for Italian unification. Bismarck used the Ems Dispatch to help provoke a war with France.

    ii. Both Cavour and Bismarck were skillful opportunists who took advantage of unfolding events. Cavour began by hoping to enlarge Piedmont-Sardinia, but ended by creating the Kingdom of Italy. Bismarck began by working for a stronger Prussia, but ended by creating a German Reich.

2. Differences

    i. Cavour recognized that Piedmont-Sardinia did not possess a powerful military. He compensated for this weakness by skillfully manipulating France to use its military for his ends. In contrast, Bismarck had access to Prussia's powerful military machine.

    ii. Cavour did not have access to significant economic resources. In contrast, Bismarck could take advantage of the economic wealth created by the Zollverein and by Prussia's growing industrial power.

VII. THE AUSTRIAN EMPIRE

A. DEFEAT AND DISCONTENT

1. Austria suffered humiliating military defeats at the hands of first France and Piedmont and then Prussia.
2. The empire's biggest problem was the discontent of the many nationalities living under Habsburg rule.
3. The Magyars were the largest and most restive national group.

B. THE DUAL MONARCHY

1. In 1867, Austria agreed to satisfy the Magyars' demands for independence by creating a dual monarchy.
2. Austria and Hungary became independent and equal states under a common Habsburg ruler. The two states still had a united army and a common foreign policy. The new empire was known as Austria-Hungary.

C. CONTINUED SLAVIC DISCONTENT

1. The dual monarchy satisfied the Magyars, but failed to solve the empire's nationality problem.
2. The Slavic regions called for, but failed to receive, a triple monarchy.
3. Slavic discontent posed a significant threat to the future of Austria-Hungary and the peace of Europe.

VIII. GREAT BRITAIN: PROSPERITY AND REFORM

A. THE "WORKSHOP OF THE WORLD"

1. Great Britain continued to enjoy unprecedented prosperity.
2. British shipyards led the world in the construction of iron ships.
3. British bankers invested surplus capital in projects all over the globe.

B. THE REFORM BILL OF 1867

1. Britain's rapidly growing working class continued to demand electoral reform.

2. Led by Benjamin Disraeli, the Conservatives (formerly the Tories) supported a new reform bill.

3. The Reform Bill of 1867 extended the suffrage to most of Great Britain's urban workers.

4. It is important to note that British women were still denied the right to vote.

IX. REALISM IN LITERATURE AND ART

A. KEY CHARACTERISTICS

1. Rejected romantic works as overly idealized and artificial.

2. Insisted on precise descriptions of the modern world. When asked to paint angels, the French artist Gustave Courbet replied, "I have never seen angels. Show me an angel and I will paint one."

3. Focused on common people, everyday activities and experiences that would have been previously unworthy of artistic attention. Realist artists often portrayed peasants and urban workers to depict what Baudelaire called the "heroism of modern life."

4. Criticized the cruelty of industrial life and the greed and insensitivity of the wealthy.

B. LEADING REALIST AUTHORS

1. Charles Dickens, *Hard Times:* described the grinding poverty endured by factory workers in Coketown, a fictitious industrial city modeled after Manchester.

2. Gustave Flaubert, *Madame Bovary*: described the story of an unfaithful wife of a French country doctor who lived beyond her means to escape the boredom of provincial life.

3. Henrik Ibsen, *A Doll's House*: aroused great controversy because of its critical attitude toward nineteenth-century marriage norms.

C. LEADING REALIST ARTISTS

1. Gustave Courbet, *Burial at Ornans:* defied tradition by using a massive 22-foot-long canvas to portray a funeral in rural France.

2. Honoré Daumier, *The Third-Class Carriage:* portrayed working-class passengers as dignified despite the dehumanizing experience of being packed together in a small railroad car.
3. Jean-François Millet, *The Gleaners:* contrasted the hard physical labor of three peasant women with the comfortable life style of wealthy landowners living in the background.

Chapter 25

Society, Mass Politics, and Culture 1871–1914

I. SOCIAL DIVISIONS IN THE "BELLE ÉPOQUE"

A. THE "BELLE ÉPOQUE"

1. Following the horrors of World War I, nostalgic Europeans would remember the period between 1880 and 1914 as the "Belle Époque" or "Beautiful Period."
2. During this time, Europeans enjoyed a period of unprecedented optimism based upon regional peace, economic prosperity, and technological progress.

B. THE UPPER CLASS

1. Just 1 to 2 percent of the European population belonged to the upper class. In the words of one French writer, its members seemed "to live upon a golden cloud."
2. An army of servants enabled upper-class ladies and gentlemen to maintain opulent urban mansions and splendid country estates.
3. Thorstein Veblen coined the term *conspicuous consumption* to describe upper-class spending habits. All of Europe was their playground. They vacationed at seaside resorts, patronized art exhibits, flocked to mountain spas, and enjoyed stays at elegant hotels.

C. THE MIDDLE CLASS

1. About 20 to 25 percent of the European population belonged to the middle class.
2. The middle class included merchants, shopkeepers, doctors, lawyers, teachers, government employees, factory workers, factory supervisors, and officer workers.

3. Cheaper foods and increases in real wages enabled middle-class families to purchase labor saving gadgets such as washing and sewing machines.

4. Electric street cars enabled middle-class families to live outside the city and commute to work each day.

5. Cities such as Paris, Vienna, and London featured broad boulevards, parks, and lighted streets. The middle class took advantage of the era's new streetcars and subways to shop in lavish department stores and enjoy cafés, dance halls, opera houses, and vaudeville shows.

6. Increasing affluence and leisure time also enabled the middle class to enjoy organized sports such as rugby, cricket, and bicycling.

D. THE WORKING CLASS

1. About 75 to 80 percent of the European population belonged to the working class.

2. Often living on the edge of poverty, the urban working class enjoyed few of the Belle Époque's wonders and advances. For example, despite major medical advances, tuberculosis and other deadly diseases remained a menace in slums and tenements from Saint Petersburg to Paris.

3. Electricity, trade unions, and slowly rising wages did improve working-class lives. It is important to note that a strong sense of nationalism, the expansion of male suffrage, and state-sponsored welfare programs all combined to weaken the revolutionary spirit envisioned by Marx and other radical socialists.

II. WOMEN'S RIGHTS

A. KEY VOICES

1. Olympe de Gouges (1748–1793)
   - i. French playwright, political activist, and early feminist.
   - ii. Wrote the *Declaration of the Rights of Woman and of the Female Citizen*, 1789.
   - iii. Demanded that French women be given the same rights as French men.

2. Mary Wollstonecraft (1759–1797)
   i. English author and early feminist.
   ii. Wrote *A Vindication of the Rights of Women*, 1792.
   iii. Argued that women are not naturally inferior to men. They only appear to be inferior because of a lack of education.
3. John Stuart Mill (1806–1873)
   i. English reformer, essayist, and influential Utilitarian.
   ii. Wrote *The Subjection of Women*, 1869.
   iii. Opposed the social and legal inequalities imposed on women. Argued that inequalities were a relic from the past and "a hindrance to human development."
4. Henrik Ibsen (1828–1906)
   i. Norwegian playwright and social critic.
   ii. Wrote *A Doll's House*, 1879.
   iii. Criticized conventional marriage roles.

The struggle for women's rights is a very important topic. Be sure that you can identify each of the four authors listed above. Each has generated one or more quotes used in multiple-choice questions.

B. ECONOMIC HARDSHIPS

1. The Industrial Revolution opened economic opportunities to women. Factory work offered higher wages than work performed at home. For example, women spinners in Manchester's cotton factories received higher pay than women who spun cotton thread at home.
2. By the mid-1850s, women and children comprised half of the labor force in the cotton industry. Women were paid about half of a man's wages for similar work.
3. Trade unions began to win better wages for working men. But these unions seldom accepted women as members. In fact, unions fought to keep women out of skilled jobs that offered higher wages.

4. During the late 1800s, many working-class women worked as shop clerks, typists, and telephone operators.
5. Opportunities for well-educated women were limited to teaching, nursing, and social work. Entrenched attitudes limited opportunities in other professions. In 1898, for example, there were only two women lawyers in all of France.

C. LEGAL DISCRIMINATION

1. Law codes in most European countries gave women few legal rights. For example, women could not sue or make contracts. If a woman's husband died, she could not act as the guardian of her children.
2. By the 1880s, women began to reverse some of these discriminatory laws. For example, divorce was legalized in Britain in 1857 and in France in 1884. However, Catholic countries, such as Spain and Italy, did not permit divorce.
3. In 1900, no country in Europe allowed women to vote. Although Marie Curie won two Nobel Prizes and was recognized as one of the world's foremost scientists, she could not vote. "Women are creatures of impulse and emotion," declared one British member of Parliament. "They do not decide questions on the ground of reason as men do."

D. THE WOMEN'S SUFFRAGE MOVEMENT

1. In the United States women such as Lucretia Mott and Susan B. Anthony launched a campaign for women's suffrage at the 1848 Seneca Falls Convention.
2. In Great Britain, women's rights activists argued that suffrage was the key to redressing legal and economic discrimination. Led by Millicent Garrett Fawcett, the National Union of Women's Suffrage Societies (NUWSS) attempted to pressure members of Parliament to grant female suffrage.
3. Infuriated by Parliament's refusal to grant females the right to vote, Emmeline Pankhurst founded the Women's Social and Political Union (WSPU) in 1903.
4. The WSPU quickly became Europe's most militant organization for women's rights. In addition to peaceful demonstrations and parades, its members cut telegraph wires, heckled government speakers, and chained themselves to gates in front of Parliament.

5. The most publicized militant action occurred when a young WSPU member, Emily Davison, committed suicide by throwing herself in front of the king's horse at the 1913 Epsom Derby. At her funeral, thousands of women in white dresses carried banners demanding the right to vote.
6. Although the women's suffrage movement commanded wide attention, it achieved few successes. In 1900, no country in Europe allowed women to vote.

E. "THE ANGEL IN THE HOUSE"

1. In his 1847 poem "The Princess," Alfred Tennyson expressed the prevailing view of European gender roles when he wrote: "Man with the head and woman from the heart. Man to command and woman to obey."
2. During the second half of the nineteenth century, men ran Europe's businesses and cast all of its votes. The widespread belief in the cult of domesticity restricted women to their homes. The stay-at-home wife was one of the chief indicators of middle-class respectability.
3. The ideal middle-class wife was an "angel in the house" who turned her home into a refuge from the hard and impersonal urban world where her husband worked.
4. Middle-class women were moral guardians who supervised the education of her children. In addition, middle-class women were expected to supervise domestic servants and manage the household.

F. THE "NEW WOMAN"

1. By the end of the nineteenth century, women lived longer and had fewer children. As a result, educated middle-class women began to enjoy more independent lifestyles.
2. A generation of middle-class "New Women" extended their role as guardian of the home to include becoming activists who fought to improve their communities.
3. The "New Woman" abandoned restrictive corsets and wore fewer petticoats. She used her newfound physical freedom by enjoying bicycling and joining sports clubs.
4. The pioneering turn-of-the-century "New Women" provided role models for the later feminist movement.

III. THE AGE OF MASS POLITICS

A. KEY TRENDS

1. Universal male suffrage
   i. Between 1871 and 1914, most European countries extended the franchise to working-class men.
   ii. Universal male suffrage led to the creation of mass political parties.
2. Trade unions and socialist parties
   i. Trade unions gained rights and played an increasingly important role in Great Britain, France, and Germany.
   ii. Workers supported socialist political parties in many European countries.
3. The welfare state
   i. Demands for reform by socialist parties and labor unions persuaded European governments to begin enacting legislation to help the lower classes. These programs laid the foundation for the welfare state.
   ii. It is important to note that a desire to counter the growing strength of socialist parties motivated many of the reforms.
4. Changing balance of power
   i. The unification of Germany and Italy ended the carefully crafted balance of power created by the Congress of Vienna.
   ii. Nationalism, the Second Industrial Revolution, and the skillful use of Realpolitik combined to create an unstable balance of power among the European states.

B. FRANCE

1. The Paris Commune, 1871
   i. The Franco-Prussian War left France defeated and humiliated. France's Third Republic began with the bitter task of ceding the provinces of Alsace and Lorraine to Germany.
   ii. The people of Paris rejected both the treaty and the new conservative government. Radicals called Communards formed a revolutionary municipal council or "Commune."

iii. Government troops besieged Paris for two months. The army finally overwhelmed the Communards and mercilessly crushed all opposition.

iv. The bloody suppression of the Paris Commune left a legacy of class hatred that poisoned French politics.

2. The Dreyfus Affair

i. Captain Alfred Dreyfus, the first Jewish officer in the French general staff, was convicted in 1894 of selling military secrets to the Germans and sentenced to life imprisonment on Devil's Island off the northern coast of South America.

ii. Although Dreyfus was innocent, a coalition of Catholics, monarchists, anti-Semites, and military officers thwarted attempts to clear his name.

iii. Émile Zola, the famed realist novelist, wrote an article called "J'Accuse" ("I Accuse"), charging that military judges had knowingly let the guilty party go, while Dreyfus remained imprisoned.

iv. Dreyfus was ultimately completely exonerated in 1906.

v. The Dreyfus Affair had a number of consequences. It created a nationwide furor that deepened political divisions and revealed widespread anti-Semitism. The Dreyfus Affair also played a key role in Theodor Herzl's decision to write *The Jewish State*, calling for a national homeland for the Jewish people.

The Dreyfus Affair has generated a significant number of multiple-choice and free-response questions on the APEURO exam. Do not neglect Émile Zola's key role in exposing injustice. You should also be able to discuss the causes and consequences of the Dreyfus Affair and place it in the context of European anti-Semitism.

C. GREAT BRITAIN

1. The Irish Question

i. Following the Act of Union in 1801, Ireland was united with Great Britain and governed by the British Parliament.

ii. Led by Charles Parnell, Irish nationalists sought to achieve home rule granting Ireland its own parliament.

iii. Prime Minister William Gladstone supported Irish home rule. However, a coalition of Conservatives and anti-home-rule Liberals defeated his home-rule bills in 1886 and 1892. Gladstone's support for Irish home rule split the Liberal Party, enabling the Conservatives to take power.

iv. Parliament finally passed an Irish home-rule bill in 1914. However, the British government suspended the bill for the duration of World War I.

2. Peaceful reforms

i. The Franchise Act of 1884 extended voting rights to rural male laborers. By 1914, 80 percent of Britain's male population was enfranchised.

ii. Parliament laid the foundation for the British welfare state by establishing a system of health and unemployment insurance.

D. GERMANY

1. Social welfare programs

i. During the 1880s, Germany became the first European country to develop a state social welfare program.

ii. Otto von Bismarck's social welfare legislation included programs for health insurance, accident insurance, and a system of old-age and disability pensions.

iii. Bismarck wanted to prove that the state was a benevolent institution and not an oppressor. He hoped that his social welfare programs would secure the loyalty of workers to the new German empire.

2. William II (reigned 1888–1918)

i. William I died in 1888 at the age of 90. His grandson, William II, became the new German kaiser. Arrogant and impulsive, William II was determined to rule on his own.

ii. William II forced Bismarck to resign in 1890. During the next 14 years, he expanded Bismarck's social reforms. At the same time, Germany's economic and military power continued to grow.

E. RUSSIA

1. Autocracy and repression

   i. The assassination of Tsar Alexander II ended Russia's brief period of reform.

   ii. Both Alexander III (reigned 1881–1894) and Nicholas II (reigned 1894–1917) were committed to the traditional policies of autocracy, orthodoxy, and Russification.

   iii. Both tsars encouraged anti-Semitic attacks on Jews called *pogroms*. Russia was the last European state to eliminate legal discrimination against Jews. Virulent anti-Semitism prompted a mass migration of Russian Jews to Western Europe and the United States.

2. Political movements

   i. Russia's program of rapid industrialization spawned a wide range of political movements.

   ii. The Constitutional Democrats or Kadets wanted a constitutional monarchy.

   iii. The Social Democrats worked for economic and political revolution. In 1903, the Social Democrats split into two factions. The Mensheviks favored gradual socialistic reform. Led by Vladimir Lenin, the Bolsheviks advocated a communist revolution spearheaded by a small elite of professional revolutionaries.

3. The Russo-Japanese War

   i. Between 1870 and 1900, the Japanese modernized their economy and built a powerful army and navy.

   ii. As Japan became stronger, it also became more imperialistic. During the 1890s, Japan expanded its influence in Manchuria, China's mineral rich northeastern province.

   iii. Japan's growing interest in Manchuria alarmed the Russians, who were also eager to control the province. In 1904, the conflict exploded into the Russo-Japanese War.

   iv. The Japanese stunned the European powers by easily crushing the Russian forces. Though still technically part of China, Manchuria was now a part of Japan's sphere of influence.

→ Russia and Japan both wanted the same region (Manchuria)

→ Russian lost

4. The Revolution of 1905

   i. Russia's humiliating defeat in the Russo-Japanese War exposed the weaknesses of the autocratic regime and led to increased unrest.

   ii. On January 22, 1905, Cossacks opened fire on a peaceful crowd of workers outside the Winter Palace in St. Petersburg. The "Bloody Sunday" massacre provoked a wave of strikes and demands for change.

   iii. Nicholas II reluctantly approved the election of a Russian parliament or Duma.

   iv. Nicholas stubbornly refused to work with the Duma, insisting that it become an advisory rather than a legislative body.

IV. SCIENCE AND THE AGE OF PROGRESS

A. THE BACTERIAL REVOLUTION

1. Louis Pasteur

   i. Conducted experiments that supported the germ theory of diseases.

   ii. Discovered that heat could destroy many harmful bacteria.

   iii. The process of heating a liquid to kill the bacteria in it is called pasteurization.

2. Robert Koch

   i. Identified the bacteria responsible for specific diseases.

   ii. Identified the tuberculosis bacteria.

3. Joseph Lister

   i. Promoted the idea of sterile surgery.

   ii. Introduced carbolic acid to sterilize surgical instruments and wounds.

4. Impact

   i. The bacterial revolution saved millions of lives, thus causing a dramatic decline in European death rates. By 1875, Europeans lived an average of 15 years longer than their grandparents.

ii. Urban residents benefited the most from improvement in public health.

B. CHARLES DARWIN AND THE THEORY OF EVOLUTION

1. The key question

   i. How can we explain the tremendous variety of plants and animals that exist on Earth?

   ii. The idea of special creation formed the most widely accepted answer to this question. According to this view, every kind of plant and animal had been created by God at the beginning of the world and remained the same since then.

2. *On the Origin of Species*

   i. Charles Darwin was a British naturalist whose book *On the Origin of Species by Means of Natural Selection* challenged the Judeo-Christian belief in special creation.

   ii. According to Darwin, within every species more individuals are born than can survive. Therefore, every living thing takes part in a constant "struggle for existence."

   iii. Only the "fittest" survive this unending struggle for survival. The fittest are determined by a process of natural selection in which new species emerge after gradually accumulating new modifications.

   iv. Darwin's idea of change through natural selection came to be called the theory of evolution.

3. The controversy

   i. Darwin's theory of evolution sparked a storm of controversy.

   ii. Naturalist Thomas Henry Huxley wrote, "It is doubtful if any single book, except *The Principia* by Newton, ever worked so great and rapid a revolution in science.

   iii. Critics accused Darwin of contradicting the biblical account of creation in which humankind was a unique creation of God. The bishop of Oxford, for example, accused Darwin of "a tendency to limit God's glory in creation."

   iv. Darwin's theory also undermined the Enlightenment belief that rational human beings lived in a tranquil and predictable world. The theory of natural selection suggested an alternate world in which aggressive individuals and groups constantly struggled with one another.

C. SOCIAL DARWINISM

1. Herbert Spencer, an English sociologist, applied the concept of natural selection to human society. Spencer argued that free economic competition was natural selection in action. The best companies make profits while inefficient ones go bankrupt. The same rules apply to individuals. This idea became known as Social Darwinism.

2. Wealthy business and industrial leaders used Social Darwinism to justify their success and explain why others fail. They strongly supported laissez-faire economic policies and opposed social welfare programs.

3. The Social Darwinists also applied the theories of natural selection and survival of the fittest to races and nations. Their theories helped rationalize and justify European imperialism, racism, and militarism.

4. Social Darwinism later influenced the development of Nazi theories about superior and inferior races.

5. It is important to point out that many critics objected to the dangerous misapplication of Darwin's biological findings to society and races. They argued that Social Darwinism was being used as an excuse for the excesses of individuals and the greed of imperialists.

V. MODERN ART

A. MODERNITY

1. New inventions such as the camera and the cinema posed a challenge to how artists traditionally portrayed people and places.

2. Artists responded with a variety of "modern" styles that marked a break with long-standing artistic traditions.

3. The newly enriched bourgeoisie provide much of the patronage for modern artists.

B. IMPRESSIONISM

1. Key characteristics

   i. Captured a moment in time; a slice of life.

   ii. Interested in the fleeting effects of light on color.

   iii. Depicted leisure activities of the Parisian bourgeoisie.

2. Key artists and works

   i. Claude Monet, *Impression Sunrise*: this view of the harbor at Le Havre gave Impressionism its name.

   ii. Claude Monet, *Gare St-Lazare*: captures the great clouds of steam and smoke as a train arrives at a Paris railway station.

   iii. Pierre-Auguste Renoir, *Le Bal au Moulin de la Galette*: depicts friends dancing and dining at a popular outdoor café.

   iv. Pierre-Auguste Renoir, *The Luncheon of the Boating Party*: depicts a carefree group of friends lunching on the terrace of the Restaurante Fournaise overlooking the Seine River.

C. CUBISM

1. Key characteristics

   i. Presented multiple views of the same object.

   ii. Fragmented forms into flat, jagged shapes.

   iii. Portrayed flat, two-dimensional space without traditional linear perspective.

2. Key artists and works

   i. Georges Braque, *Violin and Candlestick*: much of the painting is a jumble of fragmented cubes and other solid geometric shapes. Matisse reportedly remarked that Braque painted "with little cubes." This is credited with being the origin of the term *Cubism*.

   ii. Pablo Picasso, *Guernica*: depicts the confusion and horror caused by Germany's unprovoked attack on a previously peaceful Spanish village.

D. MAKING COMPARISONS: RAPHAEL AND PICASSO

1. Raphael's *School of Athens*

   i. Demonstrates the humanist interest in Greek and Roman philosophy.

   ii. Utilizes the Renaissance artistic techniques of idealized human portraits and linear perspective.

   iii. Exhibits harmony, proportion, and balance.

   iv. Painted for Pope Julius II, illustrating the importance of church patronage.

2. Picasso's *Les Demoiselles d'Avignon*
    i. Demonstrates the modernist interest in the ugly underside of real life by depicting five prostitutes inside a brothel.
    ii. Utilizes the Cubist artistic techniques of flat forms, fragmented space, and multiple views of the same person.
    iii. Exhibits a lack of harmony and proportion.
    iv. Painted for a limited group of artists, dealers, and critics.

Chapter 26

The New Imperialism

I. INTRODUCTION

A. THE OLD IMPERIALISM

1. European powers practiced an early form of imperialism between 1500 and 1800. During this period, Portugal, the Dutch Republic, and England built trading-post empires along the coasts of Africa, India, and Indonesia. For example, Portuguese traders established a mutually lucrative trade with the West African kingdom of Benin. The Portuguese prized Benin's rich supply of pepper, ivory, and gold. In return, the rulers of Benin prized Portugal's rich supply of coral beads, brass bracelets, and horses.

2. The New World was a notable exception to the pattern of coastal trading posts. Spain established an enormous empire that included the West Indies, Central America, and South America. Beginning in 1607, the English began to colonize the east coast of North America.

3. The Old Imperialists created the world's first global maritime trading network. Centered in the Atlantic Ocean, the network featured the exchange of enslaved Africans, Caribbean sugar, and Chesapeake tobacco.

B. THE NEW IMPERIALISM

1. In 1500, the European powers controlled about 7 percent of the globe's land. By 1800, they controlled 35 percent. A new Age of Imperialism began in 1870 as European powers, plus the United States and Japan, rapidly acquired vast overseas empires. By 1914, the new imperialist powers controlled 84 percent of the globe's land.

2. Led by Great Britain and France, the imperialist powers exercised increasing economic and political control over Africa and Asia. No longer content to simply trade with other peoples, European

nations now aimed to directly rule and exploit extensive regions of the globe. For example, a British force of 1,200 well-armed soldiers toppled the ruler of Benin, burned his palace, and seized 2,500 works of bronze and ivory art.

3. The imperialist powers seized direct control over some areas such as German East Africa and French Indochina. In other areas, they established protectorates where the dependent country had its own government but was still subject to the authority of the imperial power. And finally, the great powers established spheres of influence over large parts of China.

Be prepared to compare and contrast old and new imperialism. Both forms of imperialism involved varying degrees of European control over other peoples. However, the scope and speed of the new imperialism far exceeded that of the old imperialism.

II. THE TECHNOLOGY OF EMPIRE

A. EFFICIENT NEW FORMS OF TRANSPORTATION AND COMMUNICATION

1. The Second Industrial Revolution (see Chapter 22) created the tools of transportation, communication, and warfare that facilitated the rapid pace of global empire building.
2. Iron steamships fueled by coal replaced smaller wind-powered wooden sailing vessels. The new steamships could carry large cargoes of people and goods. As a result, Europeans used sea lanes to connect their colonies with the home country.
3. Insulated underwater cables revolutionized communication. In 1850, steam-powered mailboats required two to three months for a round-trip voyage from London to Bombay, India. Just 20 years later, companies in London and Bombay could exchange telegrams within hours.

B. POWERFUL NEW WEAPONS

1. The imperialist powers equipped their armies with an arsenal of advanced weapons that included repeating rifles and Maxim machine guns.

2. A Maxim machine gun could fire 11 bullets in just one second. In 1898, a small but well-armed British force needed only 5 hours to slaughter 11,000 Sudanese soldiers in a battle fought near Omdurman. Winston Churchill later described the appalling "suffering, despairing, and dying" created by "a hell of whistling metal, exploding shells, and sputtering dust."

C. EFFECTIVE NEW MEDICINES

1. Malaria is a disease caused by a parasite transmitted by the bites of infected mosquitos. Its life-threatening fever posed a formidable obstacle to European travelers attempting to explore mosquito infested jungles and swamps in Africa and Asia.
2. Quinine was first isolated in 1820 from the bark of the cinchona tree. Large-scale use of quinine as an effective treatment for malaria began after 1850. It soon played a significant role in enabling Europeans to colonize western and central Africa.

III. MOTIVES FOR THE NEW IMPERIALISM

A. ECONOMIC GAINS

1. European interest in overseas colonies began to weaken in the half century following the Congress of Vienna. In 1852, the British Prime Minister Benjamin Disraeli referred to India and other colonies as "a millstone round our necks."
2. Economic problems played a key role in changing European attitudes towards acquiring colonies. A deep economic depression gripped Europe between the mid-1870s and the mid-1890s, bringing rising unemployment and the potential for labor unrest.
3. As the Second Industrial Revolution gathered momentum, European industrialists looked to overseas colonies as sources of essential raw materials and as new markets for finished goods.
4. Economic rivalry quickly fueled a rush for colonies in Africa and Asia. By 1900, ivory and rubber from the Congo, diamonds and gold from South Africa, and rubber and rice from French Indochina provided lucrative raw materials for European economic growth.

B. GEOPOLITICAL ADVANTAGES

1. The great powers understood the importance of a strong navy to protect vital sea routes connecting a home country with its overseas colonies.

2. The great steamships required bases where they could take on coal and other needed supplies. For example, Singapore served as a strategic base for British ships. The British imperialist Lord Curzon understood the geopolitical importance of Singapore and other strategic bases when he described them as "pieces on a chessboard upon which is being played out in a game for the domination of the world."

C. NATIONALISM

1. Colonial expansion offered all citizens a vicarious share in national glory. Mass-circulation newspapers thrilled their readers with stories describing how intrepid explorers and dedicated missionaries overcame hardship and danger.

2. "Colonial fever" became a source of national pride. Imperialists proudly displayed world maps with their nation's empire highlighted in bright colors. Colored in red, a map of the British empire provided schoolchildren with patriotic visual evidence that "the sun never sets on the British empire."

D. RACIAL SUPERIORITY

1. Imperialism contradicted the European belief in local self-rule. However, imperialists ignored this inconsistency by using Social Darwinism (see Chapter 25) to justify their actions.

2. Social Darwinists assumed that some races are fitter than others. Europeans pointed to steamships, railroads, and machines guns as evidences of their superiority. They saw no reason to respect the cultures of "backward" peoples.

E. A CIVILIZING MISSION

1. It was a short mental step from a belief in racial superiority to a belief that Europeans were engaged in a "civilizing mission" to bring medicines, laws, Christianity, and other blessings of Western civilization to the people in their colonies.

2. The popular British writer Rudyard Kipling appealed not only to his readers' spirit of adventure, but also to their feelings of superiority. He saw imperialism as a beneficial mission to "civilize non-

Europeans" and urged his readers to "Take up the White Man's Burden" by modernizing "primitive" native cultures.

IV. EUROPEAN IMPERIALISM IN AFRICA

A. THE "DARK CONTINENT"

1. Inspired by Prince Henry the Navigator, fifteenth-century Portuguese sea captains began to explore the west coast of Africa. The Portuguese and other European countries established trading posts along the coast. However, they learned very little about the interior of what they called the "Dark Continent."
2. By the mid-1800s, Africa contained more than 700 different ethnic groups, each with its own language and customs. The people in this vast region could neither foresee nor prevent the irrevocable changes that the Second Industrial Revolution and imperialist rivalries would inflict on their lives.

B. KING LEOPOLD II AND THE CONGO

1. King Leopold II of Belgium began the process of exploiting the African interior. Reports of central Africa's "unspeakable riches" fired Leopold's imagination. Motivated by insatiable greed, Leopold was determined to devour "the magnificent cake of Africa."
2. Leopold formed the International Congo Association in 1875 as a private enterprise. The Congo's rubber trees provided one of the world's few sources of this increasingly valuable raw material. Leopold coerced the native population into harvesting the trees while working under brutal conditions.

C. THE BERLIN CONFERENCE, 1884–1885

1. Leopold's actions ignited European interest in Africa. Soon Britain, France, Germany, Italy, and Portugal also claimed parts of the continent.
2. Alarmed by the rising tensions, the German Chancellor Otto von Bismarck convened a conference in Berlin to establish rules for dividing Africa. Representatives from all the major European nations and the United States attended the conference. However, the European leaders did not invite a single African ruler to attend the conference.

3. The Berlin Conference opened on November 15, 1884, and concluded on February 26, 1885. The conference did not actually partition Africa. However, it did establish guidelines for regulating colonial activity in Africa. For example, the conference adopted a requirement that a country's territorial claims must be based on "effective occupation" defined as a strong actual presence in the area being claimed.

D. THE "SCRAMBLE FOR AFRICA"

1. When the new imperialism began in 1875, Europe controlled less than 10 percent of Africa. The Berlin Conference prompted a feverish "scramble for Africa." By 1900, the European powers established colonies in 90 percent of the continent. Only Ethiopia (which successfully resisted an Italian invasion) and Liberia (which had been settled by freed slaves from the United States) remained independent.
2. Great Britain controlled the lion's share of Africa. The British empire stretched from Egypt in the north to the Cape of Good Hope in the south.
3. The French empire included Morocco, Algeria, and Tunisia along with a vast expanse of the Sahara Desert.
4. The Portuguese annexed huge domains in Angola and Mozambique.
5. The Germans established colonies in German East Africa and in the Cameroons and Tongo on the west coast.
6. European diplomats created large unwieldy states that ignored traditional cultures and often forced rival tribes to occupy the same land.

V. EUROPEAN IMPERIALISM IN ASIA

A. INDIA

1. British economic interest in India began in the 1600s when the British East India Company established treaty ports at Bombay, Madras, and Calcutta. The company quickly took advantage of the growing weakness of India's ruling Mughal dynasty. By 1757, the British East India Company ruled large parts of India with little interference from the British government.

2. The British East India Company maintained an army led by British officers and staffed by sepoys or Indian soldiers. Like many Indians, the sepoys resented Britain's arrogant disregard for their cultural traditions. In 1857, word spread among the sepoys that their British-made rifle cartridges were sealed with beef and pork fat. Soldiers had to bite off the seal to use the cartridges. This outraged Hindus who were not allowed to touch beef and Muslims who were prohibited from eating pork.

3. On May 10, 1857, sepoy units rebelled against the British. Stunned British forces finally restored order after both sides suffered heavy losses.

4. The Sepoy Mutiny marked a turning point in Britain's relationship with India. In 1858, administration of India passed from the East India Company to the British crown. The British adopted a more tolerant approach towards Indian religious traditions. At the same time, the British launched a massive development program that included beginning irrigation projects, constructing schools, and building an extensive network of railroad lines.

5. India soon emerged as the cornerstone of the British empire. The Industrial Revolution had turned Britain into the world's workshop and India became a major supplier of raw materials for that workshop. India's railroads enabled farmers to ship cotton, rice, jute, and tea to coastal ports where steamships transported these products to Great Britain. In return, India absorbed one-fifth of Britain's total exports. This lucrative economic relationship prompted Prime Minister Disraeli to describe India as "the brightest jewel in Her Majesty's Crown."

B. INDOCHINA

1. Vietnam forms a long curving S on the eastern shore of the Indochina peninsula. French soldiers gradually conquered Vietnam in the years between 1857 and 1883. Ten years later, France completed the conquest by adding Cambodia (now Kampuchea) and Laos to its Indochina empire.

2. French colonists quickly exploited the region's economic resources. Huge plantations used cheap peasant labor to produce valuable crops of rice and rubber. By the early 1900s, Indochina produced all of France's raw rubber and much of its imported rice.

3. French colonists used their wealth to support a luxurious standard of living. Saigon's tree-lined streets and fashionable shops earned it the title "Paris of the Orient." French officials proudly called Vietnam "our marvelous balcony on the Pacific."

C. CHINA

1. The modern phase of European relations with China began in the early 1800s. At that time, the British traded wool and Indian cotton for Chinese tea. However, a trade imbalance occurred when Britain's thirst for Chinese tea far exceeded Chinese demand for English textiles.
2. Unscrupulous British merchants discovered that opium, a habit-forming narcotic, could be used to balance the trade deficit. British opium exports to China soared from 200 chests in 1729 to 40,000 chests in 1838. Britain prospered as Chinese addicts began to pay for the drug with silver.
3. The weak Chinese government desperately tried to halt the opium trade. In 1839, the controversy escalated into an armed conflict known as the Opium War. Outdated Chinese ships proved to be no match for modern British gunboats. In 1842, the two sides signed the Treaty of Nanking. The treaty awarded the British the strategic island of Hong Kong and the right to trade at Canton and four other ports.
4. The Treaty of Nanking marked the beginning of a century of Chinese humiliation. Between 1870 and 1914, Western nations carved China into spheres of influence. Britain, France, Germany, and Japan controlled trade, tariffs, harbor duties, and railroad rights in their respective spheres.
5. Although the United States did not take part in carving up China, American officials became increasingly alarmed that the European powers and Japan would restrict American trading opportunities in their spheres of influence. On September 6, 1899, Secretary of State John Hay dispatched a series of diplomatic notes asking the governments of these nations to respect the rights of other nations within their spheres of influence. The European powers and Japan neither accepted nor rejected Hay's Open Door notes. Hay nonetheless announced that all the powers had agreed and that their consent was therefore "final and definitive."

VI. CONSEQUENCES OF THE NEW IMPERIALISM

A. AN INTERDEPENDENT GLOBAL ECONOMY

1. The new imperialism created the beginning of an interdependent global economy with London as its financial center.

2. Foreign trade increased from just 3 percent of the world's output in 1800 to 33 percent by 1913.

3. Great Britain remained the world's biggest trading nation. However, Germany and the United States emerged as fast-growing rivals.

B. DISRUPTION OF TRADITIONAL CULTURES

1. Imperialism disrupted traditional cultures throughout Africa and Asia. For example, Kenyan farmers put aside traditional agricultural crops in order to grow coffee, tea, and sugar for European markets.

2. The process of westernization forced colonial peoples to reevaluate their traditions and adopt European legal and political practices. The adoption of Western ideas caused many non-Western peoples to call for the modernization of their societies and states.

C. DIPLOMATIC TENSIONS

1. Imperialism sharpened great power rivalries and solidified international alliance systems.

2. A new aggressive nationalism contributed to the mistrust and hostility that led to World War I.

Chapters 27–29

UNIT 8 Twentieth-Century Global Conflicts c. 1914 to Present

PREVIEW: UNIT 8 KEY CONCEPTS

- Total war and political instability in the first half of the twentieth century gave way to a polarized state order during the Cold War and eventually to efforts at transnational union.
  - World War I, caused by a complex interaction of long- and short-term factors, resulted in immense losses and disruptions for both victors and vanquished.
  - The conflicting goals of the peace negotiators in Paris pitted diplomatic idealism against the desire to punish Germany, producing a settlement that satisfied few.
  - In the interwar period, fascism, extreme nationalism, racist ideologies, and the failure of appeasement resulted in the catastrophe of World War II, presenting a grave challenge to European civilization.
- The stresses of economic collapse and total war engendered internal conflicts within European states and created conflicting conceptions of the relationship between the individual and the state, as demonstrated in the ideological battle between and among democracy, communism, and fascism.
- During the twentieth century, diverse intellectual and cultural movements questioned the existence of objective knowledge, the ability of reason to arrive at truth, and the role of religion in determining moral standards.
  - Science and technology yielded impressive material benefits but also caused immense destruction and posed challenges to objective knowledge.
- Demographic changes, economic growth, total war, disruptions of traditional social patterns, and competing definitions of freedom and justice altered the experiences of everyday life.
  - The twentieth century was characterized by large-scale suffering brought on by warfare and genocide, but also by tremendous improvements in the standard of living.

Chapter 27

War and Revolution

I. THE MARCH TO WAR

A. GERMANY AND THE NEW BALANCE OF POWER

1. Germany's industrial capacity, population, and military power all dramatically increased. In 1900, Germany produced more steel than Great Britain and France combined. Germany's population increased from 41 million in 1871 to 64 million in 1910. In contrast, France had just 40 million people in 1910.
2. European leaders from Cardinal Richelieu (see Chapter 12) to Prince Klemens von Metternich (see Chapter 20) had feared a united Germany. Their fears now became a reality. As Germany's power surged, its leaders demanded respect and a new "place in the sun."

B. BISMARCK'S NETWORK OF ALLIANCES

1. The French were humiliated by their defeat in the Franco-Prussian War and embittered by their loss of Alsace-Lorraine.
2. In an attempt to isolate France, Bismarck formed a military alliance with Austria-Hungary in 1879. Three years later, Italy joined these two countries, thus forming the Triple Alliance.
3. In 1887, Bismarck took yet another ally away from France by signing a treaty with Russia.

C. WILLIAM II'S AGGRESSIVE POLICIES

1. In 1890, Kaiser William II forced Bismarck to resign.
2. William II promptly set Germany on a new course by letting the treaty of friendship with Russia lapse.

3. William II then challenged Britain's long-standing naval supremacy by embarking on an expensive program of naval expansion that poisoned relations between the two countries.

D. THE FORMATION OF THE TRIPLE ENTENTE

1. France immediately offered Russia financial investments and diplomatic friendship. The two nations signed a Franco-Russian Alliance in 1894.
2. Alarmed by Germany's growing naval power, Britain abandoned its policy of "splendid isolation." In 1904, Britain concluded a series of agreements with France collectively called the Entente Cordiale. With French support, the British concluded a similar agreement with Russia, thus forming the Triple Entente.
3. Germany tested the Anglo-French entente by challenging France's plan to dominate Morocco. However, Germany's belligerent actions only served to draw France and Britain closer together.
4. Two rival alliances now confronted each other. A dispute between any two powers could easily escalate into a major war.

E. THE BALKAN POWDER KEG

1. As the power of the Ottoman Empire receded, the Balkan Peninsula became a powder keg of competing interests.
2. With the exception of the Greeks and the Romanians, most of the Balkan population spoke the same Slavic language. Many Slavs embraced Pan-Slavism, a nationalist movement to unite all Slavic peoples.
3. Bismarck recognized the potential danger of nationalist aspirations in the Balkans. At the 1878 Congress of Berlin, he tried to reduce tensions by supporting Serbian independence and Austria-Hungary's right to "occupy and administer" Bosnia and Herzegovina.
4. The newly independent nation of Serbia quickly became the leader of the Pan-Slavic movement. Serbian leaders hoped to unite the Slavs in the same way Piedmont had united the Italians and Prussia the Germans.
5. Austria felt threatened by the growth of Slavic nationalism within its borders and across the Balkans. In 1908, the Austrians enraged the Serbs by annexing Bosnia and Herzegovina.

6. Serbian nationalism threatened Austria. At the same time, it offered Slavic Russia an opportunity to advance its interests in the Balkans.

7. Russia and Austria-Hungary were thus on a collision course in the Balkans. As one Balkan crisis followed another, Europe teetered on the brink of war.

F. THE OUTBREAK OF WAR

1. On June 28, 1914, a 19-year-old Slav nationalist, Gavrilo Princip, assassinated Archduke Francis Ferdinand, the heir to the Austrian throne.

2. The assassination set in motion a sequence of events that plunged Europe into war. In August 1914, millions of soldiers marched off to battle, convinced the war would be over in a few weeks.

AP® European History textbooks devote lengthy discussions to the complex sequence of events that led to the outbreak of World War I. Interestingly, APEURO test writers devote very few multiple-choice questions to this topic. Don't become bogged down trying to memorize the details of the Balkan wars and the exchange of ultimatums between the Great Powers. Devote the majority of your time to studying the consequences of World War I for the home front, for Russia, and for postwar Europe.

II. THE WAR IN THE WEST

A. THE SCHLIEFFEN PLAN

1. Germany faced the daunting task of simultaneously fighting France on its western border and Russia along a lengthy eastern front.

2. In order to prevent a two-front war, General Alfred von Schlieffen drew up a master plan calling for an all-out attack against France. The Schlieffen Plan gambled that France could be knocked out of the war before Russia had a chance to fully mobilize its forces.

3. A lightning attack on France meant invading neutral Belgium.

4. Germany's unprovoked attack on Belgium outraged Britain. On August 4, 1914, Britain declared war on Germany.

B. STALEMATE

1. The Schlieffen Plan narrowly failed, making a quick victory impossible.
2. Both sides now constructed an elaborate system of trenches stretching more than 600 miles from the English Channel to the Swiss border.
3. Trench warfare produced a stalemate that lasted about four years and claimed unprecedented casualties.

C. THE HOME FRONT

1. Total war
    - i. When it became clear that the war would not be over quickly, governments mobilized all human and industrial resources in order to wage total war.
    - ii. Governments tightly controlled the news and used propaganda to rally public morale and arouse hatred of the enemy.
2. The role of women
    - i. As more and more men went to war, millions of women replaced them in factories, offices, and shops. World War I marked the first time that the employment of women was essential to a sustained war effort.
    - ii. In the decade prior to World War I, British women led by Emmeline Pankhurst waged an aggressive campaign for greater political and social rights. During the war, Pankhurst called a halt to militant suffrage activities, urging women to focus on contributing to the war effort.
    - iii. In 1918, Parliament granted the suffrage to women over the age of 30.

D. *ALL QUIET ON THE WESTERN FRONT*

1. *All Quiet on the Western Front* is a war novel written by Erich Maria Remarque, a German veteran of World War I.
2. Remarque vividly described the senseless slaughter and suffering endured by soldiers on the Western Front.

III. THE RUSSIAN REVOLUTION

A. THE END OF ROMANOV RULE

1. The poorly equipped Russian army was no match for the German war machine. By 1917, more than 7 million Russian soldiers had been killed, wounded, or taken prisoner.
2. Nicholas II proved to be an inept ruler. As an all-powerful autocrat, he was oblivious to "public opinion" and to the pressing need to withdraw from World War I. Instead, Russian battlefield losses mounted and shortages of food worsened. Nicholas moved his headquarters to the front in a futile attempt to rally his troops.
3. In early 1917, food shortages in Petrograd (formerly St. Petersburg) led to spontaneous demonstrations and strikes.
4. Nicholas ordered his troops to restore order, but the soldiers refused and instead supported the demonstrators. On March 12, 1917, Nicholas II abdicated, ending three centuries of Romanov rule.

↳ russia was dealing w/ things inside

B. THE PROVISIONAL GOVERNMENT

1. A provisional government led by Alexander Kerensky replaced the tsar.
2. As a result of tsarist political oppression, Kerensky inherited a government with no viable democratic institutions.
3. Despite mounting losses, the provisional government continued the war against Germany. This fateful decision to pursue an unpopular war weakened the provisional government and played a key role in its demise.

↳ didn't quit fighting in WWI

C. VLADIMIR LENIN AND THE BOLSHEVIK REVOLUTION

1. While the Russian army was falling apart, the Germans helped Lenin return to Petrograd. Lenin arrived at the Finland Station on April 3, 1917, and promptly urged his followers to overthrow the provisional government.
2. Lenin's key ideas
   i. Lenin denounced the extreme economic inequalities under the tsarist regime. He eschewed reform, arguing that capitalism could only be destroyed by class conflict.

ii. Lenin insisted that a communist revolution was possible in a nonindustrialized country such as Russia.

iii. Lenin argued that Russia's relatively small working class could not develop a revolutionary class consciousness. Instead, leadership would have to come from a highly disciplined group of professional revolutionaries.

3. Lenin's slogan of "Peace, Land, and Bread" captured the popular imagination and enabled the Bolsheviks to win widespread popular support.

4. Lenin sensed that it was time to act. "History will not forgive us," Lenin wrote, "if we do not seize power now." On the night of November 6, 1917, the Bolsheviks occupied most government buildings. The next day Lenin proclaimed the establishment of a new Bolshevik government.

D. THE TREATY OF BREST-LITOVSK

1. Lenin realized that the survival of the Bolshevik regime depended upon ending the war with Germany.

2. In March 1918, the Bolsheviks reluctantly agreed to the Treaty of Brest-Litovsk. Under the terms of this treaty, Russia lost a quarter of its European territory and a third of its population.

3. It is important to note that Russia later repudiated the treaty, and it was declared null and void by the Allies.

E. CIVIL WAR

1. By the summer of 1918, several "White" armies attempted to overthrow the Bolsheviks.

2. Led by Leon Trotsky, the Bolsheviks responded by forming a highly disciplined Red Army.

3. The civil war between the Whites and the Reds lasted from 1918 to 1920. The divided and poorly led Whites lost to the better-organized Red Army.

Lenin's pivotal role in the Russian Revolution has generated a significant number of multiple-choice questions on the APEURO exam. Be sure you study Lenin's key ideas. It is interesting to compare Lenin's decisive leadership with the weakness and vacillation of Tsar Nicholas II and Alexander Kerensky.

IV. THE PEACE SETTLEMENT

A. THE END OF WORLD WAR I

1. The Treaty of Brest-Litovsk enabled the Germans to transfer divisions from the east to help launch a great spring offensive.
2. Reinforced by newly arrived American troops, the British and French halted the German offensive.
3. Realizing that defeat was imminent, William II abdicated his throne and Germany became a republic. Two days later, on November 11, 1918, World War I came to an end.

B. THE FOURTEEN POINTS

1. President Woodrow Wilson became the spokesman for a just and lasting peace.
2. Wilson's Fourteen Points included a call for the following:
   - i. Open diplomacy
   - ii. Freedom of the seas
   - iii. Reduction of national armaments
   - iv. Return of Alsace-Lorraine to France
   - v. A free and independent Poland with access to the sea
   - vi. National self-determination for oppressed minority groups
   - vii. Creation of a "general association of nations" to preserve the peace and security of its members
3. Wilson's idealistic proposals were undermined by secret treaties and by a desire to punish Germany.

C. THE PARIS PEACE CONFERENCE

1. Although nearly 30 countries were represented, Great Britain, France, and the United States made the major decisions.
2. Germany and Austria-Hungary were not allowed to attend the conference.
3. Russia, which had suffered the greatest loss of life, was in the midst of a civil war and was not invited to attend the conference.

germany + austria-hungary did not go (russia also didn't go)

D. THE TREATY OF VERSAILLES

1. Germany lost 13 percent of its land, including Alsace-Lorraine.
2. Germany's territories in Africa and the Pacific were given as mandates to Britain, France, and Japan. A mandate was a territory that was administered on behalf of the League of Nations.
3. Poland once again became an independent nation. The new Poland received a large strip of German land called the Polish Corridor. This strip cut off East Prussia from the rest of Germany and gave Poland access to the sea.
4. Germany's army was limited to 100,000 men and forbidden to have artillery, aircraft, or submarines.
5. The east bank of the Rhine River was to be demilitarized, and the Allies were to have the right to occupy the Rhineland for 15 years.
6. Germany was declared guilty of starting the war and forced to pay huge payments called reparations.
7. The Allies created a League of Nations to discuss and settle disputes without resorting to war.
8. The final signing ceremony took place in the Hall of Mirrors at Versailles, the same room in which Bismarck's German empire had been proclaimed in 1871.

E. A NEW MAP OF EUROPE

1. Austria-Hungary was dissolved and the Habsburg monarchy eliminated. Austria and Hungary became separate states. In addition, territories from Austria-Hungary were given to the newly created states of Czechoslovakia and Yugoslavia.
2. The Serbs dominated Yugoslavia.
3. Finland and the three Baltic states—Estonia, Latvia, and Lithuania—emerged from the tsarist empire.

F. MAKING COMPARISONS: THE CONGRESS OF VIENNA AND THE PARIS PEACE CONFERENCE

1. The Congress of Vienna
   i. Allowed defeated France to participate in peace conference negotiations.

ii. Established a framework for future international relations based on periodic meetings, or congresses, among the great powers.

iii. Restored a conservative order based upon the institutions of monarchy and aristocracy.

iv. Created a balance of power that lasted for over 50 years.

2. The Paris Peace Conference

i. Refused to allow defeated Germany or Communist Russia to participate in peace conference negotiations.

ii. Established a framework for future international relations based on the League of Nations.

iii. Witnessed the birth of a democratic order with the elimination of monarchies in Germany, Austria-Hungary, and Russia.

iv. Created a legacy of bitterness between both the victors and the defeated, which led to a second world war in just 20 years.

Chapter 28

The Age of Anxiety

I. THE INTELLECTUAL CRISIS

A. OLD CERTAINTIES

1. Belief in the power of reason to understand the universe and discover natural laws.
2. Belief in progress and the power of science and technology to improve living standards.
3. Belief in liberty and the power of individual rights to promote a just society.

B. THE IMPACT OF WORLD WAR I

1. Caused unprecedented death and destruction.
2. Overthrew established monarchies and social orders in Russia, Germany, and Austria-Hungary.
3. Led many people to question the optimistic belief in reason, progress, and individual rights.

C. THE TERRIBLE UNCERTAINTIES

1. A widespread feeling of disillusionment, uncertainty, and anxiety.
2. New doubts about the ability of individuals to control their lives.
3. New stress on the irrational and destructive nature of humans.
4. An intellectual crisis that affected every field of thought.

II. MODERN PHILOSOPHY

A. FRIEDRICH NIETZSCHE (1844–1900)

1. Considered an important forerunner of existentialism.
2. Expressed contempt for middle-class morality, saying that it led to a false and shallow existence.
3. Argued that conventional notions of good and evil are only relevant for the ordinary person.
4. Rejected reason and embraced the irrational.
5. Believed that the "will-to-power" of a few heroic "supermen" could successfully reorder the world.

B. EXISTENTIALISM: KEY IDEAS

1. Reason and science are incapable of providing insight into the human situation.
2. God, reason, and progress are myths; humans live in a meaningless and hostile world, alone and isolated.
3. This condition of loneliness is a challenge and a call to action. Men and women give meaning to their lives through their choices. A person is therefore the sum of his or her actions and choices.

C. EXISTENTIALISM: KEY THINKERS

1. Jean-Paul Sartre, *Being and Nothingness*: argues that since there is no Creator, humans are "condemned to be free."
2. Albert Camus, *The Stranger*: a brilliantly crafted novel illustrating Camus' absurdist world view.

III. THE NEW PHYSICS

A. NEWTONIAN PHYSICS

1. From the time of Isaac Newton to the early twentieth century, physical scientists believed that unchanging natural laws governed the universe.
2. This mechanistic view of nature supported an optimistic belief in progress toward what one researcher called "a boundless future."

B. ALBERT EINSTEIN (1879–1955)

1. Theories
   i. Einstein proposed his special theory of relativity in 1905. He challenged traditional conceptions of time, space, and motion.
   ii. His famous equation $E = mc^2$ (energy = mass × the square of the speed of light) declared that mass and energy are interchangeable. This discovery laid the foundation for the development of nuclear power.
2. Implications
   i. Instead of living in a rational world with few uncertainties, humans lived in a new universe with few certainties. Everything was "relative" or dependent on the observer's frame of reference.
   ii. It is important to note that Einstein's theories did not immediately affect the average person's outlook on life. However, intellectuals and popular writers realized that by pulling the rug out from under perceived reality, the new physics contributed to the uncertainties of the postwar world.

It is very important to remember that APEURO is not AP® Physics. You will not be asked to explain the complexities of Einstein's theories. You will, however, be expected to know that the new physics challenged traditional notions of causality, time, and space. It undermined the optimistic confidence that people lived in a predictable and orderly world.

IV. THE NEW PSYCHOLOGY

A. BEFORE FREUD

1. Romantic artists and authors had explored the inner worlds of emotion and imagination.
2. Professional psychologists assumed that human behavior was based upon rational decisions by the conscious mind.

B. SIGMUND FREUD (1856–1939)

1. Theories
   - i. Freud believed that the human psyche includes three distinct parts, which he called the id, the superego, and the ego.
   - ii. The id consists of inborn sexual and aggressive urges.
   - iii. The superego acts as the conscience that seeks to repress the id. It develops as children learn their culture's moral values.
   - iv. When the superego checks the pleasure-seeking impulses of the id, it drives them into the realm of the subconscious mind. The subconscious is irrational and recognizes no ethical restrictions.
   - v. The ego is the center of reason. It attempts to find a balance between the conflicting demands of the id and the superego.
2. Implications
   - i. Freud's theories undermined the Enlightenment's belief that humans are fundamentally rational beings. Instead, humans are irrational beings capable of destroying themselves and society.
   - ii. Freud's emphasis upon the power of uncontrolled irrational and unconscious drives provided an unsettling explanation for the seemingly incomprehensible horrors unleashed by World War I.
   - iii. Freud's studies of the unconscious mind had a significant influence on modern art and literature.

V. MODERN ART, ARCHITECTURE, AND LITERATURE

A. FUTURISM

1. Key characteristics
   - i. Began in Italy when the poet F.T. Marinetti issued the Futurist Manifesto. Marinetti challenged artists to demonstrate "courage, audacity, and revolt" by glorifying war, patriotism and "the beauty of speed."
   - ii. Urged artists to abandon classical artistic traditions and embrace railroads, ocean liners, airplanes, automobiles, and other products of the new industrial age.

iii. Anticipated the growing discontent with the conventions and values of contemporary European society.

iv. Advocated war as "the only cure for the world." Marinetti praised "militarism patriotism, and the destructive gesture of the anarchist" as "beautiful ideas worth dying for." He influenced the glorification of war by Mussolini and his fascist followers.

2. Key artists and works

i. Umberto Boccioni, *Unique Forms of Continuity in Space*: sculpture that embodies Boccioni's rejection of "the blind and foolish imitation" of Greek, Roman, and Renaissance formulas.

ii. Gino Severini, *Armored Train in Action*: painting that glorifies modern technology, speed, and war.

B. DADA

1. Key characteristics

i. Received its name from a nonsensical French word chosen at random from the dictionary.

ii. Protested the madness of World War I and the absurdity of reason.

iii. Cultivated absurdity by challenging and denouncing traditional assumptions about art.

2. Key artists and works

i. Marcel Duchamp, *Fountain*: an upside-down urinal that Duchamp signed "R. Mutt" and titled *Fountain*.

ii. Jean Arp, *Collage Arranged According to the Laws of Chance*: a serendipitous composition formed by dropping pieces of torn paper on the floor and then arranging them on a piece of paper more or less the way they had fallen.

C. SURREALISM

1. Key characteristics

i. Influenced by Freud's psychoanalytic technique of free association as a means of exploring the imagination.

ii. Depicts the world of the unconscious mind as revealed in dreams and fantasies.

iii. Portrays strange, seemingly unrelated objects and symbols that express the artist's inner mind.

2. Key artists and works

   i. Giorgio de Chirico, *The Song of Love*: juxtaposes a classical head, a glove, a ball, and a building in a puzzling dreamlike combination of images.

   ii. Salvador Dali, *The Persistence of Memory*: time loses all meaning in a scene combining limp watches, a dead tree, swarming ants, and a single living fly.

D. BAUHAUS ARCHITECTURE

1. Key characteristics

   i. Architecture should be practical, useful, and above all, functional.

   ii. Architects should avoid using unnecessary exterior decorations and instead rely on clear straight lines.

   iii. Builders should use recently developed industrial materials such as glass, steel, ferroconcrete, and cantilevers.

   iv. It is important to note that the Bauhaus style originated in Germany and spread to the United States where it became known as the International Style.

2. Key architects and buildings

   i. Walter Gropius, The Fagus Shoe Factory: inspired by the principles of functionalism, the structure features a clear glass façade that gives an unprecedented feeling of openness and continuity between the inside and outside

   ii. Le Corbusier, Villa Savoye: features a flat roof on a square box illustrating Corbusier's dictum that a house is "a machine for living in"

E. TWENTIETH-CENTURY LITERATURE

1. Key characteristics

   i. Questions accepted values and practices.

   ii. Expresses discontent and alienation from middle-class conformity and materialism.

iii. Focuses on the complexity and irrationality of the human mind.

iv. Employs the stream-of-consciousness technique to explore the human psyche.

2. Key authors and works

i. James Joyce, *Ulysses*: uses a stream-of-consciousness technique to chronicle the appointments, encounters, and thoughts of a single day in the life of Leopold Bloom in Dublin, Ireland.

ii. Marcel Proust, *Remembrance of Things Past*: semi-autobiographical account of a young boy's journey through life.

iii. T.S. Eliot, *The Love Song of J. Alfred Prufrock*: utilizes a stream-of-consciousness technique to provide a dramatic monologue of an urban man overwhelmed with feelings of isolation, regret, and frustration.

F. MAKING COMPARISONS: CONCEPTIONS OF THE INDIVIDUAL IN THE RENAISSANCE AND THE AGE OF ANXIETY

1. The Renaissance

i. Displayed an interest in classical culture and a belief in human potential.

ii. Attempted to revive classical standards of beauty.

iii. Utilized perspective to create a realistic illusion of depth on a flat surface.

iv. Glorified the beauty of the human form in works such as Botticelli's *Birth of Venus* and Michelangelo's *David*.

v. Emphasized the importance of a well-rounded humanist education informed by the study of classical texts.

2. The Age of Anxiety

i. Rejected classical standards of beauty and a belief in human potential.

ii. Shocked and appalled by the unprecedented violence, destruction, and death caused by World War I.

iii. Disillusioned by Einstein's view of a universe that lacked absolute objective reality and Freud's view of human behavior dominated by irrational instinctual drives.

iv. Portrayed the meaninglessness of human existence in existential works by Sartre and Camus and in stream-of-consciousness novels by Proust and Joyce.

v. Portrayed a world of dream-like images in surrealistic works by Dali and de Chirico.

VI. THE SEARCH FOR A STABLE INTERNATIONAL ORDER

A. PROBLEMS

1. Germany resented the Versailles Treaty's harsh terms, calling it a *diktat*, or imposed settlement.
2. The United States rejected the Versailles Treaty and followed a policy of isolationism.
3. France was determined to enforce the Versailles Treaty and make Germany pay reparations for the damage it had caused.
4. Communist Russia remained outside the international system.

B. GERMANY: THE WEIMAR REPUBLIC

1. Reparations

   i. The new German republic—generally known as the Weimar Republic—faced staggering reparation payments.

   ii. When the Weimar Republic proposed a three-year moratorium on making reparation payments, the French occupied the Ruhr Valley and seized goods as payments.

2. Inflation

   i. The Weimar Republic supported itself by printing vast amounts of paper money. By December 1923, one dollar was worth 4 trillion German marks.

   ii. The 1923 inflation destroyed the savings and incomes of the German middle class. Feeling betrayed by their government, embittered Germans would later be susceptible to Nazi propaganda.

C. HOPE FOR PEACE

1. The Dawes Plan
   i. At the end of 1923, a committee of experts led by American Charles Dawes devised a plan to reestablish a sound German currency and reduce reparation payments.
   ii. The Dawes Plan provided a series of American loans to Germany. The infusion of American money revitalized the German economy, thus ending the inflationary spiral.
2. The Locarno Pact
   i. France, Germany, England, Italy, and Belgium signed the Locarno Pact, guaranteeing the borders between Germany and France.
   ii. The Locarno Pact marked an important turning point in Franco-German relations and appeared to offer the hope of a new era of peaceful relations between these two rivals.
3. The Kellogg-Briand Pact, 1928
   i. In 1928, 62 countries including the United States signed a pact promising "to renounce war as an instrument of national policy."
   ii. At the time, the Kellogg-Briand Pact appeared to bolster collective security and promote a renewed spirit of optimism.

It is easy to overlook the political events of the 1920s, since they were overturned by the tumultuous and far more famous events of the 1930s. Don't make this mistake. The Dawes Plan, the Locarno Pact, and the Kellogg-Briand Pact have all generated multiple-choice questions. Make sure that you can identify each of these agreements.

Depression, Dictators, and World War II

I. THE GREAT DEPRESSION

A. CAUSES

1. Several long-term problems negatively affected the U.S. economy:
   i. Companies overproduced consumer goods.
   ii. Consumers did not have enough money or credit to purchase goods.
   iii. Farmers overproduced agricultural products, driving down prices and incomes.
2. The American stock market crash caused enormous financial losses and triggered a global financial crisis.
3. Worried American bankers recalled loans to European banks. Austria's largest bank failed, starting a financial panic in central Europe.
4. The financial crisis led to sharp declines in global trade and manufacturing.
5. The United States raised protective tariffs, forcing other nations to retaliate.
6. Governments cut budgets and reduced spending, helping to accelerate the downward economic spiral.

B. IMPACT ON EUROPE

1. Replaced the optimistic spirit of the late 1920s with a growing sense of doubt and fear.
2. Created uncertainty and insecurity for millions of unemployed workers.

3. Prompted increased government economic programs that laid the foundation for the creation of postwar welfare states.
4. Created opportunities for demagogues and dictators to exploit people's fears.

II. CONSERVATIVE AUTHORITARIANISM AND TOTALITARIANISM

A. CONSERVATIVE AUTHORITARIANISM

1. Committed to the existing social order.
2. Opposed to popular participation in government.
3. Revived in eastern Europe, Spain, and Portugal.

B. TOTALITARIANISM

1. Exercised total control over the lives of individual citizens.
2. Used modern technology and communication to manipulate and censor information.
3. Used education to mold loyal citizens and demonize scapegoats and enemies.

C. FORMS OF TOTALITARIANISM

1. Fascism
   - i. Led by one leader and one party.
   - ii. Condemned democracy, arguing that rival parties undermine national unity.
   - iii. Supported state-sponsored capitalism.
   - iv. Glorified war and aggressive nationalism.
   - v. Exercised control over the media.
2. Communism
   - i. Led by one party, the "dictatorship of the proletariat."
   - ii. Condemned capitalism, arguing that it exploits workers.

iii. Supported state ownership of the means of production.

iv. Glorified the working class.

v. Exercised control over the media.

III. LENIN, STALIN, AND COMMUNIST RUSSIA, 1921–1939

A. VLADIMIR LENIN AND THE NEW ECONOMIC POLICY

1. Widespread famine, a deteriorating economy, and increasing unrest all plagued Russia following the civil war.
2. Lenin pragmatically realized that he needed to make a tactical retreat. In March 1921, he launched the New Economic Policy. It called for a temporary compromise with capitalism. Small businesses were denationalized, and peasants were allowed to establish free markets in agricultural products. The Communist Party still maintained control of large industries such as oil and steel.
3. The New Economic Policy successfully revived the Russian economy. By 1928, the country's farms and factories produced as much as they had before World War I.

B. JOSEPH STALIN VERSUS LEON TROTSKY

1. Lenin's death in 1924 created a power struggle between Trotsky and Stalin.
2. As a charismatic leader since 1905, Trotsky was second only to Lenin in fame. Trotsky believed that Russia should support communist revolutions around the world.
3. In contrast, Stalin was a quiet man who preferred to work behind the scenes. As general secretary of the Communist Party, Stalin placed his supporters in key positions. Stalin argued that communism should first gain a firm hold in Russia before supporting a global revolution.
4. Stalin proved to be cunning and ruthless. He successfully expelled Trotsky from the Communist Party. By 1927, Stalin stood alone as the Soviet Union's undisputed leader.

C. THE FIVE-YEAR PLANS

1. In 1928, Stalin launched the first of a series of five-year plans designed to transform the Soviet Union's economic and social structure. The plans had the following goals:
   i. End the New Economic Policy.
   ii. Create a socialist command economy in which the government makes all economic decisions.
   iii. Promote the rapid development of heavy industries.
   iv. Collectivize agriculture.
2. Stalin's commitment to a program of massive, large-scale industrialism produced results. By 1940, the Soviet Union was a major industrial power, trailing only the United States and Germany.
3. Stalin's campaign to collectivize agriculture was less successful. Conservative Russian peasants opposed surrendering their land and joining a collective farm. Stalin denounced resisting peasants as *kulaks* and ordered party officials to "liquidate them as a class." *Kulaks* and other peasants were executed, starved, and deported to forced-labor camps.

Many kulaks wrote poignant petitions describing their increasingly desperate plight. APEURO test writers often use these primary source documents to test your understanding of Stalin's policy of liquidating the kulaks and forming collective farms.

D. THE GREAT TERROR

1. Stalin was a totalitarian dictator who was more powerful than the most autocratic tsar.
2. During the mid-1930s, Stalin launched a program of state-sponsored terror that began with show trials to eliminate Old Bolsheviks. The Great Terror expanded to include intellectuals, army officers, party members, and ordinary citizens.
3. Stalin's "politics of fear" included the use of secret police and purges of political rivals. At least 8 million people were arrested. Millions of innocent people died in forced-labor camps called gulags.

E. MAKING COMPARISONS: THE REIGN OF TERROR AND THE GREAT TERROR

1. The Reign of Terror, 1793–1794
   - i. Ordered by the Committee of Public Safety led by Maximilien de Robespierre.
   - ii. Intended to save the Revolution from foreign and domestic enemies.
   - iii. Justified by the goal of creating a "republic of virtue" where all citizens would possess high moral standards and be dedicated to the public good.
   - iv. Eliminated supposed political rivals such as Georges-Jacques Danton.
   - v. Failed to create supporters for Robespierre.
   - vi. Used public executions by the guillotine to terrorize the entire nation.
   - vii. Ended when the Convention reasserted its authority by arresting and executing Robespierre.
2. The Great Terror, 1934–1938
   - i. Ordered by Joseph Stalin, general secretary of the Communist Party and dictator of the Soviet Union.
   - ii. Purged Old Bolsheviks and other supposed political rivals who threatened Stalin's power.
   - iii. Justified by claiming the existence of a plot masterminded by Trotsky along with Fascist enemies to overthrow Stalin.
   - iv. Used public show trials, executions, and mass imprisonment to terrorize the entire nation.
   - v. Ended when all supposed rivals to Stalin had been eliminated.
   - vi. Created a new Communist Party staffed with members who demonstrated total loyalty to Stalin.

IV. MUSSOLINI AND FASCIST ITALY

A. POSTWAR ITALY

1. Italy had entered World War I in hopes of winning mandates in East Africa and Austrian territory along the Adriatic Sea. When

the Treaty of Versailles rejected these claims, embittered Italian nationalists felt betrayed.

2. Italy faced a severe economic crisis that included soaring inflation, rising unemployment, and a massive national debt.
3. Italy's upper and middle classes feared that the economic crisis and growing labor unrest might lead to a communist revolt, as had just happened in Russia.

B. THE RISE OF BENITO MUSSOLINI

1. Growing numbers of Italians demanded action and waited impatiently for a strong leader.
2. Mussolini used Italy's political power vacuum to seize power. As the leader of the Fascist Party, he boldly promised to revive Italy's economy and rebuild its armed forces.
3. In 1922, Mussolini called upon his followers to march on Rome. Although the government could have stopped Mussolini with a show of force, King Victor Emmanuel III gave in and named Mussolini prime minister.

C. THE FASCIST STATE

1. Mussolini quickly consolidated his power and organized a Fascist state.
2. Mussolini outlawed all political parties except the Fascists.
3. Mussolini's propaganda encouraged Italians to accept his leadership without question. Slogans such as "Mussolini Is Always Right" covered billboards across Italy.

D. THE CORPORATE ECONOMY

1. Mussolini believed that capitalists and workers must be forced to cooperate for the good of the state.
2. He organized 22 state corporations to run all parts of the Italian economy. Each corporation included employers, employees, and government arbitrators.
3. The corporations outlawed strikes and set wages and prices.
4. It is important to note that Mussolini's corporate state combined private ownership with state control over economic decisions.

E. THE LATERAN ACCORD

1. Mussolini successfully negotiated an end to the long dispute between the papacy and the Italian state.
2. Pope Pius XII recognized the legitimacy of the Italian state. In return, Mussolini recognized Vatican City as an independent state ruled by the pope.

APEURO tests do not devote as much attention to Mussolini as they do to Adolf Hitler and Stalin. Don't be distracted by the Black Shirts, the March on Rome, and Mussolini's bombastic speeches. Instead, focus on the ideology of fascism and the characteristics of Mussolini's corporate state.

V. HITLER AND NAZI GERMANY

A. REASONS WHY THE WEIMAR REPUBLIC FAILED

1. Many Germans refused to believe that their army had been defeated in battle. They believed instead that the German army had been betrayed by socialist and liberal politicians associated with the new Weimar Republic.
2. The Versailles Treaty outraged German nationalists who resented the war-guilt clause and the loss of territory to Poland. Constant nationalist agitation undermined support for the Weimar Republic.
3. Conservatives wanted a strong leader who would restore order and reduce the power of labor unions.
4. Runaway inflation during the early 1920s destroyed middle-class savings, thus eroding confidence in the government.
5. The Great Depression had a particularly devastating impact on Germany. Millions of workers lost faith in the Weimar Republic.
6. Article 48 of the German constitution helped to undermine the republican government by allowing the president to rule by decree in cases of national emergency.

B. REASONS WHY ADOLF HITLER ROSE TO POWER

1. The weakness of the Weimar Republic helped prepare the public for a bold leader who would restore German pride.
2. Hitler concluded that he would not attempt to overthrow the Weimar Republic by revolutionary means. Instead, he would use the electoral process to legally gain power.
3. Hitler was a spellbinding demagogue who denounced the Weimar Republic and the Versailles Treaty. He skillfully used modern propaganda techniques to convince the German people to follow his leadership.
4. Hitler offered the German people an ideology that exploited their fears. The Nazi program included the following key points:
    - i. Nationalism: German national honor would be avenged by regaining the lands taken by the Versailles Treaty.
    - ii. Master race: the Germans were a master race who needed land in eastern Europe and Russia.
    - iii. Anti-Semitism: Jews were an inferior race responsible for many of Germany's problems.
    - iv. Anticommunism: Marxists were responsible for fomenting labor unrest. Much of Hitler's anti-Semitism focused on alleged Jewish responsibility for the rise of communism.
    - v. The führer: Parliamentary government produced weak, vacillating politicians. Hitler believed that Germany required an absolute leader (or führer) who would embody the national will.

C. THE NAZI TOTALITARIAN STATE

1. Hitler ruthlessly transformed Germany into a totalitarian state. A series of laws banned all political parties except the Nazis. A special secret police force called the Gestapo used sweeping powers to arbitrarily arrest anyone who opposed Nazi rule.
2. The government supervised both labor and business. New laws banned strikes and dissolved independent labor unions.
3. A ministry of culture supervised the media and shaped public opinion. Special films such as *Triumph of the Will* glorified Hitler's leadership.
4. It is interesting to note that the Nazi party's ideal German woman was a mother, wife, and homemaker.

D. ANTI-SEMITISM

1. Although Jews comprised less than 1 percent of Germany's population, Hitler blamed them for Germany's problems.
2. In 1933, the Nazis passed laws forbidding Jews to hold public office. Two years later, the Nuremberg Laws deprived Jews of German citizenship and required them to wear a yellow Star of David as identification.
3. Nazi violence against Jews steadily mounted. On November 9 and 10, 1938, the Nazis organized a "spontaneous" campaign of mob violence known as the *Kristallnacht*, or "Crystal Night," or "The Night of Broken Glass."

VI. THE MARCH OF FASCIST AGGRESSION

A. HITLER AND THE VERSAILLES TREATY

1. In 1933, Germany withdrew from the League of Nations.
2. In 1935, Hitler openly began a program of rearmament.
3. In March 1936, Hitler ordered the German army to march into the demilitarized zone of the Rhineland.

B. MUSSOLINI AND ETHIOPIA

1. In October 1935, Mussolini ordered a massive invasion of Ethiopia.
2. The invasion represented a crucial test of the League of Nations' system of collective security.
3. Although the League condemned Italy, its members did nothing. The British and French hoped that appeasing Mussolini would maintain the peace.

C. REASONS WHY THE DEMOCRACIES FAILED TO ACT

1. The Great Depression forced the United States, Great Britain, and France to focus on domestic issues.
2. The horrific loss of life in World War I created a deep desire for peace.
3. American isolationists believed that U.S. involvement in World War I had been a mistake. They wanted to avoid becoming entangled in European affairs.

4. The democracies repeatedly underestimated Hitler's thirst for power and conquest.

D. THE SPANISH CIVIL WAR

1. Spain was a deeply divided country. Between 1931 and 1936, a democratically elected government tried to cope with the Great Depression. Led by General Francisco Franco, army leaders supported by the clergy and aristocracy favored a fascist-style government.
2. The Spanish Civil War began in 1936 when Nationalist forces led by Franco rebelled against the Republic.
3. The civil war escalated into an international ideological war when Hitler and Mussolini sent men and materials to support the Nationalists. The Russians countered by supporting the Republican, or Loyalist, side.
4. During the war, a squadron of German planes bombed the defenseless village of Guernica, killing hundreds of men, women, and children. Pablo Picasso painted *Guernica* to protest this atrocity.
5. Republican resistance finally collapsed in 1939. Franco then established an authoritarian regime that remained in power until his death in 1975. It is important to note that Spain was officially neutral during World War II.

E. THE MUNICH CONFERENCE

1. In 1938, Hitler successfully annexed Austria into Germany.
2. Hitler's campaign of German expansion focused next on a mountainous region of western Czechoslovakia called the Sudetenland. This heavily fortified strategic region contained 3 million German-speaking people.
3. Hitler, British Prime Minister Neville Chamberlain, Mussolini, and French Premier Édouard Daladier held an emergency conference in Munich to negotiate Hitler's demand that Czechoslovakia give up the Sudetenland.
4. Chamberlain believed he could preserve the peace by appeasing Hitler and giving in to his demands.
5. The Munich Conference marked a turning point in European history. Filled with confidence, Hitler now made plans to attack Poland.

6. The Munich Conference quickly became a symbol of surrender. Following World War II, democratic leaders vowed they would never again appease a ruthless dictator.

VII. WORLD WAR II

A. THE OUTBREAK OF WORLD WAR II

1. In August 1939, Germany and the Soviet Union stunned the world by announcing a 10-year nonaggression pact. In addition, they secretly agreed to divide Eastern Europe.
2. On September 1, 1939, German forces attacked Poland. Two days later, Great Britain and France declared war on Germany.
3. Germany's blitzkrieg or "lightning war" combined fast-moving armor and air power to overwhelm Poland.

B. HITLER'S EMPIRE IN EUROPE, 1940–1942

1. In the spring of 1940, Hitler unleashed a second blitzkrieg that overwhelmed Scandinavia, Belgium, and France. Only Great Britain remained unconquered.
2. Led by Winston Churchill, the outnumbered British refused to surrender. Their fate rested on the skill and valor of the Royal Air Force (RAF) fighter pilots. In daily air battles beginning in July 1940, the RAF pilots proved more than equal to the challenge. By the end of 1940, Hitler knew that he could neither defeat the RAF nor break the spirit of the British people.
3. Frustrated by his defeat in the Battle of Britain, Hitler broke his pact with Stalin and, like Napoleon 150 years before, unleashed a massive invasion of Russia. By October 1941, German armies surrounded Leningrad and besieged Moscow.
4. Hitler now ruled a vast European empire stretching from the English Channel to Moscow.

C. THE HOLOCAUST

1. The Nazi nightmare did not stop on the battlefields of Europe. Hitler ordered the systematic killing of Jews and other allegedly inferior peoples. This horrible destruction of life is known as the Holocaust.

UNIT 8 | TWENTIETH-CENTURY GLOBAL CONFLICTS

2. The following factors contributed to the Holocaust:
   i. Jews were a small and vulnerable minority.
   ii. Hitler's propaganda convinced Germans that Jews were an inferior race that should be eliminated.
   iii. Hitler's secret police successfully stifled dissent.
   iv. The Nazis successfully secured collaborators in occupied territories.
3. The Nazi Holocaust claimed the lives of over 6 million Poles, Russians, Czechs, and other civilians. Of these, an estimated 5.7 million were European Jews murdered in death camps.

D. JAPAN'S EMPIRE IN ASIA, 1941–1942

1. The dramatic events in Europe overshadowed the changes occurring in Asia. In July 1941, Japanese forces overran French Indochina. President Roosevelt retaliated by ordering a total embargo of all trade with Japan.
2. On December 7, 1941, the Japanese launched a surprise attack on the United States naval base at Pearl Harbor. Within two hours, the Japanese sank or damaged 18 ships and killed 2,403 Americans.
3. The surprise attack on Pearl Harbor stunned the American people. An angry and now united nation entered World War II determined to crush Japan and Germany.
4. But reversing the Japanese advance would take time. By May 1942, Japanese forces conquered a vast Pacific empire they called the Greater East Asia Co-Prosperity Sphere.

E. THE GRAND ALLIANCE

1. Outraged Americans wanted to first avenge Pearl Harbor. However, President Roosevelt recognized that Hitler posed a greater threat than Japan. If Hitler succeeded in defeating both the Soviet Union and Great Britain, he could transform Europe into an unconquerable fortress. Roosevelt and Churchill therefore agreed upon a military strategy to defeat Hitler first.
2. The Big Three referred to Roosevelt, Churchill, and the Soviet leader, Joseph Stalin.
3. At a November 1943 meeting in Tehran, Iran, the Big Three reaffirmed their demand for the unconditional surrender of Germany and Japan.

↳ great britain + U.S. + Soviet Union

4. The Big Three held their second and final meeting at Yalta in February 1945. Churchill and Roosevelt agreed to a temporary division of Germany. In return Stalin agreed to join the war against Japan three months after the Nazis surrendered. Stalin also agreed that Poland should have a representative government based on free elections.

F. THE WAR IN EUROPE, 1942–1945

1. In the spring of 1942, German forces hoped to destroy the city of Stalingrad and then capture Soviet oil fields in the nearby Caucasus. After months of desperate fighting, the decimated German forces surrendered. Up and down an 1,800-mile front, Soviet tanks and artillery forced Hitler's armies to retreat.
2. Meanwhile, the United States and Great Britain liberated North Africa and successfully invaded Italy.
3. On June 6, 1944, American, British, and Canadian forces under the command of General Dwight D. Eisenhower forced their way onto the beaches of Normandy, France.
4. Hitler now faced the German nightmare of a war on two fronts. The once invincible German empire steadily shrank as the Soviets invaded from the east and the Allies invaded from the west. Trapped in a vise, Hitler committed suicide and Germany surrendered.

G. THE WAR IN ASIA, 1942–1945

1. The United States successfully halted the Japanese advance with a decisive victory in the Battle of Midway in June 1942.
2. American industry soon produced vast numbers of ships and warplanes. In June 1943, American forces began an "island hopping" campaign that steadily rolled back the Japanese Pacific empire.
3. By 1945, American forces reclaimed much of the Pacific including the Philippines. However, American commanders warned that an invasion of the Japanese home islands might cost a million American casualties and claim over 10 million Japanese lives.

H. THE ATOMIC BOMB

1. President Roosevelt died on April 12, 1945. Two weeks later, President Truman learned that the United States had developed a fearsome new weapon, the atomic bomb.

2. On July 26, 1945, Truman issued the Potsdam Declaration calling upon Japan to surrender unconditionally or suffer "the utter devastation of the Japanese homeland." The Japanese government ignored the warning as "unworthy of public notice."

3. President Truman authorized the use of the atomic bomb on the cities of Hiroshima and Nagasaki. First and foremost, Truman wanted to avoid a bloody invasion of Japan by shocking the Japanese government into an immediate surrender. Modern historians believe that Truman also wanted to convince Stalin to be more cooperative in postwar plans.

4. The atomic bomb destroyed both Hiroshima and Nagasaki. Aghast at the horrible loss of life, Emperor Hirohito told his war council, "I cannot bear to see my innocent people suffer any longer." Japan formally surrendered on September 2, 1945. However, hopes for a new spirit of cooperation vanished as Europe entered a new and perilous era known as the Cold War.

World War II has generated fewer AP® questions than any other major historic event. Even so, don't neglect the Nazi-Soviet Pact, the blitzkrieg, the Holocaust, and the decision to use the atomic bomb.

UNIT 9 Cold War and Contemporary Europe

c. 1914 to Present

PREVIEW: UNIT 9 KEY CONCEPTS

- Total war and political instability in the first half of the twentieth century gave way to a polarized state order during the Cold War and eventually to efforts at transnational union.
  - As World War II ended, a Cold War between the liberal democratic West and the communist East began, lasting nearly half a century.
- The stresses of economic collapse and total war engendered internal conflicts within European states and created conflicting conceptions of the relationship between the individual and the state, as demonstrated in the ideological battle between and among democracy, communism, and fascism.
- During the twentieth century, diverse intellectual and cultural movements questioned the existence of objective knowledge, the ability of reason to arrive at truth, and the role of religion in determining moral standards.
  - The experience of war intensified a sense of anxiety that permeated many facets of thought and culture, giving way by the century's end to a plurality of intellectual frameworks.
- Demographic changes, economic growth, total war, disruptions of traditional social patterns, and competing definitions of freedom and justice altered the experiences of everyday life.
  - New voices gained prominence in political, intellectual, and social discourse.

The Cold War 1946–1991

Chapter 30

I. CONTAINMENT

A. KEY POINTS

1. Once the unifying threat of Nazi Germany disappeared, the United States and the Soviet Union began to quarrel over long-standing political and ideological disputes. For example, President Truman demanded that Stalin permit free elections throughout Eastern Europe. The Soviet dictator adamantly refused, declaring, "A freely elected government in any of these East European countries would be anti-Soviet, and that we cannot allow."
2. The Soviet Union soon dominated a sphere of influence in much of Eastern Europe. Soviet-backed communist parties pushed aside opposition groups until they exercised unchallenged authority. Winston Churchill warned America that "an iron curtain has descended across the continent."
3. Truman adopted containment as a foreign policy designed to contain or block Soviet expansion.
4. Containment became the primary U.S. foreign policy from the announcement of the Truman Doctrine in 1947 to the collapse of the Soviet Union in 1991.

B. THE TRUMAN DOCTRINE

1. The immediate goal of the Truman Doctrine was to block the expansion of Soviet influence into Greece and Turkey.
2. On March 12, 1947, President Harry Truman asked Congress for $400 million in economic aid for Greece and Turkey.
3. Truman justified the aid by declaring that the United States would support "free peoples who are resisting attempted subjugations by

↳ wanted to stop the expansion of the soviet union

armed minorities or by outside pressures." This sweeping pledge became known as the Truman Doctrine.

C. THE MARSHALL PLAN

1. World War II devastated large parts of Europe. Desperate Europeans faced acute shortages of food, fuel, and industrial raw materials. In both 1946 and 1947, agricultural and industrial production in all European countries fell below pre-war levels. Economic weakness threatened political instability, making Europe vulnerable to Soviet influence.

2. The Truman administration recognized that the shattered European economy required a massive infusion of economic assistance. The Marshall Plan was a program of economic aid designed to promote the recovery of war-torn Europe while also preventing the spread of Soviet influence.

3. Marshall Plan aid began flowing into Europe in 1948. During the next 4 years, 16 Western European countries received $13 billion, the equivalent of about $200 billion in 2019. The Marshall Plan helped alleviate food shortages and stimulate industrial production.

4. The Marshall Plan was an integral part of Truman's policy of containment.

5. The Marshall Plan dramatically increased American political and economic influence in Western and Southern Europe.

D. THE NATO ALLIANCE

1. Ten Western European nations joined with the United States and Canada to form a defensive military alliance called the North Atlantic Treaty Organization (NATO). NATO coordinated defense preparations among the nations of Western Europe.

2. NATO featured an American commitment to permanently station troops in Western Europe. The NATO alliance thus marked a decisive break from America's tradition of isolationism.

E. THE WARSAW PACT

1. The Soviet Union responded to NATO by forming the Warsaw Pact.

2. The alliance linked the Soviet Union with seven Eastern European countries: Poland, East Germany, Czechoslovakia, Hungary,

Romania, Bulgaria, and Albania. The Cold War thus divided Europe into two rival blocs.

F. THE BERLIN AIRLIFT

1. The Allies failed to agree on a peace treaty with Germany.
2. In 1945, the Allies divided Germany into four occupation zones, one each for the United States, Great Britain, France, and the Soviet Union. The city of Berlin lay 110 miles inside the Soviet occupation zone. Like Germany, it was divided into four occupation zones.
3. Fearing a resurgent Germany, the Soviet Union cut off Western land access to West Berlin. This action provoked the first great Cold War test of wills between the United States and the Soviet Union.
4. President Truman ordered a massive airlift of food, fuel, and other supplies to the beleaguered citizens of West Berlin.
5. The Berlin Airlift marked a crucial and successful test of containment.
6. Following the Berlin Airlift, the United States, Great Britain, and France created the Federal Republic of Germany or West Germany. The Soviet Union responded by establishing the East German state, the German Democratic Republic.

G. MAKING COMPARISONS: THE TREATMENT OF GERMANY AFTER THE FIRST WORLD WAR AND AFTER THE SECOND WORLD WAR

1. After the First World War
    - i. The German government asked for peace based on Wilson's Fourteen Points.
    - ii. Unaware that their army had been defeated, the German people expected a lenient postwar settlement.
    - iii. The Allies excluded Germany from the peace negotiations, thus justifying the German complaint that they were coerced to sign a dictated treaty.
    - iv. The Versailles Treaty forced Germany to cede Alsace-Lorraine to France. In addition, the Polish Corridor separated part of East Prussia from the rest of Germany.
    - v. The Allies originally excluded Germany from the League of Nations.

vi. France and Great Britain demanded that Germany pay heavy reparations for the cost of the war. The reparation payments were eventually renegotiated under the Dawes Plan.

2. After the Second World War

    i. The Allies demanded and received Germany's unconditional surrender.

    ii. The United States, Great Britain, and the Soviet Union agreed to disarm Germany and divide it into four occupation zones.

    iii. Poland gained lands in East Prussia.

    iv. The Cold War led to the separation of Germany into West Germany and East Germany. West Germany became a member of the NATO alliance and East Germany became a member of the Warsaw Pact.

    v. Marshall Plan aid helped revitalize the West German economy. West Germany soon boasted a strong industrial base that contrasted with the lagging economy in Soviet-dominated East Germany.

II. THE REVIVAL OF WESTERN EUROPE

A. INTRODUCTION

1. When World War II ended, Europe faced a grim future. "What is Europe now?" Winston Churchill asked. "It is a rubble heap, a charnel house, a breeding ground for pestilence and hate."

2. Hunger and desperation stalked Europe from Bulgaria to Belgium. Tens of millions of homeless Europeans were classified as "displaced persons."

3. Despite these seemingly insurmountable problems, Europe staged a remarkable recovery that is often called an "economic miracle."

B. ECONOMIC INTEGRATION

1. The European Coal and Steel Community

    i. Jean Monnet, a French economic planner, convinced French Premier Robert Schuman that economic cooperation would be the key to future prosperity between France and West Germany.

   ii. The Schuman Plan, as the project became known, led to the creation of the European Coal and Steel Community (ECSC).

   iii. The ECSC called for tariff-free trade in coal and steel among France, West Germany, Belgium, Italy, Luxembourg, and the Netherlands.

2. The European Economic Community (Common Market)

   i. The ECSC proved to be a success. As a result, in 1957 its six member nations signed the Treaty of Rome creating the European Economic Community (EEC), popularly known as the Common Market.

   ii. The EEC eliminated trade barriers among its members, thus closely resembling a tariff union.

   iii. The EEC rapidly emerged as the driving force behind economic integration in Western Europe.

APEURO test writers have focused a number of multiple-choice questions on the creation and purpose of the European Economic Community. Although the EEC is popularly known as the Common Market, test writers prefer to use its formal name. Do not confuse the Treaty of Rome with the Treaty of Maastricht. The Treaty of Rome created the EEC. The Treaty of Maastricht transformed the EEC into the European Union.

C. THE ECONOMIC MIRACLE

1. Sparked by Marshall Plan aid and revitalized by economic integration, Europe entered a period of rapid economic growth.
2. By 1963, Western Europe produced over 2.5 times more goods than it did before World War II.
3. The booming West German economy soon dominated the European electrical, automobile, chemical, and steel industries. Between 1950 and 1980, West Germany's gross national product (GNP), or the total value of goods and services produced, grew from $48 billion to an astounding $828 billion.

D. THE WELFARE STATE

1. The term "welfare state" refers to the policy of post-World War II nations to establish safety nets for their citizens in areas of

health care, disability insurance, unemployment insurance, and retirement pensions.

2. These policies were a response to socialist demands for social justice and concerns over the strength of Communist parties in Western Europe.

3. Christian Democratic parties played a key role in supporting welfare state programs, European integration, national health insurance, aid to farmers, and political democracy.

E. CHARLES DE GAULLE'S (1890–1970) INDEPENDENT POLICIES

1. General Charles de Gaulle established the Fifth French Republic in 1958. He served as president until 1969. De Gaulle followed an independent course that opposed close ties with America and continued European political and economic union.

2. De Gaulle's key foreign policy decisions included:

    i. Granting Algeria full independence.

    ii. Withdrawing French military forces from NATO.

    iii. Developing France's own nuclear weapons.

    iv. Opposing Great Britain's entry into the EEC.

III. DECOLONIZATION

A. THE NEW IMPERIALISM

1. Between 1870 and 1914, European nations led by Great Britain and France brought much of the world under their direct control.

2. The European powers were motivated by a combination of factors including a desire to acquire raw materials, develop profitable foreign markets, protect strategic sea lanes, and bring the blessings of their superior technology to less advanced peoples.

B. BETWEEN THE WORLD WARS

1. President Woodrow Wilson's support for the principle of national self-determination inspired demands for greater independence. In addition, India and other nations expected more political sovereignty in exchange for their support in World War I.

2. The Great Powers failed to meet these expectations. Instead, they tightened control over their colonies and established a mandate system in the Middle East. The British and French empires actually increased in size during the interwar period.

C. CAUSES OF DECOLONIZATION AFTER WORLD WAR II

1. Decolonization refers to the process by which colonies gained their independence from the imperial powers after World War II.
2. Three key factors contributed to the rapid pace of decolonization. First, devastated by World War II, the imperial powers were barely able to support themselves in 1945, let alone rule expensive overseas colonies. Second, the horrors of World War II undermined European self-confidence and the moral justification for imperialism. And finally, led by a new generation of nationalist leaders, the demand for national self-determination intensified in Asia and Africa.

D. BRITISH DECOLONIZATION

1. The British Empire once included one-quarter of the world's land area and 500 million of its people. However, Britain made the most dramatic break from imperialism.
2. In 1947, Britain negotiated an end to imperial rule in India. The settlement divided the subcontinent into a predominately Hindu India and a predominantly Muslim Pakistan.
3. Britain surrendered control of Palestine to the United Nations. Israel then declared its independence, igniting a war with neighboring Arab countries.
4. Britain continued the process of decolonization in Sub-Saharan Africa. Beginning with Ghana in 1957, British Sub-Saharan colonies achieved independence with little or no violence.

E. FRENCH DECOLONIZATION

1. Unlike Great Britain, France resisted decolonization.
2. France attempted to reassert its control over Indochina. However, a resistance movement led by Ho Chi Minh declared independence after defeating French forces at the battle of Dien Bien Phu in 1954.
3. In Algeria, a bitter war broke out between French and Algerian nationalists. After a bloody struggle, French President Charles de

Gaulle accepted Algerian self-determination. After more than a century of French rule, Algeria became independent in 1962.

IV. THE SOVIET UNION UNDER KHRUSHCHEV, 1956–1964

A. STALIN'S LAST YEARS

1. Following World War II, Joseph Stalin imposed new Five-Year Plans emphasizing extensive industrialization.
2. Stalin insisted on absolute obedience. Dissent brought imprisonment, slave labor, or death.
3. Stalin's long reign of terror came to an abrupt end with his death in 1953. Stalin's legacy included industrialization, victory in World War II, expansion into Eastern Europe, and the transformation of the Soviet Union into a nuclear superpower. However, these achievements came with a heavy human price that included mass killings, the creation of a vast prison system known as the Gulag, and the building of a rigid totalitarian state.
4. After a brief period of "collective leadership," Nikita Khrushchev emerged as the Soviet Union's unrivaled leader.

B. KHRUSHCHEV'S SECRET SPEECH

1. In 1956, Khrushchev boldly attacked Stalin in a "secret speech" delivered at the Twentieth Communist Party Congress in Moscow.
2. Khrushchev denounced Stalin's reign of terror and repudiated his "cult of personality."

C. DE-STALINIZATION

1. Khrushchev's program of de-Stalinization involved all of the following:
   - i. Shifting some resources toward producing more consumer goods.
   - ii. Curbing the power of the secret police.
   - iii. Granting more freedom to writers and intellectuals.
2. De-Stalinization permitted Aleksandr Solzhenitsyn to publish *One Day in the Life of Ivan Denisovich*. This short but powerful novel described the horrors of life in a Stalinist concentration camp.

3. Boris Pasternak's novel *Doctor Zhivago* illustrated the limits of de-Stalinization. The novel celebrated the human spirit and challenged the principles of communism. Although it was published in the West, Soviet censors denounced Pasternak and refused to allow him to receive the Nobel Prize for Literature.

D. *SPUTNIK*

1. In 1957, a beaming Khrushchev proudly announced that the Soviet Union had successfully launched a 184-pound satellite named *Sputnik* into orbit around the Earth.
2. *Sputnik* quickly became a symbol of Soviet technological prowess. *Sputnik*'s success played a key role in contributing to the space race between the Soviet Union and the United States.

E. COLD WAR CONFRONTATIONS

1. The Berlin Wall
   i. Between 1949 and 1961, more than 3 million East Germans fled to West Germany by crossing into West Berlin.
   ii. On August 13, 1961, the East Germans, with Khrushchev's support, began construction of a concrete wall along the border between East and West Berlin.
   iii. The Berlin Wall stopped the flow of refugees while at the same time becoming a symbol of Communist oppression.
2. The Cuban Missile Crisis
   i. Khrushchev precipitated the Cuban Missile Crisis by constructing nuclear missiles in Cuba.
   ii. After a tense confrontation with the United States, Khrushchev agreed to withdraw the missiles in exchange for a U.S. promise not to attack Fidel Castro.
   iii. The Cuban Missile Crisis undermined Khrushchev's credibility and played a key role in his ouster from power in 1964.

F. EASTERN EUROPE

1. De-Stalinization raised hopes for more freedom in Eastern Europe. A wave of strikes and protests swept across East Germany, Czechoslovakia, Poland, and Hungary. Protestors pointed out that the Soviet model of rapid industrialization and centralized

economic planning failed to deliver economic prosperity to citizens throughout Eastern Europe.

2. The protests in Hungary quickly escalated into a major crisis when Hungary's liberal Communist leader, Imre Nagy, promised free elections and called for the removal of Soviet troops.
3. Khrushchev responded by ordering the Red Army to invade Hungary. After intense fighting, the Soviets crushed the rebellion and later executed Nagy.
4. The United States did not assist Hungary because it lay within the Soviet sphere of influence.

Nikita Khrushchev has generated more APEURO multiple-choice questions than any other Russian leader except Peter the Great. Most of the questions focus on Khrushchev's secret speech and his program of de-Stalinization. While the Berlin Wall has yet to generate a released multiple-choice question, its construction and consequences have played a role in a number of free-response questions.

V. THE SOVIET UNION UNDER BREZHNEV, 1964–1982

A. STAGNATION

1. Conservative leaders believed that Khrushchev's program of de-Stalinization posed a threat to the Communist Party's dictatorial powers and special privileges. Khrushchev's foreign policy miscalculations, failure to reform the collective farms, and attacks on the privileges of the party elite contributed to his removal from power in 1964.
2. Now led by Leonid Brezhnev, the Communist Party clamped down on Aleksandr Solzhenitsyn, Andrei Sakharov, and other outspoken dissidents.
3. Brezhnev's hard-line policies led to a prolonged period of political repression and economic stagnation.

B. CZECHOSLOVAKIA AND THE BREZHNEV DOCTRINE

1. In Czechoslovakia, a new communist leader, Alexander Dubček, initiated a program of democratic reforms saying he wanted to create "socialism with a human face."
2. Alarmed by Dubček's reforms, Brezhnev called on the other Warsaw Pact countries to invade Czechoslovakia and remove Dubček from power.
3. Brezhnev justified the invasion by claiming that the Soviet Union and its allies had the right to intervene in the domestic affairs of other Communist countries. This declaration became known as the Brezhnev Doctrine.
4. The United States refrained from taking any action because Czechoslovakia lay within the Soviet sphere of influence.

C. DÉTENTE

1. President Richard Nixon initiated a policy of détente to reduce tensions with the Soviet Union. The two superpowers agreed to limit nuclear arms and expand trade.
2. The Helsinki Accords marked the high point of Cold War détente. The accords ratified the European territorial boundaries established after World War II and committed the signers to recognize and protect basic human rights.

D. RENEWED COLD WAR TENSIONS AND CONTINUING DOMESTIC PROBLEMS

1. In late 1979 Brezhnev ordered Soviet forces into Afghanistan to save an increasingly unpopular Marxist regime. The invasion ended détente and reignited the Cold War. The Reagan administration responded with a vast American military buildup that forced the Soviet regime to increase military spending, thus exacerbating their economic problems.
2. The Soviet system of rigid centralized planning created a vast bureaucracy that discouraged innovation and reduced productivity. The economic system guaranteed employment, but the absence of incentives produced waste and inefficiency.
3. When Brezhnev died in 1982, the Soviet leadership faced a series of profound problems that included a stagnant economy, widespread political corruption, economic mismanagement, and an expensive war in Afghanistan.

VI. THE COLLAPSE OF EUROPEAN COMMUNISM

A. GORBACHEV'S REFORMS

1. In March 1985, members of the Politburo, the Communist Party's top decision-making group, selected Mikhail Gorbachev as the new leader of the Soviet Union.

2. When Gorbachev took power, the Soviet Union was still the world's most feared totalitarian dictatorship. But Gorbachev recognized that "something was wrong." Blaming poor living conditions on the country's rigid political system and stagnant economy, he launched an unprecedented program of reforms.

3. *Glasnost*

   i. Soviet leaders from Vladimir Lenin to Brezhnev created a totalitarian state that controlled the mass media and restricted human rights.

   ii. In 1986, Gorbachev introduced a new policy known as *glasnost*, or openness, which encouraged Soviet citizens to discuss ways to reform their society. Soviet citizens now began to learn the truth about poor harvests, inefficient state monopolies, and the Chernobyl nuclear disaster.

4. *Perestroika*

   i. *Glasnost* gave Soviet citizens an opportunity to complain publicly about their economic problems.

   ii. In 1986, Gorbachev launched a program called *perestroika*, or economic restructuring, to revitalize the Soviet economy by removing bureaucratic control over businesses and providing incentives for greater productivity.

5. *Demokratizatsiya*

   i. Gorbachev understood that in order for the economy to thrive, the Communist Party would have to loosen its grip on Soviet society.

   ii. In 1989, Gorbachev unveiled a third new policy called *demokratizatsiya*, or democratization. The plan called for the election of a new legislature, the 2,250-member Congress of People's Deputies.

B. MAKING COMPARISONS: STALIN AND GORBACHEV

1. Stalin
   - i. Rejected the relatively free markets created by Lenin's New Economic Policy.
   - ii. Implemented a series of Five-Year Plans that promoted state planning and industrialization.
   - iii. Forced peasant farmers to work on huge state-run and state-owned farms called collectives.
   - iv. Purged party leaders who showed the slightest degree of dissent from his policies.
   - v. Imprisoned and executed millions of Soviet citizens.
   - vi. Created a rigid totalitarian state.
   - vii. Imposed Soviet control over Eastern Europe.
2. Gorbachev
   - i. Advocated private ownership of property and free markets.
   - ii. Allowed public discussion and criticism of Communist Party policies.
   - iii. Permitted openly contested elections.
   - iv. Allowed national minorities within the Soviet Union to express pent-up grievances.
   - v. Encouraged East Europeans to reform their political systems without fear of Soviet armed intervention.
   - vi. Raised expectations in the Soviet Union and Eastern Europe for greater freedom.

C. POLAND AND SOLIDARITY

1. The people of Poland were the first to test Gorbachev's new policies.
2. Led by Lech Walesa, Polish workers formed a democratic trade union called Solidarity.
3. Pope John Paul II provided crucial support for the Solidarity labor movement in Poland.

4. In 1989, Polish voters overwhelmingly rejected the Communist Party and elected Solidarity candidates. This marked the first time the people of a nation peacefully turned a Communist regime out of power.

D. THE FALL OF THE BERLIN WALL

1. Inspired by the events in Poland, the people of East Germany demanded change in their government.
2. On November 9, 1989, a new East German leader opened the Berlin Wall. The reunification of Germany occurred less than one year later. These watershed events marked the end of the Cold War in Eastern Europe.

E. CZECHOSLOVAKIA'S VELVET REVOLUTION

1. The fall of the Berlin Wall inspired reformers in Czechoslovakia to break away from the Soviet Union.
2. A general strike led by Václav Havel resulted in the collapse of the Communist government.
3. However, ethnic differences between the Czechs and the Slovaks prevented the creation of a stable unified state. In 1993, the Czech Republic and Slovakia peacefully split into two different countries.

F. THE COLLAPSE OF THE SOVIET UNION

1. Gorbachev's reforms released forces he proved unable to control. The collapse of the Communist regimes in Eastern Europe inspired ethnic groups within the Soviet Union.
2. Gorbachev's policy of *glasnost* loosened controls, enabling ethnic protests to spread across the Soviet Union.
3. In a last desperate effort to preserve the Soviet Union, Communist hard-liners attempted to overthrow Gorbachev with a military coup.
4. The hard-liners assumed that a show of force would ensure obedience. They were wrong. Under Gorbachev's reforms, people had lost their fear of the party and were willing to defend their freedom.

5. Led by Boris Yeltsin, president of the Russian Republic, the Russian people thwarted the coup.

6. On December 25, 1991, Gorbachev announced his resignation as president of a country that by then had ceased to exist. The Soviet Union then dissolved into 15 separate republics. One former communist leader observed sadly, "Gorbachev tried to reform the unreformable."

Chapter 31

Key Trends in Post–Cold War Europe

I. INTRODUCTION

A. THE COLD WAR ERA

1. The rivalry between the United States and the Soviet Union dominated the Cold War era in Europe.
2. The Cold War appeared to permanently divide Europe into a prosperous, capitalistic West and an impoverished, Communist East.
3. However, as described in Chapter 30, the fall of the Berlin Wall, the collapse of Communism in Eastern Europe, and the disintegration of the Soviet Union ended the Cold War and opened a new era in European and world history.

B. THE NEW POST–COLD WAR ERA

1. Historians agree that we are now living in a new historic era. However, it is too soon to give the era a definitive name. It is important to remember that most periods are given labels in hindsight. For example, the Interwar Period (described in Chapters 28 and 29) got its name only after World War II bracketed World War I.
2. Although it is too soon to name the Post–Cold War era, we can identify five key trends that are currently shaping European history:
   - i. The re-emergence of Russia as a major power.
   - ii. The economic integration of Europe into the European Union.
   - iii. The transformation in women's lives caused by the movement for gender equality.

iv. The demographic changes caused by the European baby bust and the mass immigration of people into Europe.

v. The impact of revolutionary informational and digital technologies.

II. THE RE-EMERGENCE OF RUSSIA

A. BORIS YELTSIN, 1991–1999

1. Despite Gorbachev's program of *perestroika*, giant, highly centralized state monopolies still dominated the Russian economy.
2. Yeltsin was committed to adopting new policies that would place Russia on a firm course to a market economy and a pluralistic political system.
3. Advised by Western economists, Yeltsin implemented economic "shock therapy" designed to free prices and privatize industry.
4. Instead of reviving the Russian economy, shock therapy triggered runaway inflation and rampant corruption that allowed a new class of super-rich oligarchs to gain enormous power.
5. Yeltsin's problems were further exacerbated by troubles in Chechnya. A tiny republic of one million Muslims, the Chechnyans sought independence from Moscow. Tensions soon escalated into a bloody and costly civil war.

B. VLADIMIR PUTIN, 2000–PRESENT

1. The gap between Yeltsin's economic promises and actual economic performance caused widespread public disillusionment.
2. In late 1999, Yeltsin unexpectedly resigned. His chosen successor, Vladimir Putin, adopted a series of new policies that maintained relatively free markets but strengthened the power of the central government and limited media critics.
3. Aided by high oil prices, the Russian economy began to grow and its middle class began to expand.
4. Putin vowed to reassert a strong image in domestic and international affairs. He began by forcefully suppressing the independence movement in Chechnya. Putin then reestablished Russian control over the strategic Crimean Peninsula.

5. Putin's forceful policies have conveyed an image of strength that symbolizes Russia's national resurgence. From a long-term historical perspective, Putin revived Russia's long tradition of authoritarian government.

III. EUROPEAN ECONOMIC INTEGRATION

A. THE ORIGIN OF THE EUROPEAN UNION (EU)

1. In the years immediately following World War II, Jean Monnet and Robert Schuman (see Chapter 30) proposed using economic cooperation as a way to end the destructive rivalry between France and Germany. They believed that economic cooperation would build a web of interdependence that would make another war unthinkable.
2. Monnet and Schuman called for the creation of the European Coal and Steel Community (ECSC). The ECSC created a tariff-free zone in coal and steel among France, West Germany, Belgium, Italy, Luxembourg, and the Netherlands. These six nations contained most of the coal and steel resources in Western Europe.
3. As Schuman predicted, the ECSC became "the first step in the federation of Europe." The success of the ECSC led its six members to sign the Treaty of Rome, creating the European Economic Community (EEC), also known as the Common Market. The EEC encouraged the free movement of products by eliminating tariffs on all goods.
4. The EEC proved to be a huge success. During the 1950s and 1960s, all six member nations experienced economic miracles. The EEC's success prompted Great Britain, Denmark, and Ireland to join the organization in 1973.
5. During the 1980s, other European nations applied for membership in the EEC. The original core countries established economic and political criteria that included free markets, democratic politics, and respect for human rights. By 1995, the EEC included 15 nations with a combined population of 395 million people.

B. THE MAASTRICHT TREATY AND THE EUROPEAN UNION

1. In 1991, leaders of the EEC countries met in the Dutch city of Maastricht. They adopted the Maastricht Treaty, changing the name of the EEC to the European Union (EU). The treaty

committed the member nations to adopt common production standards, uniform tax rates, a single European currency, and a common EU citizenship.

2. The EU vindicated Jean Monnet and Robert Schuman's vision of an integrated European economy that permitted the free movement of goods, labor, capital, and services. On January 1, 2002, twelve of the EU member nations adopted the euro as a common currency. By 2009, 16 EU countries comprised a new "euro-zone."

C. EXPANSION TO EASTERN EUROPE

1. Following the collapse of Communism, virtually all of the Eastern European governments applied for membership in the EU. These nations viewed membership as a source of economic prosperity and a symbol of their return to Europe.

2. Between 2004 and 2013, the EU added 13 new member nations. The 28 EU nations boasted a combined population of just over 500 million people. The EU now accounts for about one-third of the world's gross national product (GNP) and about 40 percent of global exports.

D. PROBLEMS

1. Despite its impressive record of success, the EU faces formidable problems. For example, can a union of 28 sovereign countries develop a common identity and political cohesion?

2. Developments in Greece tested the unity of the Euro-zone nations. Following its admission into the EU, Greece began to develop record trade and budget deficits. A deep recession that began in the United States in 2008 and then spread to Europe exacerbated these problems. As Greece fell into a severe recession, European banks loaned it massive bailout funds that delayed, but did not solve, the Greek debt crisis.

3. Developments in Great Britain also posed a serious challenge to the long-term future of the European Union. In a referendum held in June 2016, "Brexit" supporters who wanted Britain to "exit" the EU won a surprising victory. Although Londoners opposed Brexit, older voters in the surrounding countryside expressed anger that participation in the EU created open borders that encouraged a rising tide of immigration into Great Britain. Britain's anticipated departure in 2020 poses risks for the British economy and uncertainty for the continuing strength of the EU.

IV. THE TRANSFORMATION IN WOMEN'S LIVES

A. CHANGING PATTERNS OF MARRIAGE AND CHILDBEARING

1. During the years immediately following World War II, many women left their wartime jobs and resumed their traditional roles as wives and mothers. Birthrates began to rise, creating the post-war "baby boom."
2. These traditional trends did not last. Birthrates, and thus the size of families, began to decline by the middle of the 1960s.
3. As birth rates declined, European women began to marry at an early age. The combination of early marriage and small family size meant that a new generation of young married women began to enter the workforce.
4. At the same time, Europe's booming postwar economy increased the demand for labor. The shift to white-collar service industries in government, education, and health care opened new opportunities for women.

B. SIMONE DE BEAUVOIR AND BETTY FRIEDAN

1. As more and more women entered the workforce, they began to encounter long-established patterns of discrimination in salary and working conditions. The combination of rising employment and entrenched patterns of job discrimination created a growing sense of injustice among many women.
2. The French author Simone de Beauvoir was the first European woman to publicly challenge the status quo. In her seminal book, *The Second Sex*, de Beauvoir argued that a male-dominated European society had forced women into dependent lives of housework and childbearing that denied them independent careers and creative fulfillment. She emphasized that women could only achieve genuine autonomy by escaping from their traditional inferior roles. De Beauvoir's book became a cornerstone of feminist theory.
3. De Beauvoir's argument that society trapped middle-class women in unfulfilling domestic roles had a profound influence on American housewife Betty Friedan. A college-educated journalist and mother of three children, Friedan became increasingly frustrated trying to fulfill the traditional role of "ideal housewife and mother." Friedan responded to "the problem that has no name" by publishing *The Feminist Mystique*. Released in 1963, this

landmark book criticized traditional gender roles and forcefully argued that women faced patterns of discrimination that denied them equality with men. *The Feminist Mystique* became an international best-seller that transformed Friedan into a feminist leader. In 1966, she founded the National Organization for Women (NOW), whose stated goal was to take "action to bring women into full participation in the mainstream of American society *now*."

C. THE FEMINIST MOVEMENT

1. During the late nineteenth and early twentieth centuries, the women's movement focused on overturning legal inequalities, particularly women's suffrage. Led by Millicent Garrett Fawcett and Emmeline Pankhurst, British women won the right to vote in 1918. By the end of World War II, European women received the suffrage in every country except Switzerland. The Swiss finally granted all of their female citizens the right to vote in 1991.
2. The suffrage did not change women's salaries. During the 1960s, British women earned only 60 percent of men's wages, while in France the corresponding figure was just 50 percent.
3. Continuing economic inequality prompted women to form a broad-based feminist movement focused on winning gender equality.
4. During the last three decades of the twentieth century, women activists successfully fought for "equal pay for equal work," more generous maternity leave, and affordable day care. The movement also strove to liberalize divorce laws and legalize abortion.
5. The accomplishments of the women's movement inspired other groups including gay men, lesbian women, and people with physical disabilities to organize and call for an end to legal discrimination and social harassment.

D. WOMEN AND THE GREEN MOVEMENT

1. As more and more women became social activists, they broadened their efforts to include a variety of new issues.
2. West German women played a leading role in the formation of the Green Party. Led by Petra Kelly, the Green movement fought to protect the environment and to defend human rights and equality. In 1987, the Green Party elected 42 delegates to the West German parliament.

Don't overlook the Green Party. The APEURO practice exam included a selection of statements from the Green League of Finland that generated four multiple-choice questions. It is important to remember that the Green movement opposes rampant consumerism, defends welfare-state programs, and supports expanding civil rights to gays and lesbians.

V. POPULATION TRENDS AND IMMIGRATION

A. THE BABY BUST

1. A birth rate of 2.1 children per woman is necessary to maintain a stable population.
2. Europe's postwar baby boom turned into a baby bust as birth rates began to steadily decline. By 2006, the European birth rate stood at just 1.4 children per woman.
3. The demographic impact of the baby bust can be vividly seen in Germany. If present trends continue, the German population will shrink from 82 million people in 2001 to just 62 million in 2050.
4. If it continues, the baby bust will produce serious long-term consequences. As Europe's population declines, it will also age. As a result, health care costs will sharply rise. In addition, a shrinking labor force will have to support rising social security taxes.
5. Demographers have identified a number of possible causes for the baby bust. Following World War II, European women married early, had children and then entered the labor force. An ever-increasing number of women chose not to have more children as they concentrated their energies on careers. The more educated and successful women often limited their family size to just one child.

B. GUEST WORKERS

1. Europe's booming postwar economy and declining birth rate produced a severe labor shortage.
2. The collapse of the colonial system created a vast pool of unskilled laborers eager to begin new lives.

3. During the 1960s and 1970s, millions of manual laborers from former British, French, Dutch, and Portuguese colonies entered Europe as "guest workers."
4. Europe now has an estimated 18 million foreign resident workers. Many guest workers and their families are staying in their host countries.

C. LEGAL AND ILLEGAL IMMIGRATION

1. Since the fall of Communism, poverty, political persecutions, and civil wars have combined to create waves of legal and illegal immigrants seeking opportunity and safety.
2. The arrival of millions of immigrants is straining social services throughout Europe. It is also alarming native residents who feel that immigrants threaten their jobs and undermine national unity.
3. The twenty-first century is currently witnessing a significant migration of Muslims into Europe. If this trend continues, the Muslim population in Europe will rise from about 15 million in 2006 to 30 million in 2025.
4. At the end of 2015, a tidal wave of refugees from Syria was exacerbating tensions as Europe struggled to cope with the largest refugee crisis since World War II.

The 2015 APEURO DBQ focused on how immigration is changing conceptions of French national identity and culture. The DBQ included a cover from Le Figaro Magazine *raising the provocative question, "Immigration or Invasion?" It is unlikely that the College Board test writers will feature this topic on a second DBQ. However, they may revisit the topic on either a document-based multiple-choice question or a short-answer essay.*

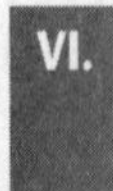

VI. REVOLUTIONS IN SCIENCE AND TECHNOLOGY

A. BIG SCIENCE

1. Before World War II, theoretical science and sophisticated engineering were largely separated.

2. During World War II, governments led by the United States, Great Britain, and Germany combined science and technology to produce new weapons. For example, British scientists developed radar, German scientists developed jet aircraft, and American scientists developed the atomic bomb.

3. The unprecedented combination of theoretical science and complex engineering under government sponsorship is called "Big Science."

4. During the Cold War, Big Science produced such significant technological breakthroughs as rockets, nuclear submarines, and spy satellites.

5. The space race between the United States and the Soviet Union provided a dramatic illustration of a Big Science project. In 1957, the Soviet Union stunned the United States by using long-range rockets to launch the first satellite, *Sputnik*, into orbit around the Earth. Four years later, the Soviet Union achieved another space milestone by successfully placing a cosmonaut into orbit. Galvanized by these Soviet firsts, the United States organized the Apollo Project to overtake the Russians by placing a man on the moon.

B. THE INFORMATION AGE

1. During the nineteenth century, innovations in the textile industry and the invention of the railroad revolutionized European society and everyday life. The late twentieth century and early twenty-first century have also witnessed revolutionary changes that are ushering in the birth of a transformative new Information Age.

2. Television signaled the birth of a new global age of shared information and images. Between the mid-1950s and mid-1970s, Europeans adopted television as an integral part of their daily lives. Television exerted a powerful cultural and political impact by shaping public attitudes toward entertainment, commercial products, national leaders, and global events.

3. The computer provides another example of how the alliance of science and technology is reshaping life in the new Information Age. Early computers were huge, expensive machines that relied on thousands of vacuum tubes. The development of tiny but powerful silicon chips dramatically shrank the size and cost of computers while vastly increasing their power. During the 1980s and 1990s, new generations of personal computers changed the pace and patterns of work and leisure.

C. THE DIGITAL WORLD

1. During the late 1990s, ongoing advances in computer and electronics ushered in a digital revolution centered around the internet and mobile phones.
2. By 2010, about one-third of the world's population was using the internet to buy goods, learn news, and connect with friends. Facebook, Twitter, and YouTube became integral parts of daily life in the new digital world.
3. The Age of Discovery in the sixteenth century witnessed the beginning of the historic process of globalization. The digital revolution is dramatically accelerating this process. Today labor, capital, ideas, services, and goods are all interconnected into complex and fast-moving social and economic webs.

PART III

KEY THEMES AND FACTS

Key Figures in European Intellectual History

NICCOLÒ MACHIAVELLI (1469–1527)

1. Renaissance political philosopher who wrote *The Prince*.
2. Believed that people are ungrateful and untrustworthy.
3. Urged rulers to study war, avoid unnecessary kindness, and always base policy upon the principle that the end justifies the means.

DESIDERIUS ERASMUS (1466–1536)

1. Northern humanist who wrote *In Praise of Folly*.
2. Wrote in Latin while most humanists wrote in the vernacular.
3. Wanted to reform the Catholic Church, not destroy it.

MARTIN LUTHER (1483–1546)

1. Protestant reformer whose criticism of indulgences helped spark the Reformation.
2. Advocated salvation by faith, the authority of the Bible, and a priesthood of all believers.
3. Believed that Christian women should strive to become models of wifely obedience and Christian charity.

JOHN CALVIN (1509–1564)

1. Protestant reformer who wrote *The Institutes of the Christian Religion*.
2. Believed in the absolute omnipotence of God, the weakness of humanity, and the doctrine of predestination.
3. Established Geneva as a model Christian community.
4. Influenced followers who were known as Huguenots in France, Presbyterians in Scotland, and Puritans in England and the New England colonies.

5. Advocated that each local congregation have a ruling body composed of both ministers and laymen who carefully supervised the moral conduct of the faithful.

It is important to understand the similarities and differences between Luther and Calvin. Both were Protestant reformers who challenged the pope and relied upon the Bible as the sole source of religious authority. Unlike Luther, Calvin formulated a systematic theology that stressed predestination. In addition, while Luther relied on state churches, Calvin devised a flexible system of church government that resisted control by the state.

MICHEL DE MONTAIGNE (1533–1592)

1. French Renaissance writer who developed the essay as a literary genre.
2. Known for his skeptical attitude and willingness to look at all sides of an issue.

NICOLAUS COPERNICUS (1473–1543)

1. Polish clergyman and astronomer who wrote *On the Revolution of the Heavenly Spheres.*
2. Helped launch the Scientific Revolution by challenging the widespread belief in the geocentric theory that the earth is the center of the universe.
3. Offered a new heliocentric universe in which the earth and the other planets revolve around the sun.

JOHANNES KEPLER (1571–1630)

1. Began his career as an assistant to the Danish astronomer Tycho Brahe.
2. Formulated three laws of planetary motion.
3. Proved that planetary orbits are elliptical rather than circular.

GALILEO GALILEI (1564–1642)

1. Italian scientist who contributed to the scientific method by conducting controlled experiments.

2. Major accomplishments included using the telescope for astronomical observation, formulating laws of motion, and popularizing the new scientific ideas.
3. Condemned by the Inquisition for publicly advocating Copernicus's heliocentric theory.

ISAAC NEWTON (1642–1727)

1. English scientist and mathematician who wrote the *Principia*.
2. Viewed the universe as a vast machine governed by the universal laws of gravity and inertia.
3. Mechanistic view of the universe strongly influenced deism.

FRANCIS BACON (1561–1626)

1. English politician and writer.
2. Formalized the empirical method into a general theory of inductive reasoning known as empiricism.

RENÉ DESCARTES (1596–1650)

1. French philosopher and mathematician.
2. Used deductive reasoning from self-evident principles to reach scientific laws.

Don't confuse Bacon and Descartes. Both contributed to seventeenth-century scientific development by articulating theories of the scientific method. Remember that Bacon's inductive method is based upon observation while Descartes's deductive method is based upon systematic doubt and the use of mathematics to express scientific laws.

THOMAS HOBBES (1588–1679)

1. English political philosopher who wrote *Leviathan*.
2. Viewed human beings as naturally self-centered and prone to violence.
3. Feared the dangers of anarchy more than the dangers of tyranny.
4. Argued that monarchs have absolute and unlimited political authority.

JOHN LOCKE (1632–1704)

1. English philosopher who wrote *The Second Treatise of Government.*
2. Viewed humans as basically rational beings who learn from experience.
3. Formulated the theory of natural rights, arguing that people are born with basic rights to "life, liberty, and property."
4. Insisted that governments are formed to protect natural rights.
5. Stated that the governed have a right to rebel against rulers who violate natural rights.

VOLTAIRE (1694–1778)

1. French philosophe and prolific author of essays and letters.
2. Championed the enlightened principles of reason, progress, toleration, and individual liberty.
3. Opposed superstition, intolerance, and ignorance.
4. Criticized organized religion for perpetuating superstition and intolerance.

JEAN-JACQUES ROUSSEAU (1712–1778)

1. Enlightened thinker best known for writing *The Social Contract* and *Emile.*
2. Believed that since "law is the expression of the general will," the state is based on a social contract.
3. Emphasized the education of the whole person for citizenship.
4. Rejected excessive rationalism and stressed emotions, thus anticipating the Romantic movement.

ADAM SMITH (1723–1790)

1. Scottish economist who wrote *An Inquiry into the Nature and Causes of the Wealth of Nations.*
2. Opposed mercantilist policies.
3. Advocated free trade and "the Invisible Hand of competition."

MARY WOLLSTONECRAFT (1759–1797)

1. British writer, philosopher, and feminist who wrote *A Vindication of the Rights of Woman.*
2. Argued that women are not naturally inferior to men.
3. Maintained that women deserve the same fundamental rights as men.

EDMUND BURKE (1729–1797)

1. English conservative leader who wrote *Reflections on the Revolution in France.*
2. Denounced the radicalism and violence of the French Revolution.
3. Favored gradual and orderly change.

JOHN STUART MILL (1806–1873)

1. English Utilitarian and essayist best known for writing *On Liberty* and *The Subjection of Women.*
2. Advocated women's rights and endorsed universal suffrage.

KARL MARX (1818–1883)

1. Scientific socialist who coauthored *The Communist Manifesto.*
2. Believed that the history of class conflict is best understood through the dialectical process of thesis, antithesis, and synthesis.
3. Contended that a class struggle between the bourgeoisie and the proletariat would lead "to the dictatorship of the proletariat," which in turn would be a transitional phase leading to a classless society.

CHARLES DARWIN (1809–1882)

1. British biologist who wrote *The Origin of Species.*
2. Challenged the idea of special creation by proposing a revolutionary theory of biological evolution.
3. Concluded that every living plant and animal takes part in a constant "struggle for existence" in which only the "fittest" survive.
4. Argued that the fittest are determined by a process of natural selection.

SIGMUND FREUD (1856–1939)

1. Austrian psychologist who formulated groundbreaking theories of human personality.
2. Theorized that the human psyche contains three distinct parts: (1) the id, which is the center of unconscious sexual and aggressive drives; (2) the superego, which is the center of moral values; and (3) the ego, which is the center of pragmatic reason.
3. Argued that human behavior is often irrational.

ALBERT EINSTEIN (1879–1955)

1. German physicist whose theory of special relativity undermined Newtonian physics.
2. Challenged traditional conceptions of time, space, and motion.
3. Contributed to the view that humans live in a universe with uncertainties.
4. Added to the feeling of uncertainty in the postwar world.

FRIEDRICH NIETZSCHE (1844–1900)

1. German philosopher whose writings influenced existentialism.
2. Expressed contempt for middle-class morality, saying that it led to a false and shallow existence.
3. Rejected reason and embraced the irrational.
4. Believed that the "will-to-power" of a few heroic "supermen" could successfully reorder the world.

ALBERT CAMUS (1913–1960) AND JEAN-PAUL SARTRE (1905–1980)

1. French existentialist philosophers and writers.
2. Questioned the efficacy of reason and science to understand the human situation.
3. Believed that God, reason, and progress are myths, and that humans live in a hostile world, alone and isolated.

Chapter 33

Key Events in European Diplomatic History

THE PEACE OF AUGSBURG, 1555

1. Ended the religious civil war between Roman Catholics and Lutherans in the German states.
2. Gave each German prince the right to determine the religion of his state, either Roman Catholic or Lutheran.
3. Failed to provide for the recognition of Calvinists or other religious groups.

THE COUNCIL OF TRENT, 1545–1563

1. Reformed Catholic Church discipline and reaffirmed church doctrine.
2. Preserved the papacy as the center of Christianity.
3. Confirmed all seven existing sacraments.
4. Reaffirmed Latin as the language of worship.
5. Forbade clerical marriage.

THE EDICT OF NANTES, 1598

1. Issued by Henry IV of France.
2. Granted religious toleration to French Protestants.
3. Marked the first formal recognition by a European national monarchy that two religions could coexist in the same country.
4. Revoked by Louis XIV in 1685.

THE PEACE OF WESTPHALIA, 1648

1. Ended the Thirty Years' War.
2. Recognized Calvinism as a legally permissible faith.
3. Recognized the sovereign independent authority of over 300 German states.
4. Continued the political fragmentation of Germany.

5. Granted Sweden additional territory, confirming its status as a major power.
6. Acknowledged the independence of the United Provinces of the Netherlands.

THE PEACE OF UTRECHT, 1713

1. Ended Louis XIV's efforts to dominate Europe.
2. Allowed Philip V to remain on the throne of Spain, but stipulated that the crowns of Spain and France should never be worn by the same monarch.
3. Granted the Spanish Netherlands (now called the Austrian Netherlands) to the Austrian Habsburgs along with Milan, Naples, and Sicily.
4. Granted England a number of territories including Newfoundland, Nova Scotia, and Gibraltar.
5. Granted England the asiento, the lucrative right to supply African slaves to Spanish America.

THE PRAGMATIC SANCTION, 1713

1. Guaranteed the succession of Habsburg emperor Charles VI's eldest daughter, Maria Theresa, to the throne.
2. Guaranteed the indivisibility of the Habsburg lands.
3. Violated when Frederick the Great of Prussia invaded Silesia in 1740.

THE CONGRESS OF VIENNA, 1815

1. Enacted a settlement that was acceptable to both the victors and to France.
2. Created a balance of power that lasted until the unification of Germany in 1871.
3. Underestimated the forces of liberalism and nationalism.
4. Used the principle of legitimacy to restore the Bourbons to the French throne.
5. United Belgium with the Netherlands to form a single kingdom of the Netherlands.
6. Created a loose confederation of 39 German states dominated by Austria.

THE BERLIN CONFERENCE, 1884–1885

1. Established rules for dividing Africa amongst the European powers. A European state could no longer simply declare a region of Africa its colony. It first had to exercise effective control over the territory.
2. Declared the Congo to be the "Congo Free State," under the personal control of Leopold II of Belgium.
3. Established rules governing the race for African colonies.

THE TREATY OF BREST-LITOVSK, 1918

1. Ended Bolshevik Russia's participation in World War I.
2. Negotiated by Vladimir Lenin because he was unwilling to risk Bolshevik gains by continuing a war that could no longer be won.
3. Nullified following Germany's defeat by the Allies.

THE TREATY OF VERSAILLES, 1919

1. Refused to allow either defeated Germany or Communist Russia to participate in peace conference negotiations.
2. Forced Germany to sign a war-guilt clause that was used to justify imposing large war reparations payments.
3. Changed the map of Europe by returning Alsace-Lorraine to France and dissolving Austria-Hungary into the separate states of Austria, Hungary, Czechoslovakia, and Yugoslavia.
4. Created the League of Nations to discuss and settle disputes without resorting to war.
5. Left a legacy of bitterness between the victors and Germany.

The Congress of Vienna and the Treaty of Versailles have generated a significant number of multiple-choice and free-response questions. Released APEURO tests contain almost 20 multiple-choice questions on these two topics. In addition, test writers have frequently asked students to compare and contrast the achievements and failures of the Congress of Vienna and the Versailles Treaty. Needless to say, it is vital that you carefully study these two key conferences in European diplomatic history.

THE LOCARNO PACT, 1925

1. Recorded an agreement between France and Germany to respect mutual frontiers.
2. Marked the beginning of a brief period of reduced tensions among the European powers.

THE KELLOGG-BRIAND PACT, 1928

1. Outlawed war as an instrument of national policy.
2. Violated repeatedly during the 1930s.

THE MUNICH CONFERENCE, 1938

1. Ceded the Sudetenland to Adolf Hitler.
2. Discredited the British policy of appeasement.

THE NAZI-SOVIET NONAGGRESSION PACT, 1939

1. Created a nonaggression agreement in which Hitler and Joseph Stalin promised to remain neutral if the other became involved in a war.
2. Divided eastern Europe into German and Soviet zones.

NORTH ATLANTIC PACT, 1949

1. Established the North Atlantic Treaty Organization (NATO) to coordinate the defense of its members.
2. Implemented Harry Truman's policy of containing the Soviet Union.
3. Forced to move its headquarters from Paris to Brussels when Charles de Gaulle withdrew French forces from the "American-controlled" NATO.

THE TREATY OF ROME, 1957

1. Created the European Economic Community (EEC), generally known as the Common Market.
2. Marked the beginning of European economic integration.

THE HELSINKI ACCORDS, 1975

1. Ratified the European territorial boundaries established after World War II.
2. Established "Helsinki watch committees" to monitor human rights in the 35 nations that signed the Helsinki Accords.
3. Marked the high point of Cold War détente.

THE MAASTRICHT TREATY, 1991

1. Created the European Union (EU), the world's largest single economic market.
2. Created a central bank for the European Union.

It is easy to neglect the Maastricht Treaty since it occurs near the end of your APEURO course. In fact, because of time constraints, many students and teachers fail to reach this topic. Don't make the mistake of failing to study this treaty. It is frequently tested and often appears as one of the last questions in the multiple-choice section.

Chapter 34

Key Events, Trends, and Figures in European Women's History

THE RENAISSANCE

1. In *The Courtier*, Baldassare Castiglione wrote that the perfect court lady should be well educated and charming. Women, however, were not expected to seek fame as men did.
2. Christine de Pizan was a prolific author who wrote a history of famous women and is now remembered as Europe's first feminist.
3. Isabella d'Este was the most famous Renaissance woman. Her life illustrates that being a patron of the arts was the most socially acceptable role for a well-educated Renaissance woman.

THE REFORMATION

1. Martin Luther believed that Christian women should strive to be models of obedience and Christian charity.
2. The Protestant Reformation reduced access to convents, thus changing the role of sixteenth-century women.
3. Quakers regularly allowed women to preach.
4. Older, widowed women were most often accused of practicing witchcraft.

THE ENLIGHTENMENT

1. Women played a leading role in hosting salons. Salons gave educated women a voice in cultural affairs. Madame Geoffrin was the most influential of the salon hostesses.
2. Support for superstition and witchcraft declined as educated Europeans turned to rational explanations for natural events.

THE EIGHTEENTH CENTURY

1. Most young married European couples lived in nuclear families. Large multigenerational households were not the norm.

2. Most couples postponed marriage until they were in their mid- to late 20s.
3. Young peasant women increasingly left home to work as domestic servants.

THE FRENCH REVOLUTION

1. Women led the march to Versailles to demand cheap bread and to force the royal family to move to Paris.
2. Women did not gain the right to vote or to hold political office.
3. Olympe de Gouges wrote the *Declaration of the Rights of Woman and of the Female Citizen.* She demanded that French women be given the same rights as men.
4. Mary Wollstonecraft wrote *A Vindication of the Rights of Women.* She argued that women are not naturally inferior to men. They only appear to be inferior because of a lack of education.
5. Napoleon Bonaparte's Civil Code reasserted the Old Regime's patriarchal system. The Code granted husbands extensive control over their wives. For example, married women needed their husband's consent to dispose of their own property. Divorce and property rights taken away by the Napoleonic Code were not fully restored until 1881.

THE NINETEENTH CENTURY

1. John Stuart Mill wrote *The Subjection of Women.* He argued that the social and legal inequalities imposed on women were a relic from the past.
2. Henrik Ibsen's *A Doll's House* criticized conventional marriage roles.
3. The ideal middle-class woman was expected to be an "angel in the house." Her most important roles were to be a devoted mother and the family's moral guardian.
4. Rising standards of living made it possible for men and women to marry at a younger age. At the same time, the rising cost of child-rearing caused a decline in the size of middle-class families.
5. Few married women worked outside the home. Most working women were single.
6. Opportunities for well-educated women were limited to teaching, nursing, and social work.
7. Law codes in most European countries gave women few legal rights. Divorce was legalized in Britain in 1857 and in France in 1884. However, Catholic countries such as Spain and Italy did not permit divorce.

8. Nineteenth-century women's rights advocates worked for the right of women to control their own property.
9. By the end of the nineteenth century, educated middle-class "new women" enjoyed more independent lifestyles.
10. As mass culture developed, fashion magazines made middle-class and working-class women more aware of style. At the same time, booksellers began to publish more fictional romances as well as articles and poems by female authors.

WOMEN'S SUFFRAGE

1. Although the women's suffrage movement commanded wide attention, it achieved few successes. In 1900, no country in Europe allowed women the right to vote.
2. Led by Emmeline Pankhurst, British women waged an aggressive campaign for women's suffrage.
3. During World War I, millions of women replaced men in factories, offices, and shops.
4. In 1918, Parliament granted the suffrage to women over the age of 30.

WOMEN IN THE SOVIET UNION

1. Marxists argued that both capitalism and middle-class husbands exploited women.
2. The Bolsheviks proclaimed complete equality of rights for women.
3. Soviet women were urged to work outside the home. Divorce and abortion were both easily available.
4. Soviet women were encouraged to become professionals. By 1950, women comprised three-quarters of the doctors in the Soviet Union.

WORLD WAR II

1. During the 1930s, Italy and Germany encouraged women to remain at home and provide their countries with more offspring.
2. During World War II, the commitment to total war caused millions of women to enter the workforce.
3. Women contributed directly to the war effort by serving as nurses and medics. In the Soviet Union, women known as "night witches" served as combat pilots.
4. Postwar reconstruction required women to continue working.
5. French and Italian women gained suffrage in 1945.

POST–WORLD WAR II FEMINISM

1. Led by Simone de Beauvoir, European feminists called attention to social problems that women faced. De Beauvoir also emphasized the need for women to control their own lives.
2. European feminists worked for liberalized divorce laws, improved access to birth control information, and expanded child-care facilities.
3. During the postwar period, European women married earlier and gave birth to fewer children.
4. Employment rates for married women dramatically increased.

PART IV

TEST-TAKING STRATEGIES AND PRACTICE QUESTIONS

Chapter 35

Strategies for the Multiple-Choice Questions

Your exam will have between 16 and 18 sets of multiple-choice questions. Each set will contain a stimulus prompt followed by 2, 3, or 4 questions. There are no sets with 1 or 5 questions. The majority of the stimulus prompts will utilize primary source passages and accounts written by modern historians. In addition, you will often be asked to evaluate a political cartoon, map, or graph.

Each of the 55 multiple-choice questions is worth 1 point. The multiple-choice section thus comprises 40 percent of 140 points on an APEURO exam. There is no guessing penalty so be sure to answer each question.

The multiple-choice questions are not designed to test your ability to recall information from long lists of names, dates, and places. Instead, test writers focus on asking you to demonstrate your ability to use historical reasoning processes such as comparison, causation, change, and continuity over time. As a result, answers focus on your ability to identify key historic trends, patterns, and influential ideas.

A SAMPLE SET OF QUESTIONS

Here is a sample primary source stimulus passage and a set of 4 multiple-choice questions:

> "Above all, Fascism . . . believes neither in the possibility nor in the utility of perpetual peace. It thus repudiates the doctrines of Pacifism—born of a renunciation of the struggle and an act of cowardice in the face of sacrifice. War alone brings up to their highest tension all human energies and puts the stamp of nobility upon the peoples who have the courage to meet it. All other trials are substitutes, which never really put a man in front of himself in the alternatives of life and death. A doctrine, therefore, which begins with a prejudice in favor of peace is foreign to Fascism . . . "
>
> Benito Mussolini,
> *The Doctrine of Fascism*, 1932

1. The Fascist movement was most clearly part of which of the following political trends during the 1920s and 1930s?

   (A) The increasing role of women as political leaders

   (B) The rise of totalitarian governments

   (C) The failure of the Bolshevik Revolution in the Soviet Union

   (D) The emergence of utopian socialism as a viable political option

2. Mussolini's scorn for "the utility of perpetual peace" was most likely a reaction to which of the following?

   (A) The growing influence of feminist agitation for greater political and social rights

   (B) The hyperinflation that struck the Weimar Republic in 1923

   (C) The decision of Great Britain and France to appease Hitler at the Munich Conference

   (D) The widespread international support for the principles embodied in the Kellogg-Briand Pact

3. Mussolini's views on war and peace are most similar to which of the following?

   (A) The commitment to the rule of law and majority rule by classical liberals

   (B) The fascination with the unconscious by Freudian theorists

   (C) The glorification of militarism by the Futurists

   (D) The disillusionment with contemporary conventions and values by the existentialists

4. Which of the following played a significant role in Mussolini's rise to power?

   (A) Italy's humiliating defeat in the invasion of Ethiopia

   (B) Punishing sanctions imposed by the League of Nations

   (C) King Victor Emmanuel's excessive use of force to suppress the Fascist Party

   (D) Embittered Italian nationalists who felt betrayed by the Treaty of Versailles

A STEP-BY-STEP APPROACH

STEP ONE: Carefully read the attribution line at the end of the excerpt.

Most students begin by carefully reading the passage. Resist this temptation. Instead begin by focusing on the information in the attribution line at the end of the passage. The brief but vital information contained in the attribution provides the historic context for the passage. For example, the attribution line in the example above tells you three key facts. First, Mussolini wrote the passage. Second, he focused on the characteristic features of Fascism. And third, he wrote the document in 1932.

These three facts are important historic clues that should focus your thinking. For example, what comes to mind when you think of Mussolini, Fascism, and the year 1932? Your thoughts could include the emergence of totalitarian dictators, the Great Depression, and Hitler's imminent rise to power. It is also important to remember that the Treaty of Versailles still remained intact and that World War II had not yet begun.

STEP TWO: Read the passage looking for the main ideas.

The passage is called a stimulus for a reason. Don't overanalyze the passage. Instead read the passage noting how the author uses key words and facts to support a main idea. In this passage, Mussolini asserts that Fascism glorifies war and renounces peace. This clearly foreshadows Mussolini's rejection of the Kellogg-Briand Pact, invasion of Ethiopia, and alliance with Hitler.

STEP THREE: Use the process of elimination.

Many times your knowledge of the topic will enable you to quickly spot the correct answer. However, there are questions in which the correct answer will not jump out and say, "Here I am!" When this happens, don't panic. Each APEURO multiple-choice question will contain answers that are clearly historically incorrect. For example, in Question 1 on page 330, you can eliminate answer choices (A), (C), and (D) because women were not yet political leaders, the Bolshevik Revolution did not fail in the Soviet Union, and utopian socialists failed to gain power in any European country. Using the process of elimination the correct answer to Question 1 is clearly (B).

Remember that eliminating at least two answer choices means that you will have a 50–50 chance of correctly answering the question. By making an educated guess, you should be able to answer at least 30 to 32 multiple-choice questions thus earning half of the 63 to 65 points you need to score a 3.

STEP FOUR: Answer each question in the set.

You should now be ready to answer each question in the set. Here are the answers to questions 1–4.

Question 1: This question is based on the historical thinking skill of contextualization. Choices (A) and (D) are incorrect because women and utopian socialists were not political leaders during the 1920s and 1930s. Choice (C) is incorrect because the Bolshevik Revolution was a success, not a failure. The Fascist movement was at least in part a reaction to the success of the Bolshevik Revolution in the Soviet Union. The correct answer is (B) because Fascism was an integral part of the growing movement towards totalitarian governments in southern and Eastern Europe.

Question 2: This question is based on the historical reasoning process of causation. Choices (A) and (B) are incorrect because the feminist movement and hyperinflation in the Weimar Republic had little or no influence on Mussolini's scorn for peace. Choice (C) is wrong because the Munich Conference took place six years after Mussolini published *The Doctrine of Fascism*. The correct answer is (D) because Mussolini scorned the Kellogg-Briand's repudiation of war as a weak and ineffectual policy that violated the militaristic tenets of Fascism.

Question 3: This question is based on the historical reasoning process of comparison. Choice (A) is incorrect because the goals of classical liberals are completely antithetical to the goals of Fascism. Choice (B) is incorrect because Freudian theorists were concerned with an internal conflict between the id and the superego. In contrast, Mussolini's view of conflict is based upon the belief that one nation must impose its will on other nations. Choice (D) is incorrect because existentialists focused on individuals giving meaning to their lives by making choices. In contrast, Mussolini's view of Fascism was based upon a supreme leader making choices for the entire nation. Choice (C) is correct because both Mussolini and the Futurists embraced militarism. For example, in the "Futurist Manifesto" Filippo Marinetti emphatically declared, "We will glorify war—the only cure for the world—militarism, patriotism, the destructive gesture of the anarchist . . ."

Question 4: This question is based on the historical reasoning process of causation. Choice (A) is incorrect because the Italian army successfully conquered Ethiopia. Choice (B) is incorrect because the League of Nations did not impose punishing sanctions on Italy. Choice (C) is incorrect because King Victor Emmanuel gave in and named Mussolini prime minister. Choice (D) is correct because Mussolini successfully appealed to embittered Italian nationalists who felt betrayed by the League of Nations.

Chapter 36

Practice Multiple-Choice Questions

Practice with the following AP®-style questions. Then go online to access our timed, full-length practice exam at *www.rea.com/studycenter*.

Questions 1–3 refer to the excerpt below.

"The painter is lord of all types of people and of all things. If the painter wishes to see beauties that charm him it lies in his power to create them, and if he wishes to see monstrosities that are frightful, buffoonish or ridiculous, or pitiable he can be lord and god thereof. . . . In fact whatever exists in the universe, in essence, in appearance, in the imagination, the painter has first in his mind and then in his hand; and these are of such excellence that they can present a proportioned and harmonious view of the whole, that can be seen simultaneously, at one glance, just as things in nature."

Leonardo da Vinci, Notebooks

1. The artistic philosophy described in the passage is best understood in the context of which of the following?

(A) The Catholic Church's emphasis upon commissioning dramatic works of art that involve worshippers

(B) The continued reliance on supernatural explanations of natural events

(C) The revival of classical learning and the development of humanism

(D) The use of realistic works of art to draw attention to pressing social problems

2. Da Vinci's discussion of the use of direct observation has the most in common with

   (A) Machiavelli's recommendations for aspiring princes

   (B) Galileo's science-based inquiries of the cosmos

   (C) Henry IV's decision to convert to Catholicism

   (D) Martin Luther's criticism of the Catholic Church in his Ninety-five Theses

3. The passage provides the most reliable information about which of the following?

   (A) The use of compositional harmony in Renaissance art

   (B) The use of precise realism and disguised subjects in Northern Renaissance art

   (C) The use of the subconscious as a source of inspiration in Surrealistic art

   (D) The use of non-European cultures in Post-Impressionist art

Questions 4–6 refer to the excerpt below.

"Thus it came about that the city [Magdeburg] and all its inhabitants fell into the hands of the enemy. . . .Then was there naught but beating and burning, plundering, torture, and murder. Most especially was every one of the enemy bent on securing much booty. When a marauding party entered a house, if its master had anything to give he might thereby purchase respite and protection for himself and his family till the next man, who also wanted something, should come along. It was only when everything had been brought forth and there was nothing left to give that the real trouble commenced. Then, what with blows and threats of shooting, stabbing, and hanging, the poor people were so terrified that if they had had anything left they would have brought it forth if it had been buried in the earth or hidden away in a thousand castles. In this frenzied rage the great and splendid city that had stood like a fair princess in the land was now, in its hour of direst need and unutterable distress and woe, given over to the flames and thousands of innocent men, women, and children in the midst of a horrible din of heartrending shrieks and cries, were tortured and put to death in so cruel and shameful a manner that no words would suffice to describe, nor tears to bewail it."

Otto von Guericke, Burgermeister of Magdeburg,
May 1631

4. The conflict described in the passage began as a result of the
   (A) formation of rival alliances in the Holy Roman Empire
   (B) emergence of Gustavus Adolphus as a charismatic leader determined to exert influence over the Holy Roman Empire
   (C) ongoing disputes over the independence of the Dutch Republic
   (D) establishment of several religiously pluralistic and tolerant states within the Holy Roman Empire

5. Which of the following was a significant consequence in Europe of the Thirty Years' War?
   (A) The unification of the Holy Roman Empire as a powerful European state
   (B) The continued ability of Spain to act as a champion of Catholicism in Europe
   (C) The continuation of increasingly destructive religious wars
   (D) The establishment of the modern system of diplomatic relations among mutually recognized sovereign states

6. The event described in the passage best illustrates which of the following aspects of the Thirty Years' War?
   (A) The creation of nationally based mass conscription armies
   (B) The ability of Protestants to make effective use of printing technology to spread their ideas
   (C) The virtual extinction of all Protestant denominations within the German-speaking regions of the Holy Roman Empire
   (D) The war's destructive impact upon the German population

Questions 7–10 refer to the excerpt below.

"So, Amsterdam has risen through the hand of God to the peak of prosperity and greatness. . . . The whole world stands amazed at its riches and from east and west, north and south they come to behold it. The Great and Almighty Lord has raised the city above all others . . . yea He has even taken from them the commerce of the east and the west and has spilled their treasure into our bosom."

Melchior Fokkens, Dutch historian,
Description of the Widely Renowned Merchant City of Amsterdam, 1662

7. The economic conditions described in the passage were most directly a result of

(A) the success of Dutch colonies in North America

(B) the success of the Dutch East Indies Company

(C) the lingering impact of the Thirty Years' War

(D) the curtailment of the African slave trade

8. The economic conditions described in the passage best explain which of the following actions by the English in the seventeenth century?

(A) The enactment of the Navigation Act of 1651

(B) The attempt by Charles I to establish an absolutist government

(C) The restoration of the Stuart rulers

(D) The enactment of the Bill of Rights

9. The Dutch historian quoted above would most likely agree with which of the following statements?
   (A) Commercial practices and laws must be based on strict adherence to religious principles.
   (B) Mining precious minerals is the most efficient way to promote economic growth.
   (C) Religious toleration promotes a free exchange of ideas.
   (D) The equitable distribution of wealth among all classes should be the paramount goal of the state.

10. A historian would most likely use the passage as evidence for which of the following seventeenth-century trends?
    (A) The emergence of a competitive state system based on new patterns of diplomacy
    (B) The competition for power between monarchs and privileged nobles
    (C) The development of a market economy based on new commercial practices
    (D) The spread of revolutionary scientific concepts and discoveries

Questions 11–14 refer to the two excerpts below.

PASSAGE 1

"I do not feel obliged to believe that the same God who has endowed us with senses, reason, and intellect has intended to forgo their use by some other means to give us knowledge which we can attain by them. He would not require us to deny sense and reason in physical matters which are set before our eyes and minds by direct experience or necessary demonstrations."

Galileo Galilei, letter to Grand Duchess Christina of Tuscany, 1615

PASSAGE 2

"First, . . . to want to affirm that in reality the sun is at the center of the world and only turns on itself without moving from east to west, and the earth . . . revolves with great speed around the sun . . . is a very dangerous thing, likely not only to irritate all scholastic philosophers and theologians, but also to harm the holy Faith by rendering Holy Scripture false. Second, I say that, as you know, the Council of Trent prohibits interpreting Scripture against the common consensus of the Holy Fathers."

Catholic Cardinal Robert Bellarmine,
letter to Paolo Antonio Foscarini, 1615

11. The two passages are best understood in the context of which of the following?

(A) The growing tension between religion and science for explanations of natural phenomena

(B) The Protestant Reformation's emphasis on individual study of the Bible

(C) The continued popularity of astrology among members of the European elite

(D) The economic growth caused by the Columbian Exchange

12. Which of the following groups in the eighteenth century would most likely have agreed with the sentiments expressed by Galileo?

(A) Scholastic theologians

(B) Swiss Calvinists

(C) French philosophes

(D) English industrial capitalists

13. Galileo's argument reflects which of the following developments during the early seventeenth century?

(A) The spread of literacy throughout Western Europe

(B) The humanist debate over the rights of women

(C) The growing influence of nationalism

(D) The emergence of scientific discoveries that challenged traditional Christian and classical authorities

14. Which of the following views would Cardinal Bellarmine have most likely agreed with?

(A) The Enlightenment's belief in the rational order of the universe

(B) The persistence of folk stories and oral traditions

(C) The right of each person to choose his or her religious beliefs

(D) The official decrees of a Church council

Questions 15–16 refer to the excerpt below.

"Such work as mine is not done twice in a century. I have saved the Revolution as it lay dying. I have cleansed it of its crimes and have held it up to the people shining with fame. I have inspired France and Europe with new ideas that will never be forgotten."

Napoleon Bonaparte, *Memoirs*, 1821

15. Which one of the following best describes an impact that the "new ideas" referenced in the excerpt would have in nineteenth-century Europe?

(A) The growing participation of women in European political life

(B) The awakening of nationalist sentiment in Germany

(C) The continued importance of hierarchy and privilege in Eastern Europe

(D) The reemergence of Spain as a major European great power

16. Historians disagreeing with Napoleon's contention that he "saved the Revolution" would most likely cite which of the following as evidence to support their argument?

(A) The support Napoleon gave to the revolution in Haiti

(B) The emphasis Napoleon placed on the rapid industrialization of the French economy

(C) The emphasis Napoleon placed on extending full legal and voting rights to French women

(D) The limitations Napoleon imposed on French newspapers, plays, and books

Questions 17–19 refer to the excerpt below.

"It was a town of red brick, or of brick that would have been red if the smoke and ashes had allowed it; but as matters stood, it was a town of unnatural red and black, like the painted face of a savage. It was a town of machinery and tall chimneys, out of which interminable serpents of smoke trailed themselves for ever and ever, and never got uncoiled. It had a black canal in it, and a river that ran purple with ill smelling dye, and vast piles of buildings full of windows where there was a rattling and a trembling all day long, and where the piston of the steam engine worked monotonously up and down, like the head of an elephant in a state of melancholy madness. It contained several large streets all very like one another, and many small streets still more like one another, inhabited by people equally like one another, who all went in and out at the same hours, with the same sound upon the same pavements, to do the same work, and to whom every day was the same as yesterday and tomorrow, and every year the counterpart of the last and the next."

Charles Dickens, *Hard Times,* 1854

17. The excerpt most clearly shows the influence of which of the following literary trends in mid-nineteenth-century Europe?

(A) Writers' rejection of overly idealized descriptions to depict social realities

(B) Writers' glorification of technological progress in the machine age

(C) Writers' turn to dreams and the subconscious as a source of inspiration

(D) Writers' use of stream-of-consciousness to portray disconnected feelings isolation, regret, and alienation

18. Which of the following mid-nineteenth-century groups would have been most likely to condemn the conditions described in the excerpt?

(A) Romantic nationalists

(B) Industrial capitalists

(C) Scientific socialists

(D) Realpolitik politicians

19. The excerpt provides the clearest evidence for which of the following features of the Industrial Revolution in Great Britain?

(A) The growth of a new consumer culture

(B) The expansion of voting rights to working-class men

(C) The environmental and social impacts of unregulated capitalism

(D) The importance of charities to provide financial assistance to people living in poverty

Questions 20–21 refer to the excerpt below.

"It was the weakness of Russia's democratic culture which enabled Bolshevism to take root. . . . The Russian people were trapped by the tyranny of their own history. . . . For while the people could destroy the old system, they could not build a new one of their own. . . . By 1921, if not earlier, the revolution had come full circle, and a new autocracy had been imposed on Russia which in many ways resembled the old."

Orlando Figes, historian, *A People's Tragedy: The Russian Revolution,* 1891–1924,
Published in 1997

20. Which of the following best supports the author's characterization of Russian political culture prior to the Bolshevik Revolution?

(A) The success of the Duma as a viable democratic institution

(B) The success of Russia's commitment to public education

(C) The growing political participation of Russian women

(D) The politically repressive nature of the tsarist government

21. Which of the following best supports the author's interpretation of Russia's "new autocracy" in the post-Lenin period during the 1920s and 1930s?

(A) The Bolsheviks' commitment to establishing democratic institutions

(B) The Bolsheviks' extensive use of repressive techniques such as the secret police and prison camps

(C) The Bolshevik regime's use of religion to justify its legitimacy

(D) The Bolshevik regime's commitment to renouncing global revolution

Questions 22 and 23 refer to the table below.

Index of Industrial Production, 1938–1967

	1938	1948	1959	1967
United States	33	73	113	168
West Germany	53	27	107	158
France	52	55	101	155
Italy	43	44	112	212
Holland	47	53	110	152
Belgium	64	78	104	153
Great Britain	67	74	105	133

Walter Laquer, *Europe Since Hitler*, 1982

22. Which of the following contributed the most to the overall trend shown in the table?

(A) The economic impact of decolonization

(B) The successful implementation of the Marshall Plan

(C) The expansion of "cradle to grave" social welfare policies

(D) The adoption of the Soviet model of rapid industrialization and centralized economic planning

23. Which of the following was a long-term consequence of the trend shown in table?

(A) An increasing discrepancy between the success of noncommunist and communist economies

(B) The growing importance of feminist ideas

(C) The shift from an industrial economy to a service-based economy

(D) The immigration of large numbers of people from former colonies to Western Europe

Questions 24 and 25 refer to the excerpt below.

"Now, woman has always been man's dependent, if not his slave; the two sexes have never shared the world in equality. And even today woman is heavily handicapped, though her situation is beginning to change. Almost nowhere is her legal status the same as man's, and frequently it is much to her disadvantage. Even when her rights are legally recognized in the abstract, long-standing custom prevents their full expression in the mores. In the economic sphere men and women can almost be said to make up two castes; other things being equal, the former hold the better jobs, get higher wages, and have more opportunities for success than their new competitors. In industry and politics men have a great many more positions and they monopolize the most important posts."

Simone de Beauvoir, *The Second Sex*, 1949

24. Which one of the following best supports the author's statement that "the situation is beginning to change?"

(A) The increasing Cold War tensions between communist and noncommunist European countries

(B) The rapid decolonization of European imperialist empires

(C) The economic impact of the postwar baby boom

(D) The extension of suffrage rights to most European women

25. Between 1970 and 2000 the growing women's movement played a significant role in which of the following political trends?

(A) Women played a leading role in the creation of the European Union.

(B) Women played a leading role in the fall of communism in Eastern Europe.

(C) Women played a leading role in supporting immigration into Europe.

(D) Women played a leading role in the formation of the Green Party.

ANSWERS AND EXPLANATIONS

1. (C) Leonardo da Vinci was one of the foremost High Renaissance artists. His work was part of the humanist revival of classical learning.

2. (B) Da Vinci's use of direct observation foreshadowed the empirical method of observation employed by Galileo and other pioneers of the scientific revolution.

3. (A) Compositional harmony was one of the hallmarks of High Renaissance art. Da Vinci's reference to "a proportional and harmonious view of the whole" underscores his commitment to symmetry and balance.

4. (A) The excerpt describes an event during the Swedish Phase of the Thirty Years' War. The war began when the Protestant and Catholic states forged rival alliances to defend their interests.

5. (D) Answer choices (A), (B), and (C) are all incorrect consequences of the Thirty Years' War. Answer choice (D) is correct because the war did lead to the establishment of the modern system of diplomatic relations among mutually recognized sovereign states.

6. (D) The "frenzied rage" that destroyed Magdeburg provides a tragic example of how the Thirty Years' War devastated the German economy and decimated its population.

7. (B) The Dutch Republic was Europe's leading commercial power during most of the seventeenth century. The Dutch East Indies Company played a key role in this economic success by displacing the Portuguese and gaining control of the lucrative spice trade in the East Indies.

8. (A) The English responded to the Dutch commercial success by enacting the Navigation Act of 1651. The act barred Dutch ships from carrying goods between other countries and England.

9. (C) Religious toleration was one of the key features of the Dutch Republic. It helped create a cosmopolitan society that promoted commerce.

10. (C) The Dutch Republic's commercial success played a key role in the development of a European market economy during the seventeenth century.

11. (A) Galileo's revolutionary discoveries challenged the Church's long-standing doctrine that God had deliberately placed the Earth at the center of the universe. The two letters reflect the ongoing tension between religious dogma and scientific discoveries.

12. (C) French philosophes such as Voltaire championed reason. They were convinced that natural laws regulated the universe.

13. (D) Galileo was one of the first scientists to use the telescope for astronomical observations. His discoveries provided irrefutable support for the heliocentric view that the Earth was a planet circling the sun. This represented a direct challenge to traditional Church and classical authorities.

14. (D) Cardinal Bellarmine specifically notes that "the Council of Trent prohibits interpreting Scripture against the common consensus of the Holy Fathers." He would therefore agree with the official decrees of a Church council.

15. (B) Napoleon unwittingly sparked a wave of German nationalism that fueled resistance to his rule. People who first welcomed the French as liberators now felt that they were being exploited by foreign invaders. Napoleon thus inadvertently accelerated the cause of German unification in the nineteenth century.

16. (D) Answer choices (A), (B), and (C) are all inaccurate statements. Historians would argue that Napoleon violated one of the French Revolution's key principles by censoring newspapers, plays, and books.

17. (A) During the mid-nineteenth century, writers and artists rejected Romantic themes as overly idealized and artificial.

The excerpt from *Hard Times* is an example of the new Realist approach to portraying the harsh realities of industrial life.

18. (C) Scientific socialists such as Marx and Engels strongly condemned the working and living conditions created by the Industrial Revolution.

19. (C) The excerpt provides a particularly vivid description of both the environmental and social impacts of unregulated capitalism.

20. (D) Answer choices (A), (B), and (C) are all historically inaccurate. The repressive tsarist government under Nicholas II provides strong support for Figes' characterization of Russia's political culture prior to the Bolshevik Revolution.

21. (B) Answer choices (A), (C), and (D) are all historically inaccurate statements. Stalin created an oppressive totalitarian state that made extensive use of secret police, purges, and prison camps.

22. (B) The Marshall Plan successfully promoted Europe's economic revival by providing needed financial aid and political leadership.

23. (A) The economic revival of Western Europe provided a stark contrast with the stagnation in the Communist bloc countries. This contrast played a key role in the popular unrest that led to the fall of Communism in Eastern Europe in 1989.

24. (D) By the end of World War II, European women received the suffrage in every country except Switzerland. This provides strong evidence supporting de Beauvoir's statement that "the situation is beginning to change."

25. (D) As more and more women became social activists, they broadened their efforts to include a variety of new issues. West German women played a leading role in the formation of the Green Party.

Chapter 37

Strategies for the Short-Answer Questions

Your APEURO exam will continue with a 40-minute section containing 3 required short-answer questions. The questions will cover topics testing your knowledge of material from the mid-1400s to the post–Cold War era in the early twenty-first century.

Short-answer question 1 is required and includes a secondary source stimulus. The topic of the question includes historical developments or processes between the years 1600 and 2001. Short-answer question 2 is required and includes a primary source stimulus. The topic of the question includes historical developments or processes between the years 1600 and 2001.

You will then be presented with two additional short-answer questions. You may select either short-answer question 3 ***or*** short-answer question 4. Neither question includes a stimulus. Short-answer question 3 focuses on historical developments or processes between the years 1450 and 1815. Short-answer question 4 focuses on historical developments or processes between the years 1815 and 2001.

Each short-answer question includes three specific sub-questions labeled a), b), and c). The three short-answer questions are worth 28 points, or 20 percent of your total exam score. Each of the three sub-points is worth 3.1 points.

STRATEGY 1

Use complete sentences to answer each sub-question. You will not be awarded points for using an outline or a bulleted list of points.

STRATEGY 2

Write succinct answers. You will be given one page for each of the three questions you choose to answer. Each page contains just 23 lines. Answers that exceed these limitations will not be scored.

STRATEGY 3

Each of the three sub-parts of a short-answer question is an all-or-nothing proposition. That is, you will either receive full credit for your answer or you will receive a zero. Remember, there is no guessing penalty. Since a blank space will receive a zero, always try to write a plausible answer.

STRATEGY 4

Most of the sub-questions can be answered in a variety of ways. Your goal is therefore not to find ***the*** answer. Instead, your goal is to find and write about ***an*** answer.

SAMPLE SHORT-ANSWER QUESTION 1: ANALYZING SECONDARY SOURCES

SOURCE 1

> "Betraying the hopes of the world, breaking treaties and commitments, the Soviet government after World War II embarked on a new course of forcible expansion and aggression. In 1945 and 1946 Russia's neighbors in Europe and the Far East, their territory occupied by the Red Army at the end of the fighting, were transformed into a new kind of dependencies, so-called satellites with the Communist Party in power. Although the United States and her Western allies protested this course, Moscow remained adamant, fully aware of the inability of the Western allies to prevent this process of expansion.
>
> David J. Dallin, "Cold War and Containment," 1956

SOURCE 2

> "Aggressive American plans to shape the postwar international economic structure along the lines of free trade and capitalist supremacy led to attempts to create a global American empire, and this in turn, caused the deterioration of relations with Communist Russia and the beginnings of the Cold War between East and West. American economic policy since 1947 has been tied primarily and increasingly to

military aid to those governments concerned with containing, repelling, or protecting themselves from Communist aggression."

Lisle A. Rose, *Dubious Victory*, 1973

Using the excerpts above, answer (a), (b), and (c).

(a) Describe one major difference between Dallin's and Rose's interpretation of the causes of the Cold War.

(b) Explain how ONE piece of evidence in the decade after World War II supports Dallin's interpretation.

(c) Explain how ONE piece of evidence in the decade after World War II supports Rose's interpretation.

SAMPLE ANSWERS

(a) Dallin blamed the Cold War on Soviet expansion in Europe and the Far East. He argued that this expansion was motivated by an implacable communist ideology that viewed capitalism as an inevitable and irrevocable historic enemy. In contrast, Rose argued that America's drive for "capitalist supremacy" turned the United States into an expansionist power that posed a threat to the Soviet Union.

(b) Dallin's argument is supported by Soviet actions in Poland. Soviet leader Joseph Stalin broke his Yalta pledges by forbidding free elections in Poland and by installing a puppet or satellite communist regime. The intrusion into Eastern and Central Europe violated the principle of national self-determination and posed a real threat to Western Europe. As the leader of the Free World, the United States had to implement a policy of containment to block Soviet expansion.

(c) Rose's argument is supported by America's economic policy, embodied in the Marshall Plan and in its military policy embodied in the NATO alliance. Although America claimed that it funded the Marshall Plan to fight poverty, it also transformed Western Europe into a lucrative market for American products. At the same time, the NATO alliance allowed the United States to encircle the Soviet Union with military bases manned by American forces backed up by B-52 bombers and Polaris submarines armed with nuclear weapons. This policy forced the Soviet Union to develop its own nuclear weapons, thus triggering a Cold War arms race.

SAMPLE SHORT-ANSWER QUESTION 2: ANALYZING PRIMARY SOURCES

> "My earliest memories are the standard postwar memories in London. Landscapes of rubble, half a street's disappeared. Some of it stayed like that for ten years. The main effect of the war on me was just that phrase, 'Before the War.' Because you'd hear grown-ups talking about it. "Oh, it wasn't like this before the war.' Otherwise I wasn't particularly affected. I suppose no sugar, no sweets and candies, was a good thing, but I wasn't happy about it. . . . The fact that I couldn't buy a bag of sweets until 1954 says a lot about the upheavals and changes that last for so many years after the war. The war had been over for nine years before I could actually, if I had the money, go and say, 'I'll have a bag of them'—toffees and Aniseed Twists. Otherwise it was 'You got your ration stamp book?' The sound of those stamps stamping. Your ration was your ration. One little brown paper bag—a tiny one—a *week*."
>
> Keith Richards, British rock musician, *Life*, 2010

Using the excerpt above, answer (a), (b), and (c).

(a) What caused the "landscapes of rubble" that formed Richards' earliest childhood memories of London?

(b) Explain the situation that led to Richard's needing to use ration books for almost a decade following World War II.

(c) Explain one factor that continued to improve economic conditions described in the excerpt.

SAMPLE ANSWERS

(a) The destruction in London was caused by a German bombing campaign known as the Blitz. Conducted between September 1940 and May 1941, the massive aerial bombardment claimed more than 20,000 lives in London and destroyed or damaged over a million homes. However, the Blitz failed to break British morale and actually enhanced Winston Churchill's stature as a courageous and inspiring leader.

(b) Britain emerged from World War II facing a dire economic crisis. Bankrupt and with nothing to export, Britain had no way to pay for imports including desperately needed food. Shortages forced the government to use ration books as an equitable way to distribute scarce goods.

(c) The Marshall Plan helped stimulate Great Britain's industrial activity and modernize its transportation and agricultural equipment. Great Britain received about one-fourth of all Marshall Plan aid, more than any other country.

SHORT-ANSWER QUESTION 3: UNDERSTANDING CAUSATION

Answer (a), (b), and (c). Confine your answers to the period from 1500 to 1700.

(a) Identify ONE cause of European colonization of the New World from 1500 to 1700.

(b) Identify ONE effect of European colonization of the New World from 1500 to 1700.

(c) Explain ONE way in which Spain's colonial policies differed from England's colonial policies from 1500 to 1700.

SAMPLE ANSWERS

(a) European demand for Asian spices and luxury items far exceeded the supply. Muslims and Venetians controlled trade routes to the East. The new monarchs in Spain and Portugal wanted to find sea routes to the lucrative Asian markets.

(b) The discovery of the New World sparked an unprecedented global exchange of agricultural products, animals, diseases, and human populations known as the Columbian Exchange. The new crops revolutionized the European diet and helped fuel a growing population. However, European diseases decimated indigenous populations.

(c) Spain created a rigid and highly centralized New World empire controlled by the crown in Madrid. In contrast, the English established a diverse group of colonies along the North Atlantic coast. Led by the House of Burgesses in Virginia and town meetings in New England, the colonies developed a tradition of self-government.

SHORT-ANSWER QUESTION 4: UNDERSTANDING CAUSATION

Answer (a), (b), and (c). Confine your answers to the period from 1870 to 1914.

(a) Identify ONE cause of New Imperialism in the period 1870 to 1914.

(b) Identify ONE effect of New Imperialism in the period 1870 to 1914.

(c) Explain ONE way in which the New Imperialism differed from colonialism in the period from 1500 to 1700.

SAMPLE ANSWERS

(a) Economic problems played a key role in changing European attitudes towards acquiring colonies. A deep economic depression gripped Europe between the mid-1870s and the mid-1890s, bringing unemployment and the potential for labor unrest. As the Second Industrial Revolution gathered momentum, European industrialists looked to overseas colonies as sources of raw materials and as new markets for finished goods.

(b) The New Imperialism disrupted traditional cultures throughout Africa and Asia. The process of westernization forced colonial people to reevaluate their traditions and adopt European legal and political practices. The adoption of Western ideas caused many non-Western people to call for the modernization of their countries.

(c) Led by Great Britain and France, the imperialist powers used steamships, railroads, underwater cables, and advanced weapons to exercise increasing economic and political control over African and Asian peoples. No longer content to simply trade with other peoples, European nations now aimed to directly rule and exploit vast regions of the globe.

Chapter 38

Strategies for the Document-Based Essay Question

After completing the short-answer questions, you will have a well-deserved 10-minute break. When you return to your desk, your exam will resume with the document-based essay question (DBQ).

The DBQ is an essay question requiring you to interpret and analyze 7 brief documents. The documents are typically excerpts from letters, speeches, diaries, reports, official decrees, and scholarly articles. In addition, the DBQ often includes a graph, map, political cartoon, or work of art.

The College Board recommends that you devote 60 minutes to the DBQ. This task typically requires about 15 minutes to read the documents, organize your thoughts, determine a thesis, and create an outline for your essay. You will then have about 45 minutes to write your DBQ essay.

Your DBQ can earn up to 7 rubric points. Each rubric point is worth 5 exam points. So a perfect score of 7 is worth 35 points, or 25 percent of your total exam score. It is important to remember that earning 5 of the 7 possible rubric points will keep you on pace to earn an overall score of 5 on your APEURO exam.

The topic of the document-based question includes historical developments or processes between the years 1600 and 2001.

THE DBQ SCORING RUBRIC

The APEURO DBQ scoring rubric is divided into the following categories:

1. **Thesis—1 point**
   - Responds to the prompt with a historically defensible thesis/claim that establishes your line of reasoning.
   - Consists of one or more sentences located in one place, either the introduction or the conclusion.

2. **Contextualization—1 point**
   - Describes a broader historic context relevant to the prompt
   - Places the prompt in its proper historic setting
   - Connects the prompt to broader historical events or trends occurring before or during the prompt's time frame

3. **Evidence: Document Content—2 points**
   - Uses the content of at least *three* documents to address the topic of the prompt. (1 point)

   OR

   - Supports an argument using at least six documents. Response must provide an accurate description, not just quotes from the documents. (2 points)

   3a. Evidence: Beyond the Documents—1 point
   - Uses at least one additional piece of specific and relevant historical evidence beyond what is found in the documents or in the contextualization paragraph.
   - Evidence must be different from the evidence used to earn the point for contextualization.
   - Evidence must be relevant to an argument about the prompt.

4. **Analysis and Reasoning: Sourcing—1 point**
   - For at least three documents explains how or why the document's point of view, purpose, historical situation, and/or audience is relevant to an argument.
   - Applies just one of these criteria to each document. For example, you can describe the point of view of one document and the intended audience of a second document.

   4a. Analysis and Reasoning: Complex Understanding—1 point
   - Demonstrates a *complex understanding* of the historical development that is the focus of the prompt using evidence to corroborate (reinforce) and/or qualify (modify) an argument that addresses the question.

- *Complex understanding* can be accomplished in a variety of ways including:
  - —Explaining both similarities and differences, or explaining both continuity and change, or explaining multiple causes, or explaining both causes and effects.
  - —Explaining nuances of an issue by analyzing multiple variables.
  - —Explaining relevant and insightful connections within and across periods.
  - —Confirming the validity of an argument by corroborating multiple perspectives across themes.
  - —Qualifying or modifying an argument by considering diverse or alternative viewpoints or evidence.

A SAMPLE DBQ AND ANNOTATED ESSAY

Practice is the key to performing well on the DBQ. The following sample DBQ is designed to illustrate how to use a guided set of seven strategies that can be applied to any DBQ.

1. Begin by carefully analyzing the assignment.

Begin the recommended 15-minute reading and planning period by carefully examining the assignment. Here is a sample assignment:

Analyze the consequences of early industrialization as seen in Manchester, England during the period 1780 to 1848.

2. Carefully examine each of the seven documents.

Your next step is to read, analyze, and organize the following seven documents:

Document 1: Source: A.P. Wadsworth and J. De Lacy, economic historians, *The Cotton Trade and Industrial Lancashire*, 1931

The idea of mechanical production had seized the cotton industry in Manchester. Scores of men were making machines, and equipping small factories; scores of inventive minds were at work, contributing a modification here, an adaptation there, which passed into common stock. There is no machine without its history of trial and error, and the men whose names have become household words were surrounded by a whole society of inventors to whom the progress of cotton machinery owes hardly less than it does to them.

Document 2: Source: William Cobbett, well-known journalist and reform politician, *Political Register*, 1824

Some of these lords of the loom have in their employ thousands of miserable creatures. In the cotton-spinning work, fourteen hours in each day, locked up, summer and winter, in a heat of from eighty to eighty-four degrees. . . . Not only is there not a breath of sweet air in these truly infernal scenes, but, for a large part of the time, there is the abominable and pernicious stink of the gas to assist in the murderous effects of the heat. In addition to the noxious effluvia of the gas, mixed with the steam, there are the dust, and what is called cotton-flyings or fuzz, which the unfortunate creatures have to inhale. . . . Can any man, with a heart in his body, and a tongue in his head, refrain from cursing a system that produces such slavery and such cruelty?

Document 3: Source: Alexis de Tocqueville, French political philosopher and historian, *Journeys to England and Ireland*, 1835

A thick black smoke covers the city. The sun appears like a disc without any rays. In this semi-daylight 300,000 people work ceaselessly. A thousand noises rise amidst this unending damp and dark labyrinth . . . the footsteps of a busy crowd, the crunching wheels of machines, the shriek of steam from the boilers, the regular beat of looms, the heavy rumble of carts, these are the only noises from which you can never escape in these dark half-lit streets. . . . From this foul drain the greatest stream of human industry flows out to fertilize the whole world. From this filthy sewer pure gold flows. Here humanity attains its most complete development and its most brutish; here civilization works its miracles, and civilized man is turned back into a savage.

Document 4: Source: *The Lancet*, British medical journal, founded and edited by Thomas Wakley, medical reformer, 1843

Average Age at Death

	Gentry/Professional	Farmer/Trader	Laborer/Artisan
Rural Districts			
Rutland	52	41	38
Bath	55	37	25
Industrial Districts			
Leeds	44	27	19
Manchester	38	20	17

Document 5: Source: James Leach, former factory worker and reformer, *Stubborn Facts from the Factories by a Manchester Operative*, 1844

In some factories none but women are allowed to labour, excepting a few men, such as managers . . . not because the women can perform the work better or turn off a greater quantity, but because they are considered to be more docile than men under the injustice that in some shape or form is daily practiced upon them. A great number of the females employed in factories are married, and not a small number of them are mothers. . . . We have repeatedly seen married females, in the last stages of pregnancy, slaving from morning till night beside these never-tiring machines, and when oppressed nature became so exhausted that they were obliged to sit down to take a moment's ease, and being seen by the manager, were fined for the offense.

Document 6: Source: Hugh Miller, Scottish geologist and writer, *First Impressions of England and Its People*, 1846

The hapless river—a pretty enough stream a few miles higher up, with trees overhanging its banks and fringes of green sedge set thick along its edges—loses caste as it gets among the mills and printworks. There are myriads of dirty things given it to wash, and whole wagon-loads of poisons from dye-houses and bleach-yards thrown into it to carry away, steam-boilers discharge into it their seething contents, and drains and sewers their fetid impurities; till at length it rolls on—here between tall dingy walls, there under precipices of red sandstone—considerably less a river than a flood of liquid manure, in which all life dies, whether animal or vegetable, and which resembles nothing in nature, except, perhaps, the stream thrown out in eruption by some mud-volcano.

Document 7: Source: Friedrich Engels, early socialist writer, *Condition of the Working Class in England*, 1845

One day I walked with one of those middle-class gentlemen into Manchester. I spoke to him about the disgraceful slums and drew his attention to the disgusting condition of that part of the town in which the factory workers lived. I declared that I had never seen so badly built a town in my life. He listened patiently and at the corner of the street at which we parted company, he remarked, "And yet there is a great deal of money made here. Good morning, Sir!"

3. Create an organizational chart.

Many students find it very helpful to organize the documents by placing them into a chart. For this assignment, your chart should focus on ecological/health, social, and economic consequences. Here is an example of what your chart could look like:

	Ecological and Health Consequences	Social Consequences	Economic Consequences
Document 1			A whole society of inventors
Document 2	Not a breath of sweet air; heat and cotton dust		
Document 3	Thick black smoke		Pure gold flows
Document 4	Mortality statistics		
Document 5		Women slaving from morning till night	
Document 6	A flood of liquid manure		
Document 7		Disgraceful slums; disgusting conditions	A great deal of money made here

4. Write an opening paragraph that establishes the historic CONTEXT of the event.

Your opening paragraph is an excellent place to establish the historic context for the event specified in your DBQ assignment. Remember that the contextualization point will contribute 5 points to your total exam score.

Your opening paragraph is very important. Use the first 2–3 sentences to establish the historic context for the topic specified in your prompt. The first two sentences in our sample introductory paragraph provide the "big picture" for the historic setting of the emergence of Manchester as an industrial center. Then use your next 2–3 sentences to present a clearly defined thesis that establishes your line of reasoning. Sentences 3–5 in our sample opening paragraph clearly establish a line of reasoning that by identifying the adverse consequences for public health, the environment, and society along with the economic benefits of early industrialization in Manchester.

Our "combo" paragraph combines contextualization and the thesis. This combination is worth 2 rubric points or 10 exam points! Given this high value plan carefully. There is no rule stating that you must begin writing after 15 minutes. It is better to take a few extra minutes to carefully construct your opening paragraph than to rush and end up with a weak thesis.

It is important to note that you should not divide this paragraph. Readers expect to see your thesis in the first paragraph. DBQ readers report that the overwhelming majority of students begin their essays with a combo approach.

Here is a sample introductory paragraph that establishes the context for the emergence of Manchester as the world's first industrial city:

Essay introduction

The political history of the years from the French Revolution to the revolutions of 1848 was dominated by the rise of liberalism and nationalism and the unsuccessful attempts to suppress them. The economic history of this period was shaped by the first phase of the Industrial Revolution that began in Manchester, England and then spread from Great Britain to continental Europe. Contemporary observers recognized that Manchester was the birthplace of profound ecological, social, and economic changes that were fundamentally transforming their world. These commentators offered scathing criticism of how industrial factories polluted Manchester's environment and divided its society into a small number of wealthy entrepreneurs and a large mass of impoverished workers. Despite these drawbacks, Manchester nurtured and rewarded a revolutionary and lasting spirit of free enterprise that energized the Industrial Revolution.

5. Support your argument with evidence from the documents (2 points)

The DBQ rubric awards you 1 point for using the content of at least three documents to address the prompt. However, you can earn 2 points by using 6 of the 7 documents to support your argument.

Most students are tempted to "plow through" the documents by addressing them one at a time. Although this strategy will earn 1 point, it will probably not earn 2 points. The most effective way to earn 2 points is to group the documents into the categories you created in your chart. Our sample essay groups the documents into 4 body paragraphs. This grouping allows for relevant and insightful connections. For example, note how the final sentence of body paragraph 2 makes a relevant and insightful connection between documents 6, 2, and 3. Similarly, the opening sentence of body paragraph 3 makes a meaningful connection between documents 5 and 7.

It is important to note that you do not have to use all seven documents. You can and should omit a document that you either don't understand or that doesn't fit into your organization.

Essay body paragraphs

(1) *Documents 2 and 4 offer compelling commentaries and alarming statistics documenting the appalling public health conditions in Manchester. William Cobbett hoped his articles in the* Political Register *would mobilize public support to arouse Parliament to address working conditions in Manchester.*

Cobbett assailed the "lords of the loom" and decried the "murderous effects of the heat" on workers forced to inhale cotton dust. (Document 2) Taken from a prestigious British medical journal, Document 4 provides mortality statistics corroborating Cobbett's concerns. For example, the average age of death of Laborers/Artisans in Manchester was 17 compared to 38 in Rutland, a nearby rural district.

(2) *The "infernal scenes" described by Cobbett (Document 2) were not limited to working conditions inside Manchester's textile mills. Alexis de Tocqueville noted that "300,000 people work ceaselessly" in a city covered by "a thick black smoke" that obscures the sun and forces people to live in "dark half-lit streets." (Document 3) Hugh Miller, a self-taught Scottish geologist, offered his concerned readers a vivid description of how industry was despoiling Manchester's natural environment. Document 6 contains Miller's memorable warning of how chemicals, dyes, and other waste products transformed the river Irwell into "a flood of liquid manure, in which all life dies." Miller's description corroborates Cobbett's and de Tocqueville's accounts of an ecological disaster that threatened to spread from Manchester to Britain's other industrial centers.*

(3) *The systematic exploitation of Manchester's factory workers outraged both James Leach (Document 5) and Friedrich Engels (Document 7). Leach focused on the deplorable working conditions endured by women laboring in Manchester's textile mills. He wrote his report to persuade Parliament to address the plight of mothers and pregnant women "slaving from morning till night beside the never-tiring machines." (Document 5) Engels did more than call for reforms. His account of Manchester's "disgraceful slums" prompted the German socialist Karl Marx to visit the city. Their experiences in Manchester fueled the overwhelming sense of indignation and urgency in* The Communist Manifesto. *Published in 1848, the polemic called upon workers to unite and forcibly create a new classless society.*

(4) *Although Manchester's deplorable living and working conditions aroused a storm of criticism, the city also had resolute defenders. The middle-class gentleman in Document 7 listened patiently to Engels' criticisms and then calmly noted, "And yet there is a great deal of money made here." Alexis de Tocqueville succinctly summarized Manchester's core paradox by observing, "From this filthy sewer pure gold flows." (Document 3) De Tocqueville was right. Manchester's textile mills produced material goods on a scale unknown in history. These products generated a river of golden profits that enabled Great Britain to become the world's undisputed industrial leader. In Document 1, two laissez-faire British economic historians praise Manchester's "society of inventors" whose entrepreneurial spirit built the world's first industrial city. The new class of successful entrepreneurs replaced the landed aristocracy as the dominant force in the process of modernizing domestic life in the nineteenth century.*

6. Provide evidence beyond the documents (1 point)

The DBQ rubric awards you 1 point for including at least one additional piece of evidence beyond that found in the seven documents. The evidence must be presented in more than a brief phrase or a passing mention and it must be relevant to an argument about the prompt.

One effective strategy for earning the beyond the evidence point is to view each document as a springboard for additional information. For example, Document 7 provides a famous anecdote written by Friedrich Engels. Note that the passage does not mention Karl Marx. This omission invites you to add information about the importance of the future relationship between Engels and Karl Marx. The last four sentences of body paragraph 3 provide relevant evidence that goes beyond Document 7.

Engels did more than call for reforms. His account of Manchester's "disgraceful slums" prompted the German socialist Karl Marx to visit the city. Their experiences in Manchester fueled the overwhelming sense of indignation and urgency in The Communist Manifesto. *Published in 1848, the polemic called upon workers to unite and forcibly create a new classless society.*

7. Sourcing documents with HIPP analysis (1 point)

The DBQ rubric awards 1 point for sourcing at least 3 documents. Sourcing means that you must explain how or why a document's historical situation, intended audience, purpose, OR point of view is relevant to an argument about the prompt. It is very important to note the word OR in this definition.

Many students use the acronym **HIPP** to help them remember the four types of ways to source a document. The **H** stands for historical setting and includes what happened at that time. The **I** stands for intended audience and includes who the document was created for. The first **P** stands for purpose and includes the author's intent. The second **P** stands for point of view and includes the author's perspective.

Our sample essay sources documents 2 (purpose), 6 (audience), 5 (purpose) and 1 (point of view). Although you only have to source 3 documents, many AP® readers recommend that you source 4 documents. This provides you with a safety in case you fail to properly source a document. Your incorrect safety will not be counted against you.

William Cobbett hoped his articles in the Political Register *would mobilize public support to arouse Parliament to address working conditions in Manchester. Cobbett assailed the "lords of the loom" and decried the "murderous effects of the heat" on workers forced to inhale cotton dust. (Document 2) (Purpose)*

Hugh Miller, a self-taught Scottish geologist offered his concerned readers a vivid description of how industry was despoiling Manchester's natural environment.

Document 6 contains Miller's memorable warning of how chemicals, dyes, and other waste products transformed the river Irwell into "a flood of liquid manure, in which all life dies." (Audience)

In Document 5, Leach focused on the deplorable working conditions endured by women laboring in Manchester's textile mills. He wrote his report to persuade Parliament to address the plight mothers and pregnant women "slaving from morning till night beside the never-tiring machines." (Purpose)

In Document 1, two laissez-faire British economic historians praise Manchester's "society of inventors" whose entrepreneurial spirit built the world's first industrial city. (Point of View)

8. Adding a conclusion (Maybe 1 point)

The DBQ rubric does not require a conclusion. However, many experienced readers recommend that you write a conclusion. Here's why: Students often have a difficult time writing a concise thesis statement in their opening paragraph. Fortunately, the rubric awards a thesis point if your thesis is in either the introduction or the conclusion. The process of writing your DBQ essay will crystallize your thoughts enabling you to write a cogent thesis in your conclusion. Here is an example from our model essay:

Manchester did produce deleterious ecological and social consequences. The industrial revolution ravaged Manchester's natural environment. It also created a callous society that exploited the city's working class. However, Manchester was also the birthplace of a revolutionary spirit of free enterprise that raised living standards and formed the foundation for a second Industrial Revolution that swept across England and America during the second half of the nineteenth century.

9. A complex understanding (1 point)

The complexity point is difficult to earn. Readers award this elusive point to less than 5 percent of all DBQ essays. Difficult does not mean impossible. Our model essay opens with a sophisticated thesis stating that Manchester's industrial experience had both adverse and beneficial consequences. It then continues this line of reasoning by grouping the documents into paragraphs discussing the public health, environmental, social, and economic consequences of early industrialization in Manchester. These categories enable the essay to provide multiple perspectives. The concluding paragraph unifies the essay's line of reasoning. Taken together, these components provide a nuanced argument that would earn the complexity point.

Chapter 39

Strategies for the Long-Essay Question

After completing the DBQ, you will yearn for a break to rest your tired writing hand. Unfortunately, there is no break. Instead, you must be resolute and focus on the next and final APEURO challenge: the long-essay question.

The long-essay section will ask you to examine three questions focusing on the same historical reasoning process. Fortunately, you only have to answer *one* of the questions. You will have 40 minutes to write your essay.

Your long essay can earn up to 6 rubric points. Each point is worth 3.5 exam points. So a perfect score of 6 is worth 21 points or 15 percent of your total exam score. It is important to remember that earning 4 of the 6 possible rubric points will keep you on pace to earn an overall score of a 4 or 5 on your APEURO exam.

THE LONG-ESSAY SCORING RUBRIC

The APEURO long-essay scoring rubric is divided into the following categories:

1. **Thesis—1 point**
   - Responds to the prompt with a historically defensible thesis/claim that establishes a line of reasoning.
   - Consists of one or more sentences located in one place, either the introduction or the conclusion.

2. **Contextualization—1 point**
   - Describes a broader historic context relevant to the prompt.
   - Places the prompt in its proper historic setting.
   - Connects the prompt to broader historical events or trends occurring before or during the prompt's time frame.

3. **Evidence—2 points**

   - Provides at least two specific examples of evidence relevant to the topic of the prompt. (1 point)

     OR

   - Supports an argument with specific and relevant examples of evidence. (2 points)

4. **Analysis and Reasoning: Historical Reasoning—1 point**

   - Uses historical reasoning to frame or structure an argument by addressing one of the following targeted historical reasoning processes: comparison, causation, or continuity and change over time. (1 point)
   - For the skill of *comparison* you can earn one point by describing similarities and differences among historic individuals, developments, or processes.
   - For the skill of *causation* you can earn one point for describing the causes and/or effects of a historical event, development, or process.
   - For the skill of *continuity and change over time* you can earn one point for describing historical continuity and/or historic change over time.

     OR

   4a. Analysis and Reasoning: Complexity—2 points

   - Demonstrates a *complex understanding* of the historical development that is the focus of the prompt using evidence to corroborate (reinforce) and/or qualify (modify) an argument that addresses the question. (2 points)
   - *Complex understanding* can be accomplished in a variety of ways including:

     —Explaining both similarities and differences, or explaining both continuity and change, or explaining multiple causes, or explaining both causes and effects.

     —Explaining relevant and insightful connections within and across periods.

     —Confirming the validity of an argument by corroborating multiple perspectives across themes.

—Qualifying or modifying an argument by considering diverse or alternative viewpoints or evidence.

—Explaining nuance of an issue by analyzing multiple variables.

THREE QUESTIONS COVERING THREE DIFFERENT TIME PERIODS

The long-essay section will provide you with three questions. Don't panic! You will be asked to answer only *one* of the questions.

The first question focuses primarily on historical developments or processes between 1450 and 1700, the second primarily on historical developments or processes between 1648 and 1914, and the third primarily on historical developments or processes between 1815 and 2001. The three questions will all address the same reasoning processes—comparison, causation, or continuity and change over time.

A SAMPLE ANNOTATED LONG ESSAY

Practice is the key to performing well on the long essay. The following sample long essay is designed to illustrate how to use a guided set of six strategies that can be applied to any long-essay question.

1. **Begin by carefully analyzing the assignment and making a pragmatic choice.**

Your first task is to select which one of the three long-essay questions you want to write about. Here are three long-essay questions that test the historical reasoning process of comparison:

- Evaluate the most significant differences between how Italian Renaissance and Northern Renaissance artists and writers viewed human beings and religion.
- Evaluate the most significant differences between how Enlightenment and Romantic thinkers viewed human beings, the natural world, and religion.
- Evaluate the most significant difference between how Romantic and Realist thinkers viewed politics and diplomacy.

Begin by taking about five minutes to evaluate the three questions. Above all, make a pragmatic choice. A common mistake many students make is to choose the question they find the most challenging thinking they could earn more points by tackling a harder task. Avoid this pitfall. Always choose the question that you know the most about.

2. The all-important first paragraph (2 points)

Your opening paragraph is very important. Use the first 2–3 sentences to establish the historic context for the topic specified in your prompt. The first two sentences in our sample introductory paragraph provide the "big picture" or historic setting. Then use your next 3–5 sentences to present a clearly defined thesis that establishes your line of reasoning.

Our "combo" paragraph combines contextualization and the thesis statement. This combination is worth 2 rubric points or 10 exam points! Given this high value, plan carefully. It is better to take a few extra minutes to carefully construct your opening paragraph than to rush and end up with a weak thesis.

It is important to note that you should not divide this paragraph. Readers expect to see your thesis in the first paragraph. Long-essay readers report that the overwhelming majority of students use a combo approach to begin their essays.

Here is a clear and fully developed opening combo paragraph for the second question above:

Evaluate the most significant differences between how Enlightenment and Romantic thinkers viewed human beings, the natural world, and religion.

Essay introduction

Isaac Newton was the last and greatest figure of the Scientific Revolution. In 1687 he published Mathematical Principles of Natural Philosophy, *a milestone book proving that gravity governs the motion of all matter on Earth and in outer space. Influenced by Newton, Enlightenment thinkers honored reason as if it were a divine force. They believed that human beings are guided by reason and that the natural world is a vast mechanism whose secrets can be discovered by reason and formulated into natural laws. In contrast, Romantic thinkers protested against the Enlightenment's excessive reliance on reason. They believed that human beings are driven by powerful and often irrational emotions. The two movements very different views of nature can be seen in their contrasting attitudes towards religion.*

3. Provide relevant supporting evidence (2 points)

Your opening paragraph established a historic context and a thesis based on a clear line of reasoning. Your next step is to provide at least two examples of specific historic evidence that support your argument that the Enlightenment and Romantic movements offered contrasting views of human beings, the natural world, and religion.

Each of the three body paragraphs contains specific historical evidence to support the thesis line of reasoning. For example, the first body paragraph uses the views of Voltaire and Diderot to illustrate the primacy of reason among Enlightenment thinkers. The second body paragraph uses Friedrich's painting to illustrate the Romantic view of nature. The third body paragraph explains the Deist view of nature and contrasts it with the growing popularity of emotional religious revivals.

Essay body paragraphs

(1) *The Enlightenment rested on a strong belief in the ability of reason to understand human nature. Enlightened writers such as Voltaire and Diderot hated ignorance and intolerance. They believed that reason was the alternative to superstition and prejudice. In contrast, Romantics stressed the primacy of the heart over the head. Romantics preferred to rely on intuition and subjective feelings. While the philosophes valued order and natural laws, the Romantics valued spontaneous feelings. Romantic artists depicted states of mind for the first time in Western art. They portrayed insanity, dreams, and nightmares. This emphasis upon states of mind anticipated Freud's work on the subconscious.*

(2) *The Scientific Revolution and the work of Newton had a strong influence on how Enlightened thinkers viewed the natural world. The philosophes believed that natural laws regulated both the universe and human society. While the philosophes investigated the natural world, Romantic artists chose to depict the natural world as a mysterious force best viewed with awe. For example, the German artist Caspar David Friedrich captured the essence of the Romantic view of the natural world in his painting, "Wanderer Looking Over a Sea of Fog." Friedrich's solitary "wanderer" stands alone on a rocky cliff pondering a landscape shrouded in thick mist.*

(3) *The Enlightened and Romantic views of human nature and the natural world affected religious thought in very different ways. Enlightened thinkers rejected faith and favored the Deist view that a distant God created the natural world and like a "divine watchmaker" stepped back and let it run according to natural laws. In contrast, Romantics embraced the wonder and mysteries of nature as a way to feel the divine presence. This stress on emotions, inner faith, and religious inspiration can be seen in the nineteenth century religious revivals and the growing popularity of Pietism and Methodism.*

4. Demonstrate the use of historical reasoning (1 point)

The long-essay rubric awards 1 point for demonstrating the use of historical reasoning to frame or state your argument. Historical reasoning processes include comparison, causation, and continuity and change over time (CCOT).

Our model long-essay uses comparison to structure its argument. Note that body paragraphs 1, 2, and 3 (see above) all use comparison to contrast relevant differences between how Enlightenment and Romantic thinkers viewed human beings, the natural world, and religion.

5. Adding a conclusion (Maybe 1 point)

The long-essay rubric does not require a conclusion. However, many experienced readers recommend that you write a conclusion. Here's why: Students often have a difficult time writing a concise opening paragraph. Fortunately, the rubric awards a thesis point if your thesis is in either the introduction or the conclusion. The process of writing your long essay will crystallize your thoughts, enabling you to write a cogent thesis as part of your conclusion. Here is a sample from our model essay:

Essay conclusion

Romanticism dominated European art and literature during the first half of the nineteenth century. The Romantic movement represented a repudiation of the Enlightened view of human nature and the natural world. Romantic authors and artists rejected reason and emphasized emotion. This new emphasis upon feeling and intuition led to the first attempts to probe the unconscious and to a widespread religious revival.

6. A complex understanding (1 point)

The complexity point is difficult to earn. Readers award this elusive point to less than 5 percent of all long-essays. Difficult does not mean impossible. Our model essay opens with a sophisticated thesis stating that Enlightenment and Romantic thinkers offered contrasting views of human beings, the natural world, and religion. The essay then continues this line of reasoning by providing detailed comparisons of Enlightenment and Romantic views of these topics. The concluding paragraph unifies the essay's line of reasoning. Taken together, these components provide a nuanced argument that would earn the complexity point.

Notes

Notes

Notes

Notes